AF553574

SMALL BUSINESS MANAGEMENT

SMALL BUSINESS MANAGEMENT

S.K. Sinha

CENTRUM PRESS
NEW DELHI-110002 (INDIA)

CENTRUM PRESS
H.O.: 4360/4, Ansari Road, Daryaganj,
New Delhi-110002 (India)
Tel: 23278000, 23261597, 23255577, 23286875
B.O.: No. 1015, Ist Main Road, BSK IIIrd Stage,
IIIrd Phase, IIIrd Block, Bangalore-560085 (INDIA)
Tel: 080-41723429
Email: centrumpress@gmail.com
Visit us at: www.centrumpress.com

Small Business Management

© Reserved

First Edition, 2010

ISBN 978-93-80540-42-9

PRINTED IN INDIA

Printed at Balaji Offset, Delhi.

Contents

Preface

Small Business Management is nothing but sales, marketing and advertising management for a small business. Sales and Marketing are lifelines of a small business. So, sales and marketing management is very much needed for the stability and growth of the small business enterprise.

Proper Analysis of Target Market-For every small business there should be a target group of customers. Identifying the specific customers and the target market for the business is very much important to take up a focused product campaign. Otherwise, the market campaign and the promotional expenses targeting all general public is a sheer waste of energy and money. If the target market is known the task of devising promotional plans become simple and affordable.

Quick Financial Investment-Firstly, owner or manager of a small business should have a well chalked out planned budget for market campaigning and he should follow the budget accordingly. Quick Financial Investment is very important in this case. There are many marketing strategies, which can be undertaken by proper and quick financial investment like TV advertisement and Banner advertisement. This kind of quick financial investment in return brings more sales and more business.

Every person longs for financial independence and desire a business of his own. The people who are born in business families, they normally join in their father's business only, whether he is a lowly vegetable seller or a top notch industrialist. They grow up in a business environment and watch their fathers and uncles in action in real life business situations. They learn by observation and by the time they are old enough to take on business responsibilities, they know the tricks of the trade. You can learn engineering, accountancy and other professions by undergoing regular courses in respective institutions. You can even learn business management. But there are few institutions, which offer courses in entrepreneurship. This book seeks to fill the gap.

The book deals with different aspects of entrepreneurship development in small scale sector. The book examines the growth and development of entrepreneurship and explains how the goal of entrepreneurship development in SSI sector can be achieved, identifies the potential areas of entrepreneurship development, analyses the problems and constraints, assesses the entrepreneurial ability of women and rural people of the state, advocates the strategy of development, highlights the role of developmental agencies and suggests the measures to create congenial environment for development of entrepreneurship.

— *S.K. Sinha*

1

Introduction

A small business is a business that is privately owned and operated, with a small number of employees and relatively low volume of sales. Small businesses are normally privately owned corporations, partnerships, or sole proprietorships. The legal definition of "small" varies historically, by country and by industry, but generally has fewer than 100 employees in the United States and under 50 employees in the European Union. However, in Australia, a small business is defined by the *Fair Work Act 2009* as one with fewer than 15 employees. By comparison, a medium sized business or mid-sized business has under 500 employees in the US, 250 in the European Union and fewer than 200 in Australia.

In addition to number of employees, other methods used to classify small companies include annual sales (turnover), value of assets and net profit (balance sheet), alone or in a mixed definition. These criteria are followed by the European Union, for instance (headcount, turnover and balance sheet totals). Small businesses are usually not dominant in their field of operation. Small businesses are common in many countries, depending on the economic system in operation. Typical examples include: convenience stores, other small shops (such as a bakery or delicatessen), hairdressers, tradesmen, lawyers, accountants, restaurants, guest houses, photographers, small-scale manufacturing etc.

The smallest businesses, often located in private homes, are called micro businesses (term used by international organizations such as the World Bank and the International Finance Corporation) or SoHos. The term "mom and pop business" is a common colloquial expression for a single-family operated business with few (or no) employees other than the owners. When judged by the number of employees, the American and the European definitions are the same: under 10 employees.

Advantages of Small Business

A small business can be started at a very low cost and on a part-time basis. Small business is also well suited to internet marketing because it can easily serve specialized niches, something that would have been more difficult prior to the internet revolution which began in the late 1990s. Adapting to change is crucial in business and particularly small business; not being tied to any bureaucratic inertia, it is typically easier to respond to the marketplace quickly. Small business proprietors tend to be intimate with their customers and clients which results in greater accountability and maturely.

Independence is another advantage of owning a small business. One survey of small business owners showed that 38% of those who left their jobs at other companies said their main reason for leaving was that they wanted to be their own bosses. Freedom to operate independently is a reward for small business owners. In addition, many people desire to make their own decisions, take their own risks, and reap the rewards of their efforts. Small business owners have the satisfaction of making their own decisions within the constraints imposed by economic and other environmental factors. However, entrepreneurs have to work very long hours and understand that ultimately their customers are their bosses.

Several organizations also provide help for the small business sector, such as the Internal Revenue Service's Small Business and Self-Employed One-Stop Resource.

Problems Faced by Small Businesses

Small businesses often face a variety of problems related to their size. A frequent cause of bankruptcy is under capitalization. This is often a result of poor planning rather than economic conditions-it is common rule of thumb that the entrepreneur should have access to a sum of money at least equal to the projected revenue for the first year of business in addition to his anticipated expenses. For example, if the prospective owner thinks that he will generate $100,000 in revenues in the first year with $150,000 in start-up expenses, then he should have no less than $250,000 available. Failure to provide this level of funding for the company could leave the owner liable for all of the company's debt should he end up in bankruptcy court, under the theory of under capitalization. In addition to ensuring that the business has enough capital, the small business owner must also be mindful of contribution margin (sales minus variable costs). To break even, the business must be able to reach a level of sales where the contribution margin equals fixed costs. When they first start out, many small business owners underprice their products to a point where even at their maximum capacity, it would be impossible to break even. Cost controls or price increases often resolve this problem.

In the United States, some of the largest concerns of small business owners are insurance costs (such as liability and health), rising energy costs and taxes. In the United Kingdom and Australia, small business owners tend to be more concerned with excessive governmental red tape.

Another problem for many small businesses is termed the 'Entrepreneurial Myth' or E-Myth. The mystic assumption is that an expert in a given technical field will also be expert at running that kind of business. Additional business management skills are needed to keep a business running smoothly.

Marketing the Small Business

Common marketing techniques for small business include networking, word of mouth, customer referrals, yellow pages directories, television, radio, outdoor (roadside billboards), print, email marketing, and internet. Electronic media like TV can be quite expensive and is normally intended to create awareness of a product or service.

Many small business owners find internet marketing more affordable. Google AdWords and Yahoo! Search Marketing are two popular options of getting small business products or services in front of motivated Web searchers. Advertising on niche sites can also be effective, but with the long tail of the internet, it can be time intensive to advertise on enough sites to garner an effective reach.

Franchise Businesses

Franchising is a way for small business owners to benefit from the economies of scale of the big corporation (franchisor). McDonald's restaurants, True Value hardware stores, and NAPA Auto Parts stores are examples of a franchise. The small business owner can leverage a strong brand name and purchasing power of the larger company while keeping their own investment affordable. However, some franchisees conclude that they suffer the "worst of both worlds" feeling they are too restricted by corporate mandates and lack true independence.

However, in some chains, such as the aforementioned True Value and NAPA, franchises may have their own name alongside the franchise's name.

Small Business Bankruptcy

When small business fails, the owner may file bankruptcy. In most cases this can be handled through a personal bankruptcy filing. Corporations can file bankruptcy, but if it is out of business and valuable corporate assets are likely to be repossessed by secured creditors there is little advantage to going to the expense of a corporate bankruptcy. Many states offer exemptions for small business assets so they can continue to operate during and after personal bankruptcy. However, corporate assets are normally not exempt, hence it may be more difficult to continue operating an incorporated business if the owner files bankruptcy.

Certification and Trust

Building trust with new customers can be a difficult task for a new and establishing business. Some organizations like the Better Business Bureau and the International Charter now offer Small Business Certification, which certifies the quality of the services and goods produced and can encourage new and larger customers. These services may require a few hours of work, but a certification may reassure potential customers. However, the most effective way to earn trust is through customer referrals.

Contribution to the Economy

In the US, small business (less than 500 employees) accounts for around half the GDP and more than half the employment. Regarding small business, the top job provider is those with less than 10 employees, and those with 10 or more but less than 20 employees comes in as the second, and those with 20 or more but less than 100 employees comes in as the third (interpolation of data from the following references). The most recent data shows firms with less than 20 employees account for slightly more than 18% of the employment.

Of the 5,369,068 employer firms in 1995, 78.8 percent had fewer than 10 employees, and 99.7 percent had fewer than 500 employees.

Sources of Funding

Small businesses use several sources available for start-up capital:

- Self-financing by the owner through cash, equity loan on his or her home, and or other assets.
- Loans from friends or relatives.
- Personal Savings.
- Private stock issue.
- Forming partnerships.
- Angel Investors.
- Banks.
- SME finance, including Collateral based lending and Venture capital, given sufficiently sound business venture plans.

Some small businesses are further financed through credit card debt-usually a poor choice, given that the interest rate on credit cards is often several times the rate that would be paid on a line of credit or bank loan. Many owners seek a bank loan in the name of their business, however banks will usually insist on a personal guarantee by the business owner. In the United States, the Small Business Administration (SBA) runs several loan programs that may help a small business secure loans. In these programs, the SBA guarantees a portion of the loan to the issuing bank and thus relieves the bank of some of the risk of extending the loan to a small business. The SBA also requires business owners to pledge personal assets and sign as a personal guarantee for the loan.

Canadian small businesses can take advantage of federally funded programs and services.

Business Networks and Advocacy Groups

Small businesses often join or come together to form organizations to advocate for their causes or to achieve economies of scale that larger businesses benefit from, such as the opportunity to buy cheaper health insurance in bulk. These organizations include local or regional groups such as Chambers of Commerce, as well as national or international industry-specific organizations. Such groups often serve a dual purpose, as business networks to provide marketing and connect members to potential sales leads and suppliers, and also as advocacy groups, bringing together many small businesses to provide a stronger voice in regional or national politics.

The largest regional small business group in the United States is the Council of Smaller Enterprises, located in Greater Cleveland.

Small Business: It's all About Relationships

As the world of business becomes more complex, a small-business owner can no longer be an expert in all of the specialized disciplines a small business needs. Despite the fact that small-business owners must necessarily focus on producing and managing enough cash flow and on getting customers in the door, it is also critically important for them to cultivate and nurture relationships with a support team. This group includes:

- Customers.
- Employees.
- A banker.
- An accountant/tax specialist.
- A lawyer.
- An insurance broker.
- A sales and marketing professional.
- A training provider.
- An enterprise systems and IT specialist.

Because it is unlikely that all of the above expertise will be available in-house, it is crucial for the owner to develop and maintain close working relationships with the outside care givers of the business before any emergency need arises.

Employees

Although thinking in terms of a "relationship" with employees might seem a little odd for a business owner, that relationship could be the most important of all of the relationships for the owner to cultivate. Because good employees represent a major resource in a small business, the time and effort the owner invests in nurturing that relationship has a huge return on investment (ROI). Employees who feel seen, respected and appreciated almost always produce more than anticipated.

Employees represent- in fact they *are*- the company to the customers. The business relationship with customers largely depends upon their experience and interaction with the employees. Happy employees tend to want to satisfy the customers, want to do a good job and want to stay in the job. This is important to the continuity of high-quality customer service and avoids the significant expense of employee turnover, employee retraining and the expensive but inevitable "rookie mistakes" of new, inexperienced employees. In addition, having trusted, long-term employees can free up the owner to handle off-site duties as needed.

Banker

A banking relationship is an obvious need, not only for routine business banking, but particularly when capital is needed to grow, increase inventory, buy a building, bridge a short-term gap between payables and receivables or to address the seasonality of the cash flow in the business. The banker that an owner goes to for a loan should know the business owner, understand the history of the business and have an understanding of the owner's judgment and credibility regarding the use and payback prospects for a loan. If the long-term relationship is there, or it is at least in the process of being built, the loan request has a much better chance of being approved. If the business has borrowed and repaid loans in the past, the established track record and relationship greatly enhance the approval prospects.

Accountant or Tax Specialist

A relationship with an accountant is equally important if the business owner is to be confident in the quality, clarity, timeliness and understanding of the financial reporting provided. A relationship with an accountant can also enhance the business's credibility with a banker when the business is seeking additional capital.

Many small businesses combine the accountant and tax-specialist functions in one outside entity for convenience, timesaving and cost reasons. This is fine if the accountant has the requisite tax experience for the industry and the tax expertise for the specific business it serves.

Lawyer

Every business owner should have a relationship with a business lawyer, liability attorney or legal firm. When an owner invests money and effort in building a business, it must be safeguarded from loss as a result of a lawsuit.

Insurance Broker

As part of business risk management, the business also should have a relationship with and the trusted advice of an insurance broker who will provide the optimal coverage in the relevant areas within the constraints of the business budget.

Marketing Professional

Depending on the owner's sales and marketing expertise, a relationship with a marketing professional is highly advised. Most small businesses start with an entrepreneur who has a specific technical skill, a trade certification or has built up a following of customers for good work done. When the owner wants to grow the business beyond the established customer base, he or she should have a well-defined marketing plan that addresses the following issues:

- Targeting the market.
- Optimizing the media used.
- Considering branding issues.
- Assessing the competition.
- Getting the best value for the marketing money spent.

Few small-business owners possess all of these skills.

Business Trainer

A similar situation often exists with training both the owner and the employees. In a small business, especially in a startup, the owner often hasn't had time to acquire the management skills necessary for managing a growing business with more employees, larger or additional computer systems, enlarged inventory, additional vehicles and more customers to manage. A relationship with independent business skills trainers can fill that need.

IT Specialist

A more recent arrival on the needed-relationship list is the enterprise systems or information technology (IT) specialist. The business owner should have someone who can come in, analyse the systems and suggest ways to effectively and efficiently manage costs. That person (or organization) should also suggest ways to keep the business competitive in terms of administrative, project-management and operating costs and maintain the scalability of the business model through process productivity and system capacity and flexibility.

Family Business

A family business is a business in which one or more members of one or more families have a significant ownership interest and significant commitments toward the business' overall well being. In some countries, many of the largest publicly listed firms are family-owned. A firm is said to be family-owned if a person is the controlling shareholder; that is, a person (rather than a state, corporation, management trust, or mutual fund) can garner enough shares to assure at least 20% of the voting rights and the highest percentage of voting rights in comparison to other shareholders.

Family businesses may have owners who are not family members. Family businesses may also be managed by individuals who are not members of the family. However, family members are often involved in the operations of their family business in some capacity and, in smaller companies, usually one or more family members are the senior officers and managers. Many businesses that are now public companies were family businesses.

Family participation as managers and/or owners of a business can strengthen the company because family members are often loyal and dedicated to the family enterprise. However, family participation as managers and/or owners of a business can present unique problems because the dynamics of the family system and the dynamics of the business systems are often not in balance.

The interests of a family member may not be aligned with the interest of the business. For example, if a family member wants to be president but is not as competent as a non-family member, the personal interest of the family member and the well being of the business may be in conflict.

Or, the interests of the entire family may not be balanced with the interests of their business. For example, if a family needs its business to distribute funds for living expenses and retirement but the business requires those to stay competitive, the interests of the entire family and the business are not aligned.

Finally, the interest of one family member may not be aligned with another family member. For example, a family member who is an owner may want to sell the business to maximize his return, but a family member who is an owner and also a manager may want to keep the company because it represents her career and she wants her children to have the opportunity to work in the business.

When the family business is basically owned and operated by one person, that person usually does the necessary balancing automatically. For example, the founder may decide the business needs to build a new plant and take less money out of the business for a period so the business can accumulate cash needed to expand. In making this decision, the founder is balancing his personal interests (taking cash out) with the needs of the business (expansion).

But balancing competing interests often become difficult in three situations. The first situation is when the founder wants to change they are involved in the business. Usually the founder begins this transition by involving others to manage the business. Involving someone else to manage the company requires the founder to be more conscious and formal in balancing personal interests with the interests of the business because they can no longer do this alignment automatically—someone else is involved.

The second situation is when more than one person owns the business and no single person has the power and support of the other owners to determine collective interests. For example, if a founder intends to transfer ownership in the family business to their four children, two of whom work in the business, how do they balance these unequal differences? The four siblings need a system to do this themselves when the founder is no longer involved.

The third situation is when there are multiple owners and some or all of the owners are not in management. Given the situation above, there is a higher chance that the interests of the two sons not employed in the family business may be different that the interests of the two sons who are employed in the business. Their potential for differences does not mean that the interests cannot be aligned, it just means that there is a greater need for the four owners to have a system in place that differences can be identified and balanced.

Successfully balancing the differing interests of family members and/or the interests of one or more family members on the one hand and the interests of the business on the other hand require the people involved to have the competencies, character and commitment to do this work.

Often family members can benefit from involving more than one professional advisor, each having the particular skill set needed by the family. Some of the skill sets that might be needed include communication, conflict resolution, family systems, finance, legal, accounting, insurance, finance, investing, leadership development, management development, and strategic planning.

Different Form of Small Business

Sole Proprietorships

The vast majority of small business start out as sole proprietorships. These firms are owned by one person, usually the individual who has day-to-day responsibility for running the business. Sole proprietors own all the assets of the business and the profits generated by it. They also assume complete responsibility for any of its liabilities or debts. In the eyes of the law and the public, you are one in the same with the business.

Advantages of a Sole Proprietorship

- Easiest and least expensive form of ownership to organize.
- Sole proprietors are in complete control, and within the parameters of the law, may make decisions as they see fit.
- Sole proprietors receive all income generated by the business to keep or reinvest.
- Profits from the business flow-through directly to the owner's personal tax return.
- The business is easy to dissolve, if desired.

Disadvantages of a Sole Proprietorship

- Sole proprietors have unlimited liability and are legally responsible for all debts against the business. Their business and personal assets are at risk.
- May be at a disadvantage in raising funds and are often limited to using funds from personal savings or consumer loans.
- May have a hard time attracting high-calibre employees, or those that are motivated by the opportunity to own a part of the business.
- Some employee benefits such as owner's medical insurance premiums are not directly deductible from business income (only partially deductible as an adjustment to income).

Partnerships

In a Partnership, two or more people share ownership of a single business. Like proprietorships, the law does not distinguish between the business and its owners. The Partners should have a legal agreement that sets forth how decisions will be made, profits will be shared, disputes will be resolved, how future partners will be admitted to the partnership, how partners can be bought out, or what steps will be taken to dissolve the partnership when needed;. Yes, its hard to think about a "break-up" when the business is just getting started, but many partnerships split up at crisis times and unless there is a defined process, there will be even greater problems. They also must decide up front how much time and capital each will contribute, etc.

Advantages of a Partnership

- Partnerships are relatively easy to establish; however time should be invested in developing the partnership agreement.
- With more than one owner, the ability to raise funds may be increased.
- The profits from the business flow directly through to the partners' personal tax returns.
- Prospective employees may be attracted to the business if given the incentive to become a partner.
- The business usually will benefit from partners who have complementary skills.

Disadvantages of a Partnership

- Partners are jointly and individually liable for the actions of the other partners.
- Profits must be shared with others.
- Since decisions are shared, disagreements can occur.
- Some employee benefits are not deductible from business income on tax returns.
- The partnership may have a limited life; it may end upon the withdrawal or death of a partner.

Types of Partnerships

General Partnership

Partners divide responsibility for management and liability, as well as the shares of profit or loss according to their internal agreement. Equal shares are assumed unless there is a written agreement that states differently.

Limited Partnership and Partnership with Limited Liability

"Limited" means that most of the partners have limited liability (to the extent of their investment) as well as limited input regarding management decisions, which generally encourages investors for short term projects, or for investing in capital assets. This form of ownership is not often used for operating retail or service businesses. Forming a limited partnership is more complex and formal than that of a general partnership.

Joint Venture

Acts like a general partnership, but is clearly for a limited period of time or a single project. If the partners in a joint venture repeat the activity, they will be recognized as an ongoing partnership and will have to file as such, and distribute accumulated partnership assets upon dissolution of the entity.

Corporations

A corporation, chartered by the state in which it is head quartered, is considered by law to be a unique entity, separate and apart from those who own it. A corporation can be taxed; it can be sued; it can enter into contractual agreements. The owners of a corporation are its shareholders. The shareholders elect a board of directors to oversee the major policies and decisions. The corporation has a life of its own and does not dissolve when ownership changes.

Advantages of a Corporation

- Shareholders have limited liability for the corporation's debts or judgments against the corporations.
- Generally, shareholders can only be held accountable for their investment in stock of the company. (Note however, that officers can be held personally liable for their actions, such as the failure to withhold and pay employment taxes).
- Corporations can raise additional funds through the sale of stock.
- A corporation may deduct the cost of benefits it provides to officers and employees.
- Can elect S corporation status if certain requirements are met. This election enables company to be taxed similar to a partnership.

Disadvantages of a Corporation

- The process of incorporation requires more time and money than other forms of organization.

- Corporations are monitored by federal, state and some local agencies, and as a result may have more paperwork to comply with regulations.
- Incorporating may result in higher overall taxes. Dividends paid to shareholders are not deductible form business income, thus this income can be taxed twice.

Limited Liability Companies (LLCs)

The LLC is a relatively new type of hybrid business structure that is now permissible in most states. It is designed to provide the limited liability features of a corporation and the tax efficiencies and operational flexibility of a partnership. Formation is more complex and formal than that of a general partnership.

The owners are members, and the duration of the LLC is usually determined when the organization papers are filed. The time limit can be continued if desired by a vote of the members at the time of expiration. LLC's must not have more than two of the four characteristics that define corporations: Limited liability to the extent of assets; continuity of life; centralization of management; and free transferability of ownership interests.

An LLC is taxed as partnership in most cases; corporation forms must be used if there are more than 2 of the 4 corporate characteristics.

Small Start Units

The word Small Start Unit (also called small start-up, or SSU) emerged as a business term to address small entities that are going to launch a innovative and specific business model in the market place. This not only on a larger geographical scale, but also with a vantage in technology they offer. In combination that gives them a sustainable competitive advantage, which they play off against (major) market competitors right from the beginning. SSU's are mainly of Western origin.

The promising business model of a Small start unit is likely to attract venture capitalists. Such VCs supply SSU's with needed capital for the get-go. With this capital SSU's are able to set up the headquarter in their home market, typically a well developed market in a Western country. Despite the disadvantage of higher costs, their competitive advantage enables them to generate new jobs in the home market by employing high-end engineers, marketing professionals and well educated managers.

Basically the characteristic of an SSU is:

1. The core competency resides in a future technology;
2. The aim is to operate on a global scale right from the beginning;
3. There is a high growth orientation within the firm;
4. A flexible network is related to them, consisting of internal and external stockholders;
5. It is able to fragment mass markets into niches;
6. Technology is built on open source technology; And
7. products are brought to markets rapidly.

By pursuing a global approach SSU's do not only exploit emerging and lucrative selling markets, but also lower their costs and boost profits more quickly by embedding their business partner in emerging markets into their value chain. SSU's take advantages out of emerging markets as well as Western markets. So globalization allows SSU's to become long-lasting and successful business entities.

Choosing to Run your own Business

Choosing to run your own business is a big step that few people take lightly. While the rewards seem self-evident, the challenges are substantial also. Learn more about what making the choice is about from assessing whether taking the step is right for you to looking at business models to help you find the right business.

Entrepreneurship

Entrepreneurism isn't just about starting a business. It is a dynamic field that covers a wide spectrum of activities and adventures. Entrepreneurial Issues gives an overview of some of the many ways entrepreneurism is practice and tells a little about the history of entrepreneurism. What is an Entrepreneur? Gives an overview of what it takes to be an entrepreneur.

Intrapreneurship

For many of you, other responsibilities in your life make it difficult to make the leap into starting your own business right now, but you are creative and are looking for ways to be entrepreneurial. Intrapreneurship, being entrepreneurial within a larger business, may be the answer to your needs.

Undecided about Taking the Step?

Making the choice to start a business can be a difficult decision. Some of the obstacles that keep people from making the choice to run your own business are:

- Do you really have what it takes to be an entrepreneur?
- Will I be able to support myself financially?
- How much money will I need to start a business?
- What is the "right" business for me?
- What are all the steps I need to take to start a business?

If you are still at the undecided stage, I have put together a simple self-scored quiz to see if you are ready to take the leap.

Decided, but don't know what Business you want to start? Perhaps you need to look at different ways to stimulate your creativity. Creativity is important in running any business. So, even if you don't find the right idea for you, know more about creativity will help you be a better business owner.

Another great resource is my list of types of businesses you can start. In Choosing the Right Business I provide a number of resources about the types of businesses you might run and what you need to know to run that business.

The actual business you pursue is not the only decision you will need to make. There are a variety of business models that you also should consider in identifying the best way to run your business. The business models article also looks at other options besides starting a business from scratch.

Want to read what other people say about starting a business? Here are some good books that provide insights into what running your own business entails.

Ready to own a Business? Think you are ready to run your own business. Visit Starting a Business.

To look at ways to not only start a business from scratch, but also to look at ways to buy into an existing business or franchise.

Advice and Ideas for a Small Business Start up

Summary: Succeeding in a small business is not at all difficult. In fact it is as simple as driving or raking the leaves. Here are some tips and ideas that might be of great use along the way.

You own a small business: You want it to succeed. You know that your competitors are many and well established. How do you make a difference? How do you ensure that your services and products are in demand?

USP, differentiators, you've heard them all and know that ultimately it may boil down to your competition offering cheaper services. You wish to succeed despite all this and need a good business plan. Well, to be frank, we've been in the small and medium segment for the past 5 years and have gathered some useful information on the way. No secrets, but useful ideas and advice that may be useful for business start ups. This article compiles them for your use.

Ideas for a Small Business Start up

- We begin by assuming that you are in the business you love. If you are not, the first tip we have for you is that you find something about it to like or move to something that you are passionate about.
- Cash! Plans! Cash forecasting and financial plans are next on the agenda. A planned budget, a measurement process, both short and long term will help your business start up. It's imperative that you know your projected income or revenue and cash expenditures to drill down to your cash flow.
- Research your business, your competition, and the industry and stay current and then define your USP. (Unique Selling Proposition) Read, and read! Get start up advice, join organizations that will help you, get on to the net and do all your homework there.
- If you can differentiate and find that USP, leverage it to the maximum.
- It helps to establish and fall back on a trustworthy mentor or advisory board. It could even be family, someone whom you can bounce ideas off, and get an objective opinion on your USP among other factors.
- Build networks-Meet with people and build a strong business support structure.
- Discipline and motivation-Plan and schedule work, execute quality project management methods. Review your business methods and ideas periodically and make the necessary changes.

- Prepare for change-an inevitable part of your business plan. Force change. Evaluate competition and benchmark against them.
- Become an agent of change. Innovate. When faced with competition, don't panic. The more the players, it simply implies that you are serving an educated market. All you have to do is to persuade customers that your services and product are better-a key factor in your business plan.
- Finally, business is all about attitude, perseverance and passion. Achieve the right balance between work, play and family to avoid losing the big picture.

More Differentiators for a Small Business Start up

- Expand customer base.
- Identify your USP (X-factor).
- Build efficient systems and a good team.
- Build reputation, momentum and market leadership.
- Identify and protect Intellectual Property.
- Promote your business through multiple channels.
- Build partnerships.
- Build trust and credibility with customers through outstanding follow-up services.
- Look for ways to increase profits.
- Give your business a web presence.
- Automate wherever possible.
- Sell based on value.
- Build on differentiators like-experience, better methodologies and a better team.
- Offer money back gurantees.

Implementing an MBO Program

To be successful, an MBO program should be part of a small business's overall system of planning and goal setting. The first step in implementing MBO is to establish long-range company goals in such areas as sales, competitive positioning, human resource development, etc. A small business owner may find it helpful to begin by defining the company's current business and looking for emerging customer needs or market trends that may require adaptation. Such long-range planning provides a framework for charting the company's future staffing levels, marketing approaches, financing needs, product development focus, and facility and equipment usage.

The next step in establishing an MBO system is to use these long-range plans to determine company-wide goals for the current year. Then the company goals can be broken down further into goals for different departments, and eventually into goals for individual employees. As goal-setting filters down through the organization, special care must be taken to ensure that individual and department goals all support the long-range objectives of the business. Ideally, a small business's managers should be involved in formulating the company's long-range goals. This approach may increase their commitment to achieving the goals, allow them to communicate the goals clearly to employees, and help them to create their own short-range goals to support the company goals.

At a minimum, a successful MBO program requires each employee to produce five to ten specific, measurable goals. In addition to a statement of the goal itself, each goal should be supported with a means of measurement and a series of steps toward completion. These goals should be proposed to the employee's manager in writing, discussed, and approved. It is the manager's responsibility to make sure that all employee goals are consistent with the department and company goals. The manager also must compare the employee's performance with his or her goals on a regular basis in order to identify any problems and take corrective action as needed.

Formulating goals is not an easy task for employees, and most people do not master it immediately. Small business owners may find it helpful to begin the process by asking employees and managers to define their jobs and list their major responsibilities. Then the employees and managers can create a goal or goals based upon each responsibility and decide how to measure their own performance in terms of results. In the Small Business Administration publication *Planning and Goal Setting for Small Business,* Raymond F. Pelissier recommended having employees create a miniature work plan for each goal. A work plan would include the goal itself, the measurement terms, any major problems anticipated in meeting the goal, a series of work steps toward meeting the goal (with completion dates), and the company goal to which the personal goal relates.

Small business owners may also find it helpful to break down employee goal setting into categories. The first category, regular goals, would include objectives related to the activities that make up an employee's major responsibilities. Examples of regular goals might include improving efficiency or the amount and quality of work produced. The second category, problem-solving goals, should define and eliminate any major problems the employee encounters in performing his or her job. Another category is innovation, which should include goals that apply original ideas to company problems. The final category is development goals, which should include those goals related to personal growth or the development of employees. Dividing goal setting into categories often helps employees think about their jobs in new ways and acts to release them from the tendency to create activity-based goals.

Another requirement for any successful MBO program is that it provide for a regular review of employee progress toward meeting goals. This review can take place either monthly or quarterly. When the review uncovers employee performance that is below expectations, managers should try to identify the problem, assign responsibility for correcting it, and make a note in the MBO files.

Small Business Owner Involvement

Given that MBO represents an unusual way of thinking about job performance for many employees, small business owners may find it best to introduce MBO programs gradually and to include a formal training component. A small business's managers can be introduced to MBO through a classroom seminar taught by the small business owner or by an outside consultant. Either way, it is important that the managers be allowed to express any doubts and reservations they may have, and that the training include preparation of an actual goal by each participant. When MBO is brought back to the small business, it may be best to start slowly, with each employee only preparing a few goals. This approach will allow employees to learn to prepare goals that are achievable, develop ways to measure their own performance, and anticipate problems that will prevent them from attaining their goals.

Another factor determining the success of MBO programs is the direct involvement of the small business owner. Pelissier noted that the small business owner needs to champion the MBO system from the beginning, as well as set an example for the company's managers, in order for it to succeed. Since managers have a natural tendency to focus their attention upon their own functions rather than on the goals of the overall organization, it can be difficult to educate them about MBO. It is also important for the small business owner to remain patient during the implementation phase: in fact, Pelissier claimed that it may take three to four years before an MBO program creates quantifiable results in a small business. As David Dinesh and Elaine Palmer indicated in their article for *Management Decision,* partial implementation is one of the major potential problems associated with MBO programs.

Implemented correctly, however, MBO can provide a number of benefits to a small business. For example, MBO may help employees understand how their performance will be evaluated and measured. In addition, by allowing them to contribute to goal setting, it may increase the motivation and productivity of a small business's employees. MBO also stands to provide a small business's employees with the means to prioritize their work on a daily basis. Although employee performance evaluation is still a complex task under an MBO system, MBO can also provide an objective basis for evaluation. However, it is important to note that an employee's failure to meet preestablished goals can be attributed to many things besides personal failure. For example, the failure to meet goals could result from setting the wrong objectives, not taking into account company restrictions that may impinge upon performance, establishing an improper measures of progress, or a combination of all of these factors.

Overall, establishing an MBO system in a small business may be difficult, but it is usually worth it. The most difficult aspect of implementing MBO may be simply getting people to think in terms of results rather than activities. Even when an MBO system is implemented well, a small business may encounter problems. For example, employees may set low goals to ensure attainment. Similarly, managers' objectives may focus on the attainment of short-term rather than long-term goals. Finally, employees and managers alike may fall victim to confusion and frustration. Some of the most common reasons for the failure of an MBO program include a lack of involvement among the top management of a small business, inadequate goal setting on a company-wide basis, implementation of an MBO system that occurs too rapidly, or the failure to instruct a company's managers and employees in the basics of MBO. But even though establishing an MBO program may be problematic, it can also offer significant rewards to small businesses.

Ethics in Small Business

Business ethics set the standard for how your business is conducted. They define the value system of how your operate in the marketplace and within your business. With legal scandals concerning insider trading and employee theft making the news, it is no wonder that businesses are increasingly giving attention to the ethical basis of their business and how to lead in an ethical way.

While the examples above seem to be clear cut breaches of ethics, many ethical dilemmas that not so clear cut are faced on a daily basis in business. In fact, there may not even be a "right" or "wrong" answer to the dilemma, but how you deal with it will say much about you and your business. These decisions are often referred to as being in the "gray" area. They are not black-or-white, but could be argued appropriately either way.

Here is an example. Jane has been operating a consulting business for about a year and has been doing very well. About a month ago, she decided she needed to hire someone to help her. After interviewing several candidates, she decided to hire the best one of the group, Sara. She called Sara on Monday to tell her she had gotten the job. They both agreed that she would start the following Monday and that Sara could come in and fill out all of the hiring paperwork at that time.

On Tuesday, of the same week, a friend of Jane's called her to say that she had found the perfect person for Jane. Jane explained that she had already hired someone, but the friend insisted. "Just meet Kim. Who knows, maybe you might want to hire her in the future!" Rather reluctantly, Jane consented. "All right, if she can come in tomorrow, I'll meet with her, but that's all." "Oh, I'm so glad. I just know you're going to like her!" Jane's friend exclaimed.

And Jane did like her. She like her a lot. Jane had met with Kim on Wednesday morning. She was everything that Jane had been looking for and more. In terms of experience, Kim far surpassed any of the candidates Jane had previously interviewed, including Sara. On top of that, she was willing to bring in clients of her own which would only increase business. All in all, Jane knew this was a win-win situation. But what about Sara? She had already given her word to Sara that she could start work on Monday.

And yet she only had the resources to hire one person at this point. Clearly, the best business decision was to hire Kim. But what about the ethical decision? If her business did poorly or Sara couldn't provide enough support, the business would suffer. As a result, her family would suffer. Money was already tight, what with two boys in college. And yet she knew Sara also had a family she was supporting. Plus, she had been so enthusiastic about starting to work.

Obviously, Jane had a problem-an ethical problem. Should she hire Sara (whom she'd already given her word) or Kim (who was obviously the best person for the job)? Questions like these touch on our deepest values. Depending on who you would ask, you would get strong arguments for both decisions. This is what we mean when we talk about "gray" area. So what is the answer?

According to Kenneth Blanchard and Norman Vincent Peale, authors of The Power of Ethical Management, there are three questions you should ask yourself whenever you are faced with an ethical dilemma.

- *Is it legal?* In other words, will you be violating any criminal laws, civil laws or company policies by engaging in this activity?
- *Is it balanced?* Is it fair to all parties concerned both in the short-term as well as the long-term? Is this a win-win situation for those directly as well as indirectly involved?
- *Is it right?* Most of us know the difference between right and wrong, but when push comes to shove, how does this decision make you feel about yourself? Are you proud of yourself for making this decision? Would you like others to know you made the decision you did?

Most of the time, when dealing with "gray decisions", just one of these questions is not enough. But by taking the time to reflect on all three, you will often times find that the answer becomes very clear.

Many businesses are developing an Ethics Policy to clearly state what employees and customers should expect. This not only defines for your employees what you consider to be inappropriate actions, but also sends a clear message about who you are and what is important to you. A number of the resources listed below in the "Related" section provide further information about training in ethics, setting up ethics policies, and ethical dilemmas faced by others and how they handled them.

Research indicates that the integrity demonstrated by your business can have a positive effect on your bottom line. The challenge is to not only believe and voice your ethical principles, but to also practice them in all your business transactions. When the world knows that your business can be trusted to act ethically, you will see the results in lower employee turnover and better customer relations-both well-documented as being critical to business survival. The old adage that "what you sow, you will reap" also supports this premise. Sow the seeds of ethical values in your business and you will see it return in value to your business.

Objectives of Small Business

When a sole trader sets up they may have some unstated aims or objectives-for example to survive for the first year. Other businesses may wish to state exactly what they are aiming to do, such as Amazon, the Internet CD and bookseller, who wants to "make history and have fun". An aim is where the business wants to go in the future, its goals. It is a statement of purpose, e.g. we want to grow the business into Europe. Business objectives are the stated, measurable targets of how to achieve business aims. For instance, we want to achieve sales of €10 million in European markets in 2004. A mission statement sets out the business vision and values that enables employees, managers, customers and even suppliers to understand the underlying basis for the actions of the business.

Business Objectives

Objectives give the business a clearly defined target. Plans can then be made to achieve these targets. This can motivate the employees. It also enables the business to measure the progress towards to its stated aims.

The most Effective Business Objectives meet the Following Criteria:

- *S – Specific* – objectives are aimed at what the business does, e.g. a hotel might have an objective of filling 60% of its beds a night during October, an objective specific to that business.
- *M-Measurable* – the business can put a value to the objective, e.g. €10,000 in sales in the next half year of trading.
- *A*-Agreed by all those concerned in trying to achieve the objective.
- *R-Realistic* – the objective should be challenging, but it should also be able to be achieved by the resources available.

- *T-Time specific* – they have a time limit of when the objective should be achieved, e.g. by the end of the year.

The main Objectives that a Business might have are:

- *Survival* – a short term objective, probably for small business just starting out, or when a new firm enters the market or at a time of crisis.
- *Profit maximization* – try to make the most profit possible – most like to be the aim of the owners and shareholders.
- *Profit satisficing* – try to make enough profit to keep the owners comfortable – probably the aim of smaller businesses whose owners do not want to work longer hours.
- *Sales growth* – where the business tries to make as many sales as possible. This may be because the managers believe that the survival of the business depends on being large. Large businesses can also benefit from economies of scale.

A Business may find that some of their Objectives Conflict with one and other:

- *Growth versus profit:* for example, achieving higher sales in the short term (e.g. by cutting prices) will reduce short-term profit.
- *Short-term versus long-term:* for example, a business may decide to accept lower cash flows in the short-term whilst it invests heavily in new products or plant and equipment.
- Large investors in the Stock Exchange are often accused of looking too much at short-term objectives and company performance rather than investing in a business for the long-term.

Alternative Aims and Objectives

Not all businesses seek profit or growth. Some organisations have alternative objectives.

Examples of other Objectives:

- *Ethical and socially responsible objectives* – organisations like the Co-op or the Body Shop have objectives which are based on their beliefs on how one should treat the environment and people who are less fortunate.
- Public sector corporations are run to not only generate a profit but provide a service to the public. This service will need to

meet the needs of the less well off in society or help improve the ability of the economy to function: e.g. cheap and accessible transport service.

- Public sector organisations that monitor or control private sector activities have objectives that are to ensure that the business they are monitoring comply with the laws laid down.
- *Health care and education establishments* – their objectives are to provide a service – most private schools for instance have charitable status. Their aim is the enhancement of their pupils through education.
- *Charities and voluntary organisations* – their aims and objectives are led by the beliefs they stand for.

Changing Objectives

A Business may change its Objectives over time due to the Following Reasons:

- A business may achieve an objective and will need to move onto another one (e.g. survival in the first year may lead to an objective of increasing profit in the second year).
- The competitive environment might change, with the launch of new products from competitors.
- Technology might change product designs, so sales and production targets might need to change.

If you own a small business but are struggling to make it successful you might want to think about changing some things. There are a lot of things that go into a small business so the reason why your business is struggling could come from numerous things. One thing might be because you haven't set any business objectives. If you don't know how setting business objectives will improve your small business here is some information to make it a little more clearly for you.

The first thing is to know what type of objectives to set. You will want to take into consideration what type of small business you are first. Because depending on what type of small business you are might depend on what type of business objectives you have. You will want to make sure that your business has goals. Goals are an important thing to have because it makes you have something to work towards. Without goals you might not have the spark you need to keep your business going. Goals are something that helps you to decide where to take your business and what steps you need to get to the next level. You will want to make sure that you have both short and long term goals as well. The reason for this is so that you don't always feel like you have to do something more to achieve your goals by just having long term goals.

The second thing is to make sure that your objectives are spelled out. You want to make sure that your objectives are specific so that your employees and other people that are in with your small business know what you are talking about and what is expected of them.

The third thing is to be realistic in your objectives. You will want to make sure that you have objectives that do with quantities and qualitative. The reason for this is so that you know what you need to do to meet both of these criteria's. If you only have the object of quantities then your quality might not be that great because you are only focused on getting a certain number of products out the door. Same thing with just concentrating on the quality, doing this might make it so you don't put out as much which lowers your output.

The fourth thing to do is to make sure that you write down or document all of your objectives. The reason for this is because you might get off track and not remember what you first started out with wanting to achieve or how long you gave yourself to achieve different objectives. But if you write them down you will be able to refer back and see exactly what expectations you have had from the start. You will want to make sure that when you write them down that you include time limits. You will want to make sure that you put things on there that are both short range and long range targets as well.

These are just some of the examples of setting business objectives. If you set business objectives such as these ones your small business will improve. The reason for this is because you will be able to see what needs to change and what things need to improve to help you to reach different objectives which in return will help you to improve your small business. One thing that you might want to do before you set your business objectives is to do some research and see what type of things other small businesses are doing to help them improve their business. Doing this will also give you a better idea of how setting business objectives will improve your small business.

Why does a Good Business Relationship Rely on Having some Common Business Objectives?

As you attend networking events, you will gradually find ways that make it easy for you to mingle and be heard. Your message will need to be clear, focused and consistent each time. You will find that many of the people you met at one event will attend others you go to. These are the people that you will likely form a kind of bond with. It is these people you can work with to brainstorm on the best networking events to attend and those that have not panned out. This is also a way to start new business relationships. If you had not found anything in common with them before, you now have something to discuss. You can ask questions as to the type of business they are looking for and who their best customer is. You can also find out more about their business objectives and how they may mesh with what you are doing at the present time. The ultimate goal here is to get to the first appointment to explore possibilities. They may want to do business with you as much as you want to do business with them. Once you focus on commonalities between each company and commonalities between individuals, the business relationship has an opportunity to form. You are not selling at this point; you are simply trying to establish a good business relationship. Each of you may try a little of what the other has to offer in order to test the waters before the relationship can be solidified. The word business "pain" is flaunted regularly in marketing and sales circles and sometimes has very little meaning. Most organizations will not reveal their pain to anyone except an insider. If you are able to form a solid business relationship within the company, then you will be closer to finding out what improvements the company is striving for.

Business Possibilities

When choosing a what business you want to pursue, there are not only many different kinds of businesses you can run, but there are also a wide variety of business models that you should consider when deciding what is the right business for you. A good overview of all the kinds of businesses you could start can be found by looking at how the federal government classifies businesses. All federal data are now collected using the North American Industrial Classification System (NAICS) of Businesses. This system identifies 1170 industries each of which include a number of specific types of businesses. The 1170 industries are grouped into general categories: construction, education and health services, financial activities, government, information, leisure and hospitality, manufacturing, natural resources and mining, other services, professional and business services, transportaion and utilities, and wholesale and retail trade.

How Small Businesses can Achieve their Financial Objectives?

How small businesses can achieve their financial objectives? Not an easy question to answer. This becomes even harder to small business owner who's not literally with financial works. But there is some good clues that you can follow. There are no dark, deep secrets to financial management. The techniques are straightforward. Your accountant can help you in executing your financial management strategy. You can hire outside consultants to advise you on occasion. But it really comes down to you. You should understand and take the time to perform your critical strategy to achieve financial objectives of your business.

Financial Strategy-1. Understand Profit Mechanics

It may seem unnecessary to say so, you are in a business for profit, so you must understand how to make profit. You need a good business model to make profit, of course. And you need a profit model that you see clearly in your mind's eye.

Your regular profit and loss [P&L] report is indispensable for tracking your profit performance. But the P&L has too much detail for strategic level profit analysis. A good profit model should be small enough to reveal the following three key factors drive profit:

Key Factor-1: Unit margin (or, margin per unit): Equals the net price received from selling one unit of product or service, minus all variable expenses of selling the unit.

- Net price equals list price less all sales price reductions (discounts, rebates, and so on) and less expenses that come off the top of sales revenue (sales commissions, credit card fees, and so on).
- The main variable expense of a business that sells products is cost of goods (products) sold. A business may have other significant variable expenses, such as packing and shipping costs.

Key Factor-2: Sales volume: Equals the total quantity sold during the period. Unit margin times sales volume generates the margin earned from each product and service sold. All sources of sales combined generate the total margin of the business for the period, which equals profit before fixed expenses are considered.

Key Factor-3: Fixed expenses: Equals total amount of cost commitments that you can't escape or decrease during the period.

Examples are rents paid under lease contracts, depreciation, employees paid fixed salaries and wages, property taxes, and so on. Fixed costs provide sales capacity, which is the maximum volume that you can sell during the period.

Increasing sales volume increases profit — as long as you don't sacrifice unit margins on the products/services you sell and assuming that you stay within the sales capacity provided by your fixed expenses. Of course, it's better to increase sales of higher unit margin items than lower unit margin items.

Improving unit margin is challenging: You have to increase sales prices or reduce the variable costs of making sales, which are daunting tasks. But improving unit margin by say, 5 percent, may be more realistic than improving sales volume 5 percent. And, besides, you don't have to worry about crowding the limit of your sales capacity by improving unit margin.

Financial Strategy-2. Know Your Sources of Profit

Most small businesses consist of two or more parts. Our local cleaner, for example, does both laundry and dry cleaning, and the prices are very different between the two. Clothing stores have men and women's departments. New car dealers operate a service department as well as sell new and used vehicles. Many restaurants and coffee houses sell T-shirts and other souvenirs. You got the point.

Your accounting system should be organized to provide information for each major profit centre of your business. Basically, a profit centre is a separate source of sales revenue that you can assign direct costs to, in order to determine the margin earned for each part of your business. Margin is a measure of profit before considering the fixed expenses of the business. You need a P&L report [or income statement] for your business as a whole, of course, but it's just the tip of the iceberg. What's under the water line is just as important. You need to know the profitability of each location, each product line, and each department for each mainstream revenue source of your business. In a nut-shell, you should know the margin ratios and the amount of margin earned for every significant part of your business. The problem is how much detail to delve into. A local hardware store carries more than 100,000 different items.

The general manager doesn't have the time (or patience) to read through margin reports for all 100,000 items, of course. Generally, profit centres reflect the organizational structure of the business. For example: if you have two locations, you should get a separate margin report for each. If you make both wholesale and retail sales, you should treat each as a separate profit centre. Within each profit centre, you need further breakdown by products, customers, or on some other basis of making sales (over the Internet versus in-store, for example). Dividing your business into the right categories of sales and profit centres for management analysis and control is never easy. Consider getting the opinion of an outside consultant on how best to organize the reporting of profit centres.

Financial Startegy-3. Analyse Year-to-Year Profit Change

Suppose that your profit decreased 50 percent this year compared with last year. Shouldn't you know why? Shouldn't you find out the exact reasons for such a large drop in profit? Did sales volume shrink in some profit centres? Did unit margins change significantly? What happened to fixed expenses? I don't mean that you should take the time to do the detailed analysis. Ask your accountant to sort out the big changes from the small changes and to prepare a neat explanation of the key changes that caused the significant change in your profit.

In my experience, small business managers don't ask their accountants for a detailed year-to-year comparative analysis of profit. They rely on their gut feeling regarding the main reasons for the profit change. But without a thorough analysis, you can't be sure what caused the profit change. Spending time analysing the change in profit from period to period is quite valuable. For one thing, it encourages you and your accountant to develop an analytical profit model. Furthermore, doing a comparative profit analysis helps in budgeting next year's profit plan.

Financial Strategy-4. Budget Profit and Cash

I have discussed about budgeting and forecasting a lot [you can find them through categories available on the right side-bar]. So I won't repeat them here. I just want to remind you of the critical importance of forecasting and budgeting profit, cash flow, and financial condition for the coming year.

Your budgeted statement of cash flow for the coming year is especially important. It may reveal that you'll have to raise additional capital to finance your growth, and the earlier you get started on this task, the better.

I strongly urge you to give your accountant at least estimates of sales volume, sales prices, costs, and major changes you're planning in the coming year. With this information, your accountant can whip out an impressive set of pro forma budgeted financial statements for the coming year.

Financial Strategy-5. Understand the Cash Flow

Hypothetically, you can run your business so that cash flow equals profit [or loss] for the period. A dollar of profit would yield a dollar of cash inflow, or a dollar of loss would cause a dollar of cash outflow. You wouldn't own any fixed assets on which depreciation is recorded; rather, you'd have to lease all your long-term operating assets. You'd make only cash sales, or if you extend credit to customers, you'd have to collect all receivables by the end of the period. You'd carry no inventory of products for sale, or if you did, you'd have to sell all products by the end of the period. You wouldn't prepay any expenses. And you'd pay all expenses by the end of the period and have no accounts payable or accrued expenses payable on the books. In this theoretical case, cash flow equals profit (or loss).

Of course, you can't really restrict your business that way. You may have to carry inventory; you may have receivables from credit sales; you may invest in fixed assets; and you may have unpaid bills and other unpaid expenses at the end of the period. These factors cause cash flow to differ from your bottom line profit or loss for the period.

Here are two principal examples of why cash flow differs from profit:

- Suppose that your accounts receivable (uncollected receivables from credit sales) increases $50,000 during the year, and annual sales revenue is $1,000,000. Therefore, cash flow from sales through the end of the year is $50,000 less than sales revenue. In other words, profit includes $50,000 of uncollected sales revenue.
- Suppose that $85,000 depreciation expense is recorded for the year. The cost balance of your fixed assets was written down $85,000 to recognize the use of your fixed assets during the year, and the fixed assets moved one year closer to their eventual disposal. The fixed assets were bought and paid for years ago. Therefore, profit includes an expense that required no cash outlay during the year.

The bottom line on cash flow is this;

- Start with net income or loss for the period, as if this amount were your cash flow for the period (but remember that it isn't).
- Next, add back depreciation. Don't stop here.
- Deduct increases in accounts receivable, inventory, and prepaid expenses.
- Or, add back decreases in these assets.
- Add back increases in accounts payable and accrued expenses payable.
- Or, deduct decreases in these two types of operating liabilities.

Now wasn't that easy? Of course, you don't do all this arithmetic; that's the job for your accountant. Your job is to understand why these adjustments are made to profit to determine cash flow.

Financial Strategy-6. Keep Sizes of Assets Under Control

Marketing types like to say that nothing happens until you sell it. Sales and marketing is the heart of every successful business. You make profit by making sales. But you can't make sales without assets. You need a working cash balance. You need inventory if you sell products and receivables if you sell on credit. You need to own a variety of fixed assets (although you can lease many of them). Your short-term operating liabilities (accounts payable and unpaid accrued expenses) supply part of your total assets. The rest comes from debt and equity capital. Suppose that your total asset minus your total operating liabilities equals $500,000. So you have to raise $500,000 capital. The owners [the partners in a partnership, the share owners in a limited liability company, or the stockholders of a corporation] can put up the entire $500,000 capital. However, you probably would go to debt sources for part of your total capital. Both sources of capital have a cost. The cost of debt is interest, as you know. The cost of equity capital is higher; it's the rate of return that you should earn on the equity capital invested in the business. If your interest rate on debt is 8 percent, the owners expect you to earn an annual profit equal to 10, 15, or an even higher percent of return on their capital.

Don't overindulge in assets. Keep the sizes of your assets to no more than they have to be to make sales and conduct the operations of the business. Like people, businesses tend to get fat if they don't watch their weight.

Financial Strategy-7. Stabilize Your Sources of Capital

Raising capital is always a challenge for most startup business ventures. Raising capital during the early days of a business may be done in fits and starts and often lacks an overall cohesion and sense of continuity. This situation may be unavoidable during the hectic startup period of a new business. Once your business gets traction, it's very important to settle down on a steady policy for your sources of capital. Your lenders and owners will demand that you develop a predictable capital strategy for operating and growing your business.

Financial Strategy-8. Choose the Right Legal Entity

Certain types of legal organizations are treated as pass-through entities for income tax purposes. The business doesn't itself pay income tax. A pass-through entity must determine its annual taxable income. Its taxable income is divided up among its owners in proportion to the ownership shares of each, and the owners include their shares of the business's taxable income in their individual income tax returns.

In contrast, a regular, or so-called C-corporation doesn't have this advantage. It's subject to income tax on its taxable income. Distributions from its after-tax net income to its stockholders are subject to a second income tax in the hands of the individual stockholders. As you probably know, the income tax law is complex. You should get the advice of an income tax professional on the best legal form of organization.

Strategy-9. Understand Internal Controls

Last [but not least] is internal control. I have talked about internal controls a lot too. Small businesses are notorious for having weak internal controls and, therefore, are vulnerable to errors and fraud. Your business may be the exception, but don't bet on it. Although this strategy is on the last paragraph, it does not necessarily mean it is the least important. You lock the doors at the end of the day, don't you? In like manner, you should institute protective procedures to prevent fraud and establish checks and balances to minimize errors. My advice [if you need it] is to hire a CPA to do a critical examination of your internal controls. It is money well spent.

2

How to Plan and Organize a Small Business

How to Become a Fearless Small Business Owner

Step 1: Go Fishing for the Real You.

It's time to focus on what you do better than anyone else and put that out there to your customers and prospects. You have to peel away all the layers that have made you a jack of all trades and hone your skills to become an expert at something that's valuable right now. Perhaps you own a boutique ad agency and you can design anything, but what you do best work is build b-to-b websites. That's your vein of gold, and where you can drive revenue to your customer's bottom line.

Step 2: Use Your Differences as a Lure.

In extraordinary economic times like these, the natural tendency is to just hunker down, do the work, cut back on expenses and try not to lose the business you have. News flash: That's exactly the strategy that will probably hang you. Because if you're not standing up, standing out, and standing for something important, your days may be numbered. Use the strengths of what makes you different to make a difference with your customers.

Step 3: Find a Few Fish like You.

Step 3 on the path to fearlessness is to build relationships so that you can anchor yourself in these rough seas. Now is the time to reward your customers for their loyalty, get on an airplane and see them, take them out to lunch (nothing fancy or you'll look out of touch), and stay connected through social networking sites. This is the moment to deepen customer relationships to ensure your security and your company's future.

Step 4: Swim in Their Ocean Your Way.

Every time you pitch a prospect you are a fish out of water. When you finally get inside, it's important to learn how to be part of the culture without getting lost in it. As a small business owner, it can be deadly to get so entrenched with someone else's culture or demands that you can't find the real you. Instead look for what resonates with you and don't buy into what doesn't feel right. Stay true to your core values. If you don't, at the end of this recession, you may not recognize yourself or your own company.

Step 5: Put Yourself Out on the Line.

Businesses who shine a light on what's different about them are perfectly positioned to make a difference. It's not the wallflower who's going to help their customers go green, or the conformist who will invent the new business model. Getting behind a cause is good for business and makes you look like a hero. Volunteer, join a board, make a major donation. You may be paralysed by fear and feel like every minute you need to push that rock up the hill. Shake it off. Give to others instead and watch what you receive in return.

Step 6: Evolve by Casting a Wide Net.

Conformity is not distinguishing. The way to live deeply is to keep reinventing yourself, changing with the times and with the your customers. Holding onto the essential you while updating your style, your website, your advertising and your thinking is the fastest way to the top. Step 6 of being a Fearless Fish asks that you use your place outside the circle to always be relevant to your customers and industry. It's about staying true to the essence of who you are, and then recasting your image to feel brand new.

Step 7: Reel in Your Unique Power.

Uncertainty makes everyone question their personal value and the value of their business. The fearless among us overcome these doubts by practicing their ABCs—action, belief, and courage. It's time to stop wringing your hands and start raising your hand to make a difference. Believes in ourselves can either propel us, or hinder us. The story that you tell about your company is what others will believe. Use your unique power to make them believe that you are indispensable and that is exactly what you will be!

Planning Organizing and Managing of Small Business

Starting/Buying a Small Business

Starting a business is a busy time. Not only are you trying to produce a product or service that is marketable, but you are also putting together all the organizational details that are the basis of the business. The information here is presented to help you make certain you have covered all the bases on your way to a successful business venture.

Once you have decided that you want to own a small business, you need to decide whether you want to buy a business, buy a franchise, get involved in a multi-level marketing (MLM) business, or start from scratch. If you are buying a business, franchise or MLM business, do check to make certain it is not a scam before making any commitments.

Many of you may know that you want to start a business, but don't know what exact business you want to start. Take a look at the list of business possibilities to get ideas for businesses you might run and what the investment, financially and time-wise would be.

Whatever choice you are making for your business, there are a variety of business models, such as whether it is home-based or office-based, that will have some bearing on how you run the business. The more specific you can be at this stage about what will work for you, the higher your probability of success. You certainly don't want to get into a business, and then discover that you have not considered something that makes a vital difference in how you feel about running this particular business.

If you are buying a business, you will have a functional business in place. You may wish to change how it operates, but you will not have the startup concerns that a new business implies. I have put together a Startup Checklist for those of you who are starting fresh. The checklist includes the steps you need to cover to help you make certain you have covered all the bases.

Business Models

There is more to deciding on the right business other than settling on the actual product or service you will be producing. Here are a number of other factors that may be a consideration in identifying the right model for your business.

Buy a Franchise vs. Join a Direct Marketing Business vs. Start from Scratch

This is a question of how ready you are to plan and implement every aspect of your business. Direct marketing businesses and franchises train and support you, but your flexibility of what you offer is limited. It also can be costly to buy into an established business. Franchises do usually have a track record and marketing that can be a bonus to get your business going.

Look carefully into any direct marketing businesses you might consider. They can require tremendous investments that often cannot be recovered if you decide it is not the right path for you.

Home-based vs. Office-based

Some people are looking for a business they can operate out of their home; others feel more productive when they separate their business from their home life. Zoning laws may limit the types of businesses you can do from your home. You also may have space limitations that limit your choices. Home-based businesses can be lonely. Office-based businesses may bring hassles with other tenants if you are renting or cashflow if you purchase.

Invent Something New vs. Produce a Product vs. Offer a Service vs. Consult as an Independent Contractor

Inventions are usually solitary activities that require a lot of creativity. Products require manufacturing facilities, supplies, and distribution; services are more people-oriented, often facing deadlines not of your own choosing. Independent contracting can be the best of all worlds, although continually finding new contracts can cause cash flow problems.

Long Term Commitment vs. Build a Business to Sell

Some people have every intention of staying in this business forever. It is the realization of a dream. Others dream of making their money through starting new businesses, then selling them. The rush for them is the joy of starting something new over and over. Such folks are sometimes called "serial entrepreneurs." Each way of operating requires a very different financial model. Be honest with yourself about what is right for you so that you can structure your business plan accordingly.

Not-for-profit vs. Profit-based

Not-for-profits can be very emotionally rewarding, but are often low pay, although as with any business you can set your own pay within the budget of the business. There also extra legal hoops to jump through to run a not-for-profit business. If you dream of a solid nest egg or even fame and fortune, a profit-based business may be the best path for you.

Online vs. Physical Business (or Both)

Online businesses are often the choice of people who want a home-based business, but they are not synonymous. Online businesses can be any size and in any location. They can be worldwide or local. Physical businesses are almost always local unless there is a mail-order or commerce component. Each of these types of businesses is different to manage and run. Don't let other factors like wanting to be home-based influence your decision on this. If you like activity and hate computers, the internet is not the right spot for you. Grow vegetables instead.

Sell Your Product or Service in a Physical Location vs. Contracting Your Goods or Services Out to the Federal or State Government Selling as a contractor has lots of rules, regulations, and paperwork, but can provide a lot of flexibility and a great cash flow. Selling locally (or nationally) is a totally different kind of marketing effort, but in many ways less hassle. One of the biggest areas of contracting is the federal government. The Small Business Administration has a number of programs to help with selling to the government. So, do take a look at some of the pros and cons if you think this might be something of interest to you.

Size of Business

Some entrepreneurs simply want to make enough to live simply. Others are looking to build another Microsoft. There are two components to consider in size. What is a comfortable size to start for you and how big do you eventually want to get? Some folks who are new to business want to be on their own to learn the ropes before adding employees, others who have managed before may be more comfortable having at least a few employees to share the workload. Your strengths and weaknesses will help you assess your short-term objective. Your own personal goals will help you determine your long-term objective.

Skills Needed

You may have a dream of what business you want to have eventually, but not have the skills yet. Education may need to be part of your business plan. Even for those of you who have a basic idea of what the business entails, the more you can learn about it, the better a business you will have. Make certain you know what skills are required for a business and how your strengths and weaknesses fit with those skills.

Urban vs. Rural

Urban businesses and rural businesses frequently have different constraints and different models. Marketing can be very different. It can make a difference in what business you choose. You may have always wanted to move to a rural location or vice versa and are taking the opportunity of starting a business to explore such a change. Do be aware of the differences in population density, consumer behaviour and zoning laws, to name only a few of the differences you will experience by changing location. Learn as much as you can before taking this leap.

Buying a Business

For many entrepreneurs the idea of starting a business from scratch may seem overwhelming. For them, buying an existing business or a franchise is often a viable alternative.

Finding profitable businesses for sale at reasonable prices can be difficult. Business owners often have an inflated idea of the market value of the business. There are, however, many resources for finding profitable businesses for sale. Depending upon the type of business you are interested in buying you can find many listed in local and online classified ads. Business brokers are also available locally and online.

Do watch out for business opportunities that are scams. The Federal Trade Commission provides a substantial amount of information about scams and false business opportunities. The Better Business Bureau is also a good resource about deceptive practices that a business may have engaged in. You also may want to take a look at Business Opportunity Scams and Work at Home Schemes.

Advantages of Buying a Business

Among the many favourable aspects to buying an existing business is the drastic reduction in start-up costs. In addition, cash flow may be immediate because of existing inventory and receivables. Other positive side effects include existing goodwill and easier financing opportunities.

Disadvantages of Buying a Business

Among the biggest downsides to buying a small business is the initial cost of the purchase. Because developing the business concept, customer base, brands and other fundamental work has already been done, the costs of acquiring an existing business may greater then starting up a new business. Other possible disadvantages include hidden problems associated with the business and receivables that are valued at the time of purchase, but later turn out to be non-collectable.

Once you have found a business you might want to buy, you will need to research the business to determine whether the stated reasons for selling are valid and whether it is valued appropriately. Additionally, you need to conduct due diligence and draw up an airtight sales agreement.

It is important during the closing to make sure that you have legal counsel available to review all of the documentation necessary for the transfer of the business. Consult this checklist to make certain everything is in order before you close the sale.

Choosing Your Business Name

For some people business names come easily, for others finding the right one is a major challenge. In How to Name Your Business I have listed the basic steps to follow in naming a business. If you are feeling really stymied, you may need to examine ways to inspire your creativity to give you an initial list of names. There are multiple "rules-of-thumb" that tend to be contradictory. Some insist that a business name should be descriptive of the business, others suggest being unique is the best way to be remembered.

Keep in mind that your business name is an important part of your marketing effort. It is a major component of how customers' perceive your business. Your business image is based on this perception. So, it is critical that it reflect the image that you want customers to have of your business.

My tendency is to go with what your inner voice (also referred to more primitively as "your gut") says is right for you. You are the one who has to live with this business day and night for a long time to come. So choose something you feel good about. One test might be to think about the name being splashed across a major headline (how about "Your Business Reports Phenomenal Profits"?). How does it feel to see that name in print representing your business? If it feels good, go with it.

If all else fails, there are businesses available that will help you find the right name and even provide an overall branding image for you. If you decide to go this route, look for a good fit for you. A positive first impression helps. How does their website fit with how you would like to be perceived? While not definitive, it certainly expresses their "style." Also, take time to think through what are the critical components of the name for you before approaching any business name vendor. You want this to reflect your concept, not someone else's. Keep in mind this is one of the most important decisions you will make about our business. It will determine how others perceive your business from now on.

As part of naming your business, you may also want to design a logo for your business. Again, if creativity is not your long suit, many of the businesses that help in naming will also design a logo. While all this may seem excessive, you will never regret the time you have spent on this part of setting up your business. This is the first piece and most critical part of marketing your business. Do it right and your future marketing will be much easier to plan and implement.

Legal Issues

Picking a name for your business requires much more than just creativity and a working knowledge of your target market. First, you'll need to decide which business structure you will use, since each structure has its own peculiarities. For example, many states require a sole proprietor to use their own name as the business name unless they formally file another name as a trade name, or "fictitious name."

Of equal importance if finding out whether your name or a very similar name is being used by another business, and if so, what rights they may or may not have to use the name in the area where you do business. Keep in mind that some businesses only file trademarks within their locality, so it's possible that the same name can be used elsewhere.

Search and Registration

Trade names can be registered through state Secretary of State offices, and for wider marketplace protection, through the U.S. Patent and Trademark office (USPTO). Businesses should first use the USPTO's online system to search all state and federal trademark registers to see if their proposed name is being used.

Domain Names

For many businesses that operate on the Web, trade names are synonymous with domain names, such as Amazon.com and Monster.com. Domain names are not registered through state or local government. Rather they can be obtained through online businesses, which will allow you to conduct a name search prior to purchase to make sure your chosen name isn't taken.

Equipping your Business

The equipment choices for any business these days is enormous-answering machines, cell phones, videoconferencing, telephones with multiple services built in, fax machines, digital cameras, folding machines, xerox machines, and more.

Do you need all of these? Each business differs in answering that question. Tools I vowed I would never buy are now a powerful part of my everyday work process. For me, the primary consideration is how much time is the tool going to take to learn to use well as compared to time lost to finding other solutions to replace that function.

A simple example is a fax machine. Not having a fax machine can mean lost business opportunities, but the addition of machine means learning to use the machine, maintaining it, keeping supplies on hand, and deciding whether it warrants an additional phone line. There are now multipurpose machines on the market that can handle more than one of these functions.

The downside of multifunction machines is that if it is broken, you lose not only your fax capabilities, but also your copy capabilities and perhaps even your printing capabilities. Whereas if you had both a fax machine and a copy machine, you could always make copies on the fax machine should the copier be broken. Making backup plans for down time on all your equipment is critical because it will happen no matter how well you take care of your equipment.

Making the right choices for your business means you need to think through some typical transactions for your business and what you will need to make them happen. Most importantly, set a budget and live within it. Decide on the minimum you can live with to start. List the

Plantation Crop Based Farming System

The monoculture in small holdings is a nightmare during the year of slump and epidemic of pest and diseases. Raising more than one crops alongwith a particular plantation crop not only reduce the gestation period but also ensure steady and higher farm income even in the period of slump. Seasonal crops like vegetables in the formative years of the plantation crops and permanent crops like orange, arecanut, agar, tree beans, black pepper, gooseberry etc. could be grown in the matured plantation to augment productivity and profitability. Intercropping also stands as insurance against crop failure and price slump.

Premium Organic Farming

The organically, grown products have been gaining popularity worldwide and fetching premium price both at the domestic as well as international market. Since the virgin soil in the hill areas is favourable for tea cultivation, the natural production condition in the NE India could be highly gainful in the production of user-friendly tea. On account of high amount of organic matter and other plant nutrients in these soils, the plantation crops can be grown organically with minimum of agro-chemicals. The strategy to produce organic tea and popularize among the consumers would pay high dividend.

Such innovation in value-addition of tea is potentially economically remunerative and helps conserve the precious soil and water resource.

Constraints

The cultivation of these plantation crops in the region has been traditionally a corporate activity. The production system is also highly knowledge intensive and scale biased. Therefore, the expansion of small-scale tea in the recent period confronts number of constraints including lack of information and extension services, timely supply of processing facilities and lack of required knowledge of agronomic practices. Inadequate training infrastructure to prepare the required skills among the farmers is also a reason for slow growth. Thus, the early stage of transition in the plantation economy requires effective planning strategies.

The post-harvest management in plantation crops is very crucial. The green leaves require quick processing facility and then necessary market facilities must follow, or else there could be total loss of production due to quality deterioration.

Perfect knowledge is essential in every stage of the production of tea; viz, production, harvesting, processing and marketing. Hence information technology becomes crucial. Capital requirement is particularly very high in the initial period. The common farmers find it difficult to invest the high amount without adequate institutional financial assistance, which is essential for the promotion of small-scale tea cultivation. In recent years, Tea, Coffee and Rubber Boards have introduced a number of schemes to promote the crops under small sector. NABARD also assists the tea growers. But indepth studies on the subject is severely lacking. It makes the information system on the knowledge on financial requirement, availability of credit and other constraints extremely scarce.

There is vast scope for expansion of tea, coffee and rubber in the region. Adequate policy support is needed to intensify small-scale cultivation of these crops in suitable areas. The production of tea could be enhanced if certain management practices are improved. The commodity boards such as Tea, Coffee and Rubber Boards have already taken various schemes to popularize respective crops in the region. More promotional schemes are essential as majority of the existing large tea gardens in Assam have crossed the economic age and some are over 70-80 years old. As a result, this has caused steep shortfall in production of tea. Thus scheme of replacing the older trees and replanting or expansion planting should be implemented. If the system is modernized and adequate technological changes are brought about, the sector could enhance the export earnings substantially.

Cluster Village Plantation: Emergence of Small-scale Tea Cultivation

With the emergence of small-scale tea cultivation, the nature of technological requirement has changed tremendously. The demand for efficient plant type, improved crop management practices and post-harvest technology would grow substantially in due course of time. This would require concerted effort in terms of private-public interface on R&D including the promotion of delivery system. The prestigious corporate bodies should invest more on effective demand-driven R&D on these crops. The limitation of the plantation crops is that processing is time-demanding and urgent. The harvest must be processed into marketable forms within a specified time to preserve the quality. Thus growth of plantation sector must be tagged with the establishment of need to be following. For businesses operating in other countries, there are a wide variety of regulations. Check with international resources for locating the regulations that may apply for the country you are in or would like to do business in.

Not only are there laws and regulations governing the actual registration of the business and the business name, but there may also be licenses and permits needed to operate certain types of businesses. For instance, a restaurant may need health department or liquor licensing, a hair stylist may need to be licensed within their profession, or a child care service may need to have special permits from social service or educational agencies. You can find out more about such regulations from your state business resource offices.

You also may want to trademark your business name and/or logo. Take a look at Patents, Copyrights, and Trademarks to find out how to protect that valuable name you worked so hard to choose.

The one step we have ignored so far, but that is an integral part of your legal structure is what kind of business do you want to have? Your choices are a sole proprietorship, a business partnership, a limited liability company (LLC) or a corporation. Follow the simple How to Choose the Legal Form of a Business if you have no idea which would be right for you. The legal structure you choose is not permanently binding, but there can be complications in changing so consider it carefully. One final step you may want to take to provide a good legal base for your business-and that is to identify a good attorney that you can use should you need legal advice. Establishing a relationship now can be good for opening opportunities in the future as well as having someone well versed in your business goals as an advisor as your business develops. To find a good attorney, ask your banker, your accountant or other professionals in your field for recommendations. Then put together a list of questions and interview more than one finalist to see who is a good fit for you and your business.

Organizing a Small Business

Your business plan states the objectives for your business. Your next step is to figure out how you are going to accomplish those objectives. Without organization timelines are not going to be met and goals will not be accomplished. Organization needs to happen on both a macro-and a micro-level; i.e., the macro-level is how you structure the business itself, the micro-level is how you run the business on a daily basis. An organization chart is a good to thing to have even for one person organizations, as silly as that might sound. A good organization chart details the processes that need to occur to produce the product or service for your business. It is a good visual way to see the overview of your business on a macro-level. Another important part of organizing is having a good time management system. Small business owners always have too much to do. Time management is a critical to literally keeping sane. Set yourself up with a system you can live with and live it. On the micro-level there are a lot of little things you can do to make the business function effectively. Here are some simple how-tos that will help you organize better on a day-to-day basis.

How to Organize Meetings

Meetings can be the most dreaded part of business, yet they are essential to good communication. Make them a positive part of your business operation by organizing them well.

How to Set Your Priorities

Do you get to the end of the week and wonder what you got done? None of the items on your list have been completed. Here are some ways to set priorities and follow them.

Organization Charts

Even if you are a one person business, constructing some kind of organization chart will help you see what functions need to be performed so that you can make certain everything is getting done. To show you how this is done, here is an example of a simple organization chart for a one-person retail business.

Retail Business

The Buying Function	*The Selling Function*	*The Controlling Function*
Checking catalogs	Advertising	Cashiering
Finding suppliers	Doing inside displays	Checking invoices
Placing Orders	Maintaining a clean store	Issuing credit
Receiving and stocking	Pricing	Keeping records
Seeing salespersons	Selling	Making bank deposits
Taking inventory	Trimming windows	Paying bills
Viewing showrooms		Securing loans

How to Organize Meetings

Meetings can be the most dreaded part of business, yet they are essential to good communication. Make them a positive part of your business operation by organizing them well.

To Organize a Meeting:

1. Decide exactly who should attend the meeting.
2. Schedule a time for the meeting with the persons attending, making it clear what the meeting is about and how long it will take.
3. Schedule a place for the meeting that is conducive to discussion and does not allow interruptions.
4. Plan an agenda with a time schedule for addressing each issue.
5. Distribute the agenda well in advance of the meeting, asking for any modifications or additions.
6. Once the meeting starts there should be one person in charge who manages the meeting and facilitates discussion.
7. The meeting leader should stimulate and clarify communication, summarizing points made.
8. Consensus should be encouraged, but don't make that the endpoint.
9. If more information is needed for making decisions, schedule another meeting with homework assignments.
10. At the end of the meeting clarify what has transpired and what the next steps are.
11. Distribute a summary of decisions reached at the meeting, including the date and time of any future meetings.

Tips:

1. It is important to include all critical parties for a meeting, but any number greater than eight reduces the meeting's effectiveness.
2. The person running the meeting should be a facilitator who is there to listen, not an active participant.
3. Meetings do not need to be held for lengthy reporting. Reports can be written and circulated for comments.

How to set your Priorities

Do you get to the end of the week and wonder what you got done? None of the items on your list have been completed. Here are some ways to set priorities and follow them.

To set Priorities:

1. Make as comprehensive a list as possible of everything you can think of that needs to be done.
2. Make another list of your personal goals for the business, for example, have a certain profit level or number of clients over a certain time frame.
3. Make one more list of what you want from this business. Lots of money? Personal satisfaction? Steady income and a good reputation.
4. Compare list two and list three. Are they basically in agreement? If not, revise number two. Your business goals need to agree with what is important to you.
5. Now go back that big long list from step one. Relate each of those items to list two, giving each job a priority based on how closely they align with the goals you are hoping to achieve.
6. Now take one more pass through list one rating each of the high priority items by A: this needs to happen right away and B: these are not crucial immediately.
7. Take the A items and choose three to work on in the next 24 hours.
8. Don't even think about the other items unless you finish all three in that 24 hour period.
9. Revisit your lists for a brief period at the same time each day, revising based on new information.
10. When revising your lists, check off the items that are done by placing them on a done list. Then at intervals you can see visible proof of what you have accomplished!
11. If you feel you are not making the progress on reaching your priorities at the pace you would like, it may be time to hire someone to help.

Tips:

1. Some businesses do not need daily lists. Weekly or even monthly

can be sufficient in ventures that operate in a slow market with longer time frames.

2. Keeping your lists on a computer allows you add, delete and move items around easily.
3. Make certain your first list includes items like 'start planning for taxes. Don't wait for the deadline for something to give it a high priority. Give early planning a place on the list.

Operating a Small Business

There are a wide variety of ways to put together the operations of your business so that it functions effectively and efficiently. The model that works best for you will be related to your objectives, what your product or service is, and your personal operational style. However, there are a number of functions that every business needs to address simply as part of doing business. Here are some topics that you need to know about to keep your business running with minimal effort:

Financial Management

The bookkeeping and accounting systems, record keeping, taxes, collecting money, insurance, budgeting, and managing risk are all part of keeping your business financially solvent. While many people consider this the most painful part of running a business, it needs to handled well if you are going to stay in business.

Legal Management

You don't need to have a lawyer in house, but you definitely need to make certain that all the operations of your business are legal. Some of the issues to consider are business licenses, determining the correct legal form of your business, alliance agreements, copyrights, trademarks, patents, contracts with suppliers, and employment law.

Management of the Business as a Whole

Someone needs to be in charge of keeping the business functioning on a day-to-day basis and planning for its future. The manager, CEO, boss-whatever you want to call that function-sees that the business objectives are met. Planning, organizing, staffing (human resources), directing (leadership), and controlling are the traditional realms of management. Learn what those functions really involve.

Marketing

Marketing involves getting the message out to customers about your product or service. The traditional nomenclature in marketing are the four P's: product, price, promotion, and place (distribution). Each of these functional areas involves a lot of coordination and planning to arrive at the best advertising, public relations, and sales package to best present your product or service to the customer.

Office Management

You have to have a place to operate your business and the proper equipment to accomplish its tasks. Putting together the right space, furniture, and equipment to make your business operate efficiently is something that needs careful consideration.

Production

Whatever your business, you are producing something that you hope to sell. That means you need to have a production process in place that will help you make certain that you have a quality product when you need it, produced the way you planned it. Lackadaisical production is costly. There are some standard production models that can help make this part of your business operate efficiently and economically.

Financial Management

Financial Management is the process of managing the financial resources, including accounting and financial reporting, budgeting, collecting accounts receivable, risk management, and insurance for a business.

The financial management system for a small business includes both how you are financing it as well as how you manage the money in the business.

In setting up a financial management system your first decision is whether you will manage your financial records yourself or whether you will have someone else do it for you. There are a number of alternative ways you can handle this. You can manage everything yourself; hire an employee who manages it for you; keep your records in-house, but have an accountant prepare specialized reporting such as tax returns; or have an external bookkeeping service that manages financial transactions and an accountant that handles formal reporting functions. Some accounting firms also handle bookkeeping functions. Software packages are also available for handling bookkeeping and accounting.

Bookkeeping refers to the daily operation of an accounting system, recording routine transactions within the appropriate accounts. An accounting system defines the process of identifying, measuring, recording and communicating financial information about the business. So, in a sense, the bookkeeping function is a subset of the accounting system. A bookkeeper compiles the information that goes into the system. An accountant takes the data and analyses it in ways that give you useful information about your business. They can advise you on the systems needed for your particular business and prepare accurate reports certified by their credentials. While software packages are readily available to meet almost any accounting need, having an accountant at least review your records can lend credibility to your business, especially when dealing with lending institutions and government agencies.

Setting up an accounting system, collecting bills, paying employees, suppliers, and taxes correctly and on time are all part of running a small business. And, unless accounting is your small business, it is often the bane of the small business owner. Setting up a system that does what you need with the minimum of maintenance can make running a small business not only more pleasant, but it can save you from problems down the road.

The basis for every accounting system is a good Bookkeeping system. What is the difference between that and an accounting system? Think of accounting as the big picture of how your business runs — income, expenses, assets, liabilities — an organized system for keeping track of how the money flows through your business, keeping track that it goes where it is supposed to go. A good bookkeeping system keeps track of the nuts and bolts — the actual transactions that take place. The bookkeeping system provides the numbers for the accounting system. Both accounting and bookkeeping can be contracted out to external firms if you are not comfortable with managing them yourself.

Even if you outsource the accounting functions, however, you will need some type of Record keeping Systems to manage the day-to-day operations of your business-in addition to a financial plan and a budget to make certain you have thought through where you are headed in your business finances. And, your accounting system should be producing Financial Statements. Learning to read them is an important skill to acquire.

Another area that your financial management system needs to address is risk. Any good system should minimize the risks in your business. Consider implementing some of these risk management strategies in your business. Certainly, insurance needs to be considered not only for your property, office, equipment, and employees, but also for loss of critical employees. Even in businesses that have a well set up system, cash flow can be a problem. There are some tried and true methods for Managing Cash Shortages that can help prevent cash flow problems and deal with them if they come up. In the worst case you may have difficulties meeting all you debt obligations. Take a look at Financial Difficulties to learn more about ways to manage situations in which you have more debt than income.

It is possible you may even be at the a point where you want to sell the business or simply close it and liquidate assets. There are financial issues involved for these circumstances too. So, be certain that you know what steps you need to take in order to protect yourself financially in the long run.

Clearly, financial management encompasses a number of crucial areas of your business. Take time to set them up right. It will make a significant difference in your stress levels and in the bottom line for your business.

Accounting Systems

Your accounting system should provide an accurate picture of your business and how it is doing. Setting up a good accounting system and understanding the numbers producd can make a major difference in how your business fares in the long run. The financial statements produced from your accounting system will help you with:

Pricing your Product Accurately

Pricing your product is the first single most important thing you have to do in business. It's a simple equation, which says that you have to charge more than it costs you, right?? So tell me, what about paying back that loan that you opened last winter when you couldn't meet your workers compensation bill? What about the tools you put on your MasterCard for the last job? What about product liability insurance? There's a long list you're likely forgetting, or if not forgetting, discounting beyond reality. Nearly anyone can figure out the direct costs of their product or service-a good set of books will tell you just what ought to go into that equation for overhead, which is the difference between making a profit or loss.

Know If you are Making Money

Are you making money? Well, even after you price your product, you have to know how your pricing compares with reality. If you are making some bad decisions with your pricing, and you wait until next April 14th to find out whether you've lost or made money, it may be too late to do anything about it. Running a business profitably is tough. It can take a long time for some of your decisions to prove right or wrong, even with good books. Give yourself a break and at least be paying attention so you see things happening soon enough to correct them.

Work with Bankers

As much as possible, have your numbers organized on a cash flow spreadsheet before you go to the bank. If you're already working with a bank, impress them with good numbers. I don't mean good in the sense of whitewashed, at all. I mean good in the sense of accurate. With good books, you will see problems coming before they happen. Go talk with your banker about them in advance, and you will have a better chance of getting and keeping that person on your side. A side note about relationships-never go in thinking that your relationship with your banker is adversarial by definition. The opposite is true-that relationship has to be one of teamwork and understanding. To look at your banker as an adversary from whom you should hide bad information is a huge mistake. Find a banker you can talk to and work with, and keep him/her posted, good or bad. Develop those relationships, and they'll stick by you as long as they can.

Taxes

Use books that you've prepared for your decision making, and maybe the results won't be a surprise. If your books are done and you know before the end of the year what taxes you have to pay, chances are you can save yourself money by paying ahead, or by buying tools that you know you will need. At any rate, your tax accountant can help you do whatever planning you need to do, but you cannot do that in the absence of good information.

Cash vs. Accrual Accounting

There are two ways handling your accounting records: cash or accrual. The cash method does not account for payments due or bills due. When you write the check, you enter the expense. When you receive money, you enter the sale. The accrual method keeps track of what expenses actually apply to the current period.

As an example of the differences, in the cash method if you receive a check for deposit on a house in December, and start the work in March, you are going to be taxed one year on the money you have taken in, and the next year show a loss because of your expenses of building the house. With the accrual method, on the other hand, you put the money in the accounting period where it actually is used. You pay the expenses the same month as you enter the sale, so it all makes sense.

Most small businesses will want to use the accrual method of accounting. Even if you aren't required to do so for tax purposes, you will have a better idea of where you stand month to month if you record your expenses as they are incurred.

Financial Statements

To appreciate bookkeeping and accounting, you need to understand why you are doing what you're doing with these numbers, and what knowledge your results will give you. The result you are working toward is good information that which will be available to you from your financial statements. There are a wide variety of financial statements you can generate with the most common ones being a balance sheet and an income statement. These each take a different view on what is essentially the same information.

The Income Statement (also called a profit and loss statement) simply shows income and expenses for a given time period. It gives you a picture of you are making money or losing money over that time interval.

The Balance Sheet looks at the bigger picture of your business comparing all your assets to all your liabilities. It tells you if you closed the business and sold everything today, how much money would you have (or how much would you owe). The reason this is called a Balance Sheet is that Assets need to balance (equal) the Liabilities. The amount you would have if everything were liquidated today is called Net Worth and is listed under Liabilities. If have more Liabilities than Assets, the Net Worth is negative.

Although some business owners want to see the income statement and may ignore the balance sheet, you need to use both together to see the total picture of what is happening in your business. What makes accounting useful is the relationship between the numbers on the financial statements, and the things you can learn when you understand them.

Here are some other financial statements that are useful to have:

Operating Budget

A budget projects sales and expenses for each month of a year to estimate the flow of cash. This helps you predict times that you may have cash shortfalls and prepare for them. It also allows you to compare over the year how you are performing in relation to your projections.

Cash flow Statement

This may be one of the most critical and least understood documents you can prepare. Some of the information that can be gained from this statement is:

- Are the operating activities generating cash? It is not critical if they are not, but it is a good sign if they are.
- Which working capital components have large uses of cash? What might be happening to cause this? This helps you understand how the cash got used.
- How much cash is provided for or used in investing activities? Compare this year's capital expenditures to last year's capital expenditures. Were there any significant increases or decreases? A reduction in capital expenditures may indicate a cash flow problem.
- What cash is provided by or used in financing activities? This will tell you how much debt has been paid (or borrowed.) It will indicate if you are using more debt or have paid down your credit line in the past year. It will also tell you if there were other unusual financing activities which were not highlighted elsewhere in the analysis.

Ratios and Quality Indicators

Financial ratios look at relationships between various numbers generated by your financial statements. The ratios allow you to analyse how different aspects of your business are functioning. If there are problems, they help you locate what is causing the problems. The ratios give you a deeper look into specific parts of your business so that you can see what is working and what is not.

Developing a set of Financial Statements

To develop a set of financial statements, you have to start with a plan for how you will organize the information. This plan is called your Chart of Accounts. It is the framework upon which the financial statements are built. In your business, you have expenses that are going directly into your product-labour, materials, freight. There are also indirect costs that are more supportive (and ongoing) in nature-utilities, telephone, and the cost of bookkeeping. An easy way to distinguish the two is that direct expenses stop when you don't have work. Indirect expenses, also called overhead costs, don't.

A chart of accounts uses a numbering system to organize the information so that it is easy to understand. All the information in your accounting reports is in numerical order. The first digit of each account indicate what sort of account it is. The digits that follow put the accounts in order. As your system develops and you want to get more intricate, you can further refine this system, but the basic outline is as follows:

Balance Sheet Accounts

- 1000 Asset Accounts: What you own.
- 2000 Liability Accounts: What you owe.

1000 Asset Accounts, what your own, has two sub categories: current assets and fixed assets. Current assets are cash or things you can convert to cash readily, like inventory that could be sold and accounts receivable which you've billed for and should be in the mail. All of that gets an early number and gets put at the top of the page on your balance sheet under Current Assets. You need to make certain that you have enough current assets on hand to pay current bills.

Fixed Assets are the big tools, equipment, computers, vehicles, and the building you operate in. All major items are entered in your accounting records with their purchase price.

2000 Liability Accounts also has two sub categories: current and long term. If the liability needs to be paid within the year, it is entered in the current category. If you have a loan you pay out over time, you put it under long term. However, you will have to take one year's worth of principal on each loan and enter it under current liabilities, because you do, in fact, owe that within a year.

Current liabilities also contains customer deposits. Until the product is made or service rendered, you are holding money that belongs to someone else. Even if you have spent money on contracts that is non-refundable, it still isn't earned.

Income Statement Accounts

- 3000 Income Accounts Sales.
- 4000 Direct Expense Accounts: Labour and materials: expenses that will stop if you're not working.
- 5000 Indirect Expense Accounts: Expenses they just keep going, whether you're working or not; also called overhead.
- 7000-8000 Non-Operating Accounts: Numbers whose meanings are pretty obvious (interest income, and income tax), but which are kept at the bottom of the page separate from normal operating expenses or incomes.

Keeping the Direct Expenses separate from Indirect Expenses is very important. You will need to know what your overhead (indirect expense) is when you price your work. Having them clearly defined is also important when you want to calculate your gross profit. As manage your accounting entries, make a concerted effort to separate your direct from your indirect expenses to save yourself headaches down the line.

In terms of employees, overhead is the support staff-office and sales, primarily. If you are in retail sales, the wage for your salesperson is a direct expense. Shop and design are direct expenses.

Most accounting software packages come with preset charts of accounts for various businesses, which you can use to get you started, and modify as needed.

Office Space, Equipment, and Supplies

Choosing the right office space can be a critical decision for any business. You have to have a place to operate your business and the proper equipment to accomplish its tasks. Office space as it is referred to here means not only where you manage your accounting functions, but also where you do your actual production. Sometimes this is referred to as your business premises.

Many small businesses start out in the owner's home so the biggest question for these folks is How to Design Your Home Office. However, even folks who are operating out of their homes need to adhere to zoning laws and other legal restrictions, so cruise through some of the articles below to see if any of them may pertain to you. If you are looking for space outside your home, finding a good place to do business is important. Certainly visibility, accessibility and functionality of the space are crucial to your financial success; however, failing to adhere to zoning restrictions and building codes, or neglecting to properly read a commercial lease, can shut down your business before it starts. And, once you have the space, organizing it well so that you operate efficiently and effectively becomes important.

The Right Office for your Business

The most important factor in choosing your space is the old adage-location, location, location-whether it is within your home, your community or a larger region. Being conveniently located for your customers is key, but the location should also meet your business and personal needs.

Whether at home or another location, the space needs to be capable of serving both your present and projected needs. Before actively looking for space, your first move should be to map out your facility needs in some detail. Carefully consider the functions that the facility must perform for your business.

Once your needs are clear, alternatives can be explored. Think about the interior space that will be needed. Does it need to be subdivided into rooms or work areas? What types of work will be done in the space. For the exterior, what should the appearance and surroundings convey about your business? What about parking and loading docks?

For the home based, it is important to set up a distinct place for business activities that separates your personal and professional lives. Can you grow from this space? Other possibilities are leasing or buying space, sharing a facility or joining a business incubator.

Gather as much information as possible about the community in which you wish to locate, looking at prospective sites and buildings. Allow yourself time to conduct a thorough search. Network, testing your plans out on trusted associates. This is a critical decision to the business so take ample time to think through all the ramifications of cost, space and location.

Designing your Office Space

Designing your space should happen simultaneously with choosing the space. The most efficient layout will make a major difference in your space requirements. Map out an efficient work flow. Group the equipment you use most frequently closest to you. If at all possible, plan flexibility into the space with movable equipment and desks and adjustable shelving. Then as work flow changes, the space can rearranged appropriately.

Consider how systems work together. Multiple pieces of equipment can work at odds with each other. For instance, most equipment requires some type of electrical outlet. Be certain that the circuits do not get overloaded and that adequate outlets are available.

Good lighting is critical, but different lighting is needed for different tasks. Arrange lights so you can turn them on and off in various work areas as the need arises.

Noise can be a major distraction, especially if you need to make numerous phone calls. Place noisy equipment away from work areas that need quiet. There may be other special needs for your particular business. Look at the equipment you will be using, not only from a convenience standpoint, but also from what it needs to function properly and what type of output it produces.

Don't forget comfort. We all should be very aware by now of the consequences of long-term exposure to poorly designed environments. Ergonomics, the study of the spatial design of job requirements and work sites in relation to human physical and psychological capabilities and limitations, has become a critical component in any work environment.

Two of the most important ergonomic considerations are the human interaction with equipment and the range of motion each job entails. Human interaction problems relate to how working with a particular piece of equipment affects the human using it. For instance, chairs at the wrong height for working at a computer keyboard. Range of motion problems arise from maintaining the same position or repeating the same physical motions for a long time. A key appears to be movement. Introduce variety into activities to allow the muscles to stretch and move. Variety also is good for mental activity.

Making the work space an enjoyable place will pay off many times in productivity and positive attitude towards work.

Production

Production is an activity that converts materials into useful forms. The materials may be raw materials, semiprocessed or semifinalist goods, or even finished products. Machinery, equipment, methods, and processes are the basic elements of production.

Using the formal definition of production, there are four types of manufacturing processes:

- *Analysis:* The breaking down of raw materials, such as crude petroleum, into their components.
- *Extraction:* The removal of substances from other materials, as in the extraction of copper from ore.
- *Fabrication:* Changing the form of materials in some way such by pressing, weaving, or cutting. Examples include the manufacture of clothing, shoes, and metal bolts.
- *Synthesis:* Combining materials to form new products, as in the manufacture of glassware, metal products, or synthetic fibers.

Another type of synthesis is assembly, whereby various fabricated parts are place together to form a new product (as in the manufacture of automobiles).

Small businesses usually use fabrication or synthesis for their manufacturing. While you may not consider your business as manufacturing, if it produces a product that is precisely what you are doing. For instance, a small printer is practicing synthesis in its production of the printed products it produces.

The reason that this is an important concept to small businesses is that the organizational concepts that are used for production on a large scale are equally pertinent on a small scale. In order to produce your product efficiently and economically, you need to consider purchasing, receiving, shipping, quality control, research and development, maintenance, and stock keeping.

Purchasing refers to the obtaining the raw materials, components, machinery, equipment, supplies and necessary services needed in the production process. Some of the items that need to be considered in setting up a purchasing operation are:

- Ascertaining what needs to be ordered.
- Sources of supply.

- Quotations, prices and terms for supplies.
- Contracting for the supplies or services.
- Verifying that what has been ordered has been delivered on time.
- Inventory.

Receiving the supplies needs to be coordinated with purchasing. If the items are delivered to the precise area that they are needed, someone needs to verify that what was received is what was ordered, and that it is undamaged. A good record keeping system is critical to this process so that you don't add costs to production by receiving the wrong or inappropriate materials and equipment.

3

Marketing Plan: Marketing Objectives and Strategies

Meeting Marketing Objectives should lead to sales. (If not, you need to set Different Marketing Objectives.) They should:

- be clear.
- be measurable, and
- have a stated time frame for achievement.

Examples of Marketing Objectives Follow:

- Increase product awareness among the target audience by 30 percent in one year.
- Inform target audience about features and benefits of our product and its competitive advantage, leading to a 10 percent increase in sales in one year.
- Decrease or remove potential customers' resistance to buying our product, leading to a 20 percent increase in sales that are closed in six months or less.

If you have multiple objectives, make sure they are consistent and not in conflict with each other. Also, be sure that the remainder of your marketing plan components-the marketing strategy, budget, action programs, controls and measures-support your marketing objectives.

Setting your marketing objectives and finalizing the remaining components of your marketing plan may serve as a reality check: Do you have the resources necessary to accomplish your objectives?

The marketing strategy section of your plan outlines your game plan to achieve your marketing objectives. It is, essentially, the heart of the marketing plan. The marketing strategy section should include information about:

- Product-your product (s) and services.
- Price-what you will charge customers for products and services.
- Promotion-how you will promote or create awareness of your product in the marketplace.
- Place (distribution)-how you will bring your product(s) together with your customers.

These are the "4Ps of Marketing":

- Product.

Product

Products may be described in terms of their features and benefits.

Features are product characteristics that deliver benefits; we buy products for their benefits. Stated another way:

- Features are product characteristics such size, colour, horsepower, functionality, design, hours of business, fabric content, and so forth.
- Benefits answer the customer's question: Why would I want to own it?

A Feature is:

- Physical size.
- A 75 horsepower motor.

Patented box spring design A Benefit is:

- Small enough to fit in your raincoat pocket.
- A mower that takes the work out of yard work.
- A restful night's sleep.

While product features are usually easy to detect and describe, product benefits can be trickier because they are often intangible. The most compelling product benefits are those that provide emotional or financial rewards. It is not the brighter smile that the toothpaste offers that is its benefit; it is what the smile might bring you.

Emotional rewards run the gamut of human emotions but basically allow the buyer to feel better in some way. For example, sending flowers to a friend or family member allows the buyer to express love. Buying products made from recycled materials offers the buyer the chance to be environmentally responsible.

Products that Deliver Financial rewards allow the buyer to:

- Save money (a discount long-distance phone plan).
- Make money (computer software for managing a home-based business).
- Gain convenience and time (micro waveable meals).

To identify your product's benefits, you need to consider the customer's viewpoint. Besides putting yourself in your customer's shoes mentally, talk to or survey them asking them to tell you why they like the product. They might see benefits in the product that you had not considered-or, conversely they may not be seeing the benefit in the product that you had designed it for.

Look at the customers who have purchased your product in the past. What does that customer profile tell you about your product's benefits? If you don't have that information, in the future you might set up a few systems to develop and track the following information:

- Ask customers for suggestions for improvement.
- *Pay attention to customer complaints and prospect inquiries:* Listen to what your customers say. Train and reward employees for listening to customers and prospects to learn what they want and what they don't like about your product. Analyse and learn from this input.
- *Watch your competitors:* Do the changes in their product offerings suggest desired product benefits?

Understanding product features and benefits helps you develop your marketing strategy to better:

- Describe your products in marketing brochures, publications or in a personal selling situation in a way that is most relevant to customers.
- Differentiate-explain how your product is differs from other products in the market.
- Use a variety of pricing and positioning strategies effectively.

Products may be highly unique (speciality products) or virtually indistinguishable from competitor's products (known as commodity products). Speciality products are not necessarily better than commodity products, but they do require different marketing strategies. An important strategy for speciality products is differentiation. A company differentiates its products when it sets them apart from the competitor's products in the minds of customers. Having a thorough understanding of how your product's benefits compare to your competitors allows you to compete with them through differentiation.

Commodity Products

Few, if any, perceived differences among competing products <———————————————————> Speciality Products. Highly unique features compared to other products competing for buyers' dollars.

Strategies that are Based upon Features

Introducing

Being the first to offer a new product feature is a proven competitive strategy. For example, being known as the first organic body lotion to have Vitamin E will position your company as a leader, at least for a while.

Improving/Modifying: Instead of being at the head of the pack with a totally new feature, you might simply modify and/or improve your product's features. Improving your product creates the impression that your company cares about satisfying its customers.

Modifying product features is a strategy many businesses use to compete with a competitor who lowers their price. For example, if the maker of one organic body lotion lowers its price, the maker of another may add Vitamin E as a new improved feature, but keep its price the same.

Modifying features usually leads to changes in benefits. Find out what the perceived benefits your product offers so you can communicate them in your marketing messages.

Grouping

Features are frequently grouped into different product models-and prices-starting with a basic model to a deluxe model. Automobiles, many electronic devices, vacation packages and many other products offer a variety of features to add to a basic product model. This can even be true of services. For example, if you are an accountant you might offer a certain fee for preparing annual tax returns, another fee to additionally process payroll, and another to manage all of a client's financial affairs

Price

Pricing your product or service is one of the most important business decisions you will make. You must offer your products for a price your target market is willing to pay-and one that produces a profit for your company-or you won't be in business for long. There are many approaches to pricing, some scientific, some not. Here is one framework for making pricing decisions that takes into account your costs, the effects of competition and the customer's perception of value.

Definitions:

- Cost is the total of the fixed and variable expenses (costs to you) to manufacturer or offer your product or service.
- Price is the selling price per unit customers pay for your product or service.

So, the price you set is the cost to the customer. Ideally, it should be higher than the costs you incurred in producing the product.

Think of your cost as the surface of the ocean. You must set your price above the surface to cover costs or you will quickly drown. Of course, there will be times when you decide to set prices at or below cost for a temporary, specific purpose, such as gaining market entrance or clearing inventory.

How the customer perceives the value of the product determines the maximum price customers will pay. This is sometimes described as "the price the market will bear." Perceived value is created by an established reputation, marketing messages, packaging, and sales environments. An obvious and important component of perceived value is the comparison customers and prospects make between you and your competition.

Somewhere between the your cost and "the price the market will bear" is the right price for your product or service-a price that enables you to make a fair profit and seems fair to your customers. Consequently, once you understand your costs and your maximum price, you can make an informed decision about how to price your product or service.

However, while costs are important in setting your prices, don't limit your thinking only to cost-based pricing. Value-based pricing makes you think about your business from the customer's perspective.

If the customer doesn't perceive value worth paying for at a price that offers you a fair profit, you need to re-think your game-plan.

Promoting your Business

Promotion refers to marketing activities that create awareness of your business and/or product. These activities get the word out so potential customers know what you have to offer. Promotion also includes activities such as community involvement, sponsorship of special events and giving away speciality items (keychains, hats, pens). These activities allow you to subtly promote your product or company because the focus is on the event or speciality item. Your company's name is simply associated with the event or speciality item.

The type of promotional activities you choose helps to create and affirm your company image. For example, if you offer free water bottles (with your company logo on them) to participants in a race to raise funds for breast cancer research, your company will be associated with caring about health issues affecting women.

Community Involvement and Special Events

Because your community supports your business, it is a good business practice to support your community. Community means more than just a location. Community also can refer to specific groups of people, such as the Hispanic community. The great thing about participating in community events and programs is that it's a win-win for both you and the community.

When choosing an event or program to support, set specific goals for your participation that provide tangible results. For example, if you choose to serve on the board of directors of a local woman's shelter, your goal may be to network with other board members for business opportunities. Or, sponsoring a highway cleanup for a portion of a well-travelled road puts your name in front of potential customers. You should also look for events and programs with natural tie-ins that reinforce the image you want to have. For example, sponsor a golf tournament if you run a sporting goods store.

You should also consider the resources you have available for community relations, such as time, equipment, products, facilities or money. If all you have is time, find an organization or program that needs your skills. If you have a product or facilities to offer, but no time, find an organization that would be helped by using your facility or product.

Types of Community Involvement and Special Events

Shows, displays and exhibits: The most typical of these is the trade show at which you host an exhibit, speak, and/or host an event.

Road shows: An exhibit or presentation that you take on the road or to several locations in your town.

Fairs: Consumer job fairs, health fairs.

Parades or pageants: Depending on the type of your business, this might be a fun and economical promotional outlet for you.

Athletic Competitions: Fun runs, bike races, and sponsored walks.

Entertainment and cultural events: Shakespeare in the Park or a Designer Show house.

Commercial displays: If you have a store front, you might use your window display to tie into seasonal themes or community activities.

Stunts: Your imagination is the only limit here. But be careful-stunts backfire as often as often as they succeed. Be sure to adequately publicize your stunt and make it unusual enough to gain attention.

Banquets, luncheons, style shows or meetings: Sponsor or co-sponsor an event for a local chapter of an organization (whose members are your target audience). Volunteer (or accept a nomination) to serve on the board of directors of a not-for-profit organization. Not-for-profit organizations are always looking for people interested in supporting their cause. Not only will you feel good about what you do, but it is a great networking opportunity.

Participate in community activities: Cinco de Mayo, Mardi Gras or Earth Day celebrations.

Speciality Items

Your office and home are probably full of them. A keychain with a realtor's name stamped on it, a cap with a company's name embroidered on it or a yardstick with the local hardware store's name. These are speciality items, also called give aways or promotional items. Speciality items are a way to get-and keep-your name in front of prospects. You can spend a few cents to thousands of dollars for a speciality item. One thing is certain: there's a speciality item you can use to promote your business if that is part of your promotional plan.

Place (Sales and Distribution)

Place in the marketing model refers to how your product or service reaches the customer. It involves not only how you make the sale, but how your distribution system.

There are many factors to consider in sales and distribution. You need a well-thought-out plan for conducting the sale and distributing (delivering) your product to the customer. Here are some questions to consider:

- Is your sales approach highly persuasive and emotional? Or, is it informational and low-keyed?
- What is the average length of the sales cycle?
- How many products can you produce in what time frame?
- How many products can you store, or what is your inventory capacity? Use sales forecasts to decide what your inventory levels *should* be in order to meet customer demands.
- How often will you "turn" or replenish your inventory? How does this compare with the standards in your industry?
- What are the cyclical fluctuations or seasonal changes that affect the demand for or production of your products? For example, if you produce Christmas decorations, how will you manage peak production and sales periods as well as slow periods?
- Describe your distribution channel. In other words, how will your products be delivered or distributed to the customers?

For relatively small sales, such as selling your paintings through a local gallery, the distribution method is such a routine part of the sales contact that it requires only a small amount of thought and description. (In this scenario, the painting is displayed and stored at the gallery, the sales approach is probably low-pressure and informational, and the painting is given to the customer at the time of the sale.)

At other times, such as when an order is taken over the Internet and the product is mailed, more planning and description of the entire approach is in order.

Product Availability

At first glance, it may seem like the more convenient and available your product is, the better. This isn't always true, however. Often, it's better to be more selective, even exclusive, about sales locations for your product. Take every opportunity to think strategically.

Product Description

A product can be a physical item, a service, or an idea.

- Describe in detail your products or services in terms of the features and benefits they offer customers.
- Describe what you need to have or do to provide your product or service (how it's produced).

Pricing

List the price of your products and describe your pricing strategy. List price ranges for product lines. For example, if your product is a line of cosmetics, include information in this strategy section about your lipsticks "ranging in price from $5.00 to $15.00 per item" rather than a detailed product price list. (You should, however, consider including a detailed price list in the Supporting Documents section.)

Describe any price flexibility or negotiating room, as is common with large purchases such as houses or cars. Outline any discounts you offer for long-term customers, bulk purchases or prompt payment. Also, include the terms of sale, such as "net due in 30 days," extended payment plans, and whether you accept credit cards.

Promotion Plan

A promotion plan describes the tools or tactics used to accomplish your marketing objectives.

If your marketing objective is to:

Then tools or tactics might be:

- Create awareness of baby care products among mothers of newborns.
- Advertise in baby care or motherhood magazines.
- Distribute product samples to obstetricians.
- Offer free baby care seminars to expectant mothers.
- Increase sales of potato chips to teens.
- Distribute free samples or discount coupons at high school football games.
- Sponsor an event attended by teens.

In your Action Programs section, you will describe the steps that need to be taken in detail, when they should be done, who will do them, and so on.

Placement (Sales and Distribution)

In this section, describe how your products and customers "meet" or come together through sales and distribution.

Describe your sales philosophies and methods. Do you employ an aggressive sales method for a large number of quick sales, or a relaxed method where the emphasis is on having customers feel comfortable to come back another time even if they don't buy now? Do you use contract sales people or employees? Explain your approach to sales issues.

Describe your distribution system. (Where will your product be placed so customers have access to it?) A few points about distribution to address in your marketing plan are:

- Is the exchange of the product made in a store? Through the mail? Through a direct sales representative?
- What are your production and inventory capacities? (How quickly can you make products and how many can you store?)
- Are there cyclical fluctuations or seasonal demands for your products? For example, if you produce Christmas decorations, how will you manage peak production and sales periods as well as slow periods?
- Do you sell to individuals or to re-sellers? Your company may use more than one method. For example, you may sell directly to customers who place large orders but also sell to customers who buy small quantities of your product through retail outlets.

Small Business Marketing Strategies

The small business marketing strategies you'll discover in the coming months are all based on or related to several simple foundations. Frankly, effective marketing "ain't rocket science" and involves a lot of good old fashioned common sense. To keep it all together and organized, I created my MARKETING TRIANGLE more than 20 years ago. It has, obviously, three components, no one more or less important than the other two...

- Right Message.
- Right Markets.
- Right Media.

Most small business owners start with Media, often under pressure-an urgent need to stimulate business or a media salesman in the doorway screaming about a deadline. A lot of bad advertising decisions and a lot of bad advertising happens this way. So we'll approach this a bit differently and start by thinking about *what* you have to say (that might be interesting!) *before* we worry about *how* you will say it. So, let's start with Message.

Three Choices: No Message, Wrong Message, Right *Message!*

A lot of advertising and small business marketing messages are really No Messages at all. They're just "business cards." Name, rank and serial number. Who we are, what we do, where we are. As Joe Friday used to say on Dragnet,' "Just the facts, ma'am." I say this is no message, because it lacks Differentiation and it lacks Reason to respond now.

Then there are Wrong Messages. These are boring and plain vanilla, "me-too-ish," cheapest price as only lure, or focused on your product or service instead of customers and their needs, desires and interests. These also typically lack Differentiation and reason to respond now.

The worst reason to advertise is your need for customers. The best reason is having something exciting, bold, interesting, Different (and differentiating) to say, structured to produce immediate response. I can get you moving toward this kind of Right Message by posing the single most important (tough!) question anybody will ever ask you about your business as long as you're in it...my own proprietary, copyright protected question, incidentally, invented in 1979 and used since then to help tens of thousands of business owners find and develop their own "USP," unique selling proposition,' an invaluable asset. Here's the Question:

"Why should I, your prospective customer/client/patient, choose to do business with you vs. any and every other option available to me?"

And a catchy slogan is NOT a sufficient answer. Developing a really clear, strong, compelling answer isn't necessarily easy or instant. It tends to evolve. But it can be a huge breakthrough worth millions. Think: "fresh, hot pizza delivered in 30 minutes or less, guaranteed" or my client Craig Proctor's "if we don't sell your home in 90 days, I'll buy it for cash at the pre-agreed price." They both happen to rely on time-specific guarantees-a good path to a USP but, by far, not the only one. You will learn much more about USP and related message devices' as you continue with us as a Member, and you'll be able to "borrow from" or be inspired by the examples to continually improve and strengthen your own Best Marketing Message. This is an Evolutionary Process Of Continual Improvement, and many of our Members can show you truly awful Messages replaced again and again and again, over months and years, with better and better Messages. One student' who's been with me for 20 years, a chiropractor, Dr. Gregg Nielsen sent me as a gift a 3-ring notebook starting with his ads, mailings and newsletter Before Glazer-Kennedy,' the improved versions each year, to present, and the continuous improvement is amazing.

The second biggest message issue' you will see hammered home in the NO B.S. Marketing Letter and our other resources coming your way is: direct-response offers. This kind of marketing is the polar opposite of the brand/image advertising you see most big, dumb corporations doing-and the worst move you could ever make is copying them! We teach you to establish a process by which your ideal prospective customers/clients raise their hands and identify themselves by requesting widgets' (like free information, reports, etc.) from you, take baby steps' toward you...and let you follow-up with them effectively. This combines classic lead generation advertising'; something called permission marketing' (if you've read Seth Godin's books, that term will be familiar), and effective multi-step, multimedia follow-up to develop the new customer. If all that sounds "like Greek" to you, don't be concerned. You'll quickly "get it"-and as a result, finally, be able to do measurable, accountable advertising. Whether you use a lot of online/internet marketing or off-line marketing, these small business strategies apply. Further, for new and old customers alike, you'll discover the power of well-crafted irresistible' offers.

For now, let's assume you can develop really exciting Marketing Messages. Next,

The 'Who' is even more Important than the 'What'

Most advertising and marketing is UN-focused....mud thrown against the wall...and therefore loaded up with costly waste. When you move to *Targeted Marketing* aimed at and put together for exactly who you want as your customer or client, you can get a lot more bang for your buck!

As an example, consider this: as a professional writer of sales letters and direct-mail, I have a confession: the who' is more important than the what.' In fact, a poorly written sales letter offering a proposition perfectly and exactly matched to the needs, desires, fears and problems of a targeted group of people can get great results...but a great sales letter, expertly written, offering a proposition to people with no interest in it fails. One of the biggest moneymaking discoveries ahead for you is how to obtain lists or attract web site traffic or otherwise locate and connect only with your Ideally Matched prospective customers/clients who have strong interest in what you offer. This changes everything!

The Media you use to get your Message into the Hands (and Minds) of your Targeted Customers/Clients

No media is inherently good or bad. Newspapers, Val-Pak(R), radio, imprinted snow scrapers and baseball caps, postcards, web sites. Most small business owners think picking the right media will solve all their problems, so it's a shock to hear that there is no such things as a right or wrong, good or bad media...any more than a hammer is a good or a bad tool; it depends on what it's used for and the way it is used. In fact, as you understand more and more "Glazer-Kennedy Style Marketing" you'll be able to use more kinds of media profitably and have many more choices for promoting your small business than you do now-and that's fun, exciting and liberating.

This can also give you a strong competitive advantage. Here's why: a friend of mine, the late Joe Cossman, found that most manufacturers only distributed their products by one to three methods-but, on average, there were ten to twenty different viable distribution opportunities. He took over ten different products and quickly made millions with each one simply by plugging it into the ten or twenty instead of just three. In a very similar way, most businesses advertise and promote, attract customers, and sell more to present customers using only about three to, at most, five different media. (Make the list-how many do you use consistently?) Imagine if you can double or triple the number of different media you can profitably use! Your competitors will still be where you were: using one, three, at most five, while you use ten or twenty. Soon, you'll be amazing yourself, your employees and your family-and confounding your competition-by your much more *diverse* marketing of your business!

So, those are the "puzzle pieces" we'll be putting together: Message, Markets, Media.

"But, My Business is Different!"

Platinum Member Dr. Tom Orent had this made as a big wall poster for my conference room because I hear it so often from so many-",

But MY Business Is Different." Thinking this way is a huge temptation. But it is also a huge roadblock to any progress. If you insist on paying attention only to examples, ideas and information from your specific business, you guarantee status quo; continuing to get the same results you get now. Most businesses sequester themselves, only read their industry trade journals, only look at the other ads in their section of the Yellow Pages. Breakthroughs in sales, income and growth are only possible for the business owner who eagerly looks at EVERY example and idea of effective marketing that we deliver to find something he can translate and transfer. That's your role and responsibility in this partnership of ours. Our job is to show you the very best, most amazing, most powerful small business marketing strategies and ideas we can find from wherever we can get them. Your job is to look past the fact that the example comes from the pet grooming business and you are a financial planner or vice versa, extract the core strategies, translate and transfer to your business. Quite frankly, any idiot paid minimum wage can be given an issue of *The No B.S. Marketing Letter* and told to make a list of at least 100 reasons why nothing in it this month applies to a plumber and he may very well get the job done. It's the smart entrepreneur deserving of maximum profit that can examine the examples from a plumber and find something to use in his restaurants. This "translate and transfer whatever works" mindset is a very valuable, personal asset you can develop with time by hanging around us!

Success Magazine once said that I "move with remarkable ease applying my small business marketing strategies to one very different business after another." That I do. And that's exactly the sort of "power skill" you can develop with us. *It's telling that, in 2007, two of our Members' companies were recognized on INC. Magazine's prestigious list of "The 500 Fastest Growing Companies In America." They are in very different fields. One is a software company. One is a mortgage company. They both made the list with Glazer-Kennedy style marketing!*

Your Biggest Hurdle in profiting to the max as a Member will be getting over "my business is different thinking." Your Biggest Gain can be in acquiring the "translate and transfer mindset."

The Importance of a Target Market in Small Business

When it comes to your customers keep in mind the importance of target marketing. The reason this is important is that only a proportion of the population is likely to purchase any products or service. By taking time pitch your sales and marketing efforts to the correct niche market you will be more productive and not waste your efforts or time.

It's important to consider your virtual segmentation by selecting particular verticals to present your offerings to. Those verticals will have the particular likelihood of purchasing your products and services. Again, this saves you from wasting valuable time and money.

Small Business Marketing and Large Business Marketing are Different

If you are like the majority of small business owners your marketing budget is limited. The most effective way to market a small business is to create a well rounded program that combines sales activities with your marketing tactics. Your sales activities will not only decrease your out-of-pocket marketing expense but it also adds the value of interacting with your prospective customers and clients. This interaction will provide you with research that is priceless.

Small businesses typically have a limited marketing budget if any at all. Does that mean you can't run with the big dogs? Absolutely not. It just means you have to think a little more creatively. How about launching your marketing campaign by doing one of the following:

- Call your vendors or associates and ask them to participate with you in co-op advertising.
- Take some time to send your existing customers' referrals and buying incentives.
- Have you thought about introducing yourself to the media? Free publicity has the potential to boost your business. By doing this you position yourself as an expert in your field.
- Invite people into your place of business by piggybacking onto an event. Is there a concert coming to town, are you willing to sell those tickets? It could mean free radio publicity. If that is not your cup of tea, how about a walkathon that is taking place in your area, why not be a public outreach and distribute their material?

When you do spend money on marketing, do not forget to create a way to track those marketing efforts. You can do this by coding your ads, using multiple toll-free telephone numbers, and asking prospects where they heard about you. This enables you to notice when a marketing tactic stops working. You can then quickly replace it with a better choice or method.

15 Basics Points

Focus on one Contact

Marketing Strategy For Small Business: Target one decision maker you'd like to meet and invite him to share his expertise. Ask for a (very) short article for your newsletter or a quick phone interview for your podcast. Follow up by sending, or better yet dropping by with a copy of your finished production with a thank-you and of course, more information about your product & services.

Create Relevant Content

Marketing Strategy For Small Business: Promote your business online via creating content areas on your website that would attract users and position your business and brand as a source of valuable knowledge. Creating these content pages does not require any additional budget, but they do require time and creativity. For example, a children clothes store can dedicate a page to 'Tips on keeping your child busy on school vacation' and through that page, attract parents to the site.

Write for trade Magazines

Marketing Strategy For Small Business: If you want people to call you, there is nothing like writing an article for a trade magazine (for B2B) or local magazine (for B2C) to gain credibility and exposure. You can demonstrate your expertise and position yourself as the go-to person for your product or service. This strategy generates responses from people who are the ready-to-buy stage.

Google Add Words on the Cheap

Marketing Strategy For Small Business: Run market research on the cheap by using Google Adwords to target an audience, with the landing page being a question survey. A snappy question to attract people, along with Google's Geo-targeting can provide great results, for next to nothing.

Sponsor your Local Sport Teams

Marketing Strategy For Small Business: Sponsor a local sports team. For less than the cost of a 1/4 page ad in a local paper, you can buy team uniforms for a local soccer, basket ball, baseball or other sports teams. This a sure fire way to get the team, and their friends, family and fans that your business is a genuine part of the local community. It's a great PR technique too, as your local press will be very interested that you're taking this action and will probably send a photographer round to photograph you with the team and their new strips!

Its all Keywords

Marketing Strategy For Small Business: Statistically, 3 out of 4 internet users live in North America, making exposure on the web critical. Having a website that is keyword optimized for what your small business does and where you are located works as an online brochure as well as a "24 hours a day" sales person for your services and products.

Get out of the Dark Ages

Marketing Strategy For Small Business: Business owners should look beyond the brick and mortar and reach out to a bigger audience with the web. Establishing a presence online is key, whether it's by creating an interactive, regularly updated site or blog, or by building informative yet informal profiles on social networking sites like Facebook or Twitter. Opening communication channels online will not only increase brand awareness, it'll also boost your company's rank on search engines, and prove that you're a business that "gets it" and doesn't live in the dark ages.

Go To The Chamber

Marketing Strategy For Small Business: Make yourself the expert in your field. Volunteer to teach seminars through your local Chamber of Commerce about your area of expertise. Your business will receive promotion through the event itself, as well as through all marketing for the event. Your association with the Chamber will boost your credibility, as well.

Create an E-News for your Biz

Marketing Strategy For Small Business: As a relatively new start up, it may sound "old fashioned" in today's Twitter world, but having a great e-news with valuable content is key for our business. E-News is more than a sales pitch, rather, the opportunity to position your business as an expert, provide relevant information, and to add another layer in relationship building. Building a strong database with a focus on media/bloggers, giving your clients the opportunity to subscribe, and publishing frequently (but not obtrusively) is still one of the best, and least expensive, marketing tools in our arsenal. You would be surprised how often your content is tweeted on twitter, covered by bloggers, or open the door to a more extensive PR pitch.

The "Wow" Factor

Marketing Strategy For Small Business: Marketing gurus often refer to it as "differentiation." Academics who fancy themselves as marketers – they're the ones who write marketing text books – prefer to call it a USP, your Unique Selling Proposition. What they're both taking about is more correctly described as "Wow!" Whatever it is that separates your Stuff – your products or services – from the similar Stuff your competition is selling, that's your Wow!, what makes your Stuff better.

Leverage Online Forums

Marketing Strategy For Small Business: Many communities now have online forums/bulletin boards that offer varying levels of paid memberships. Purchase a membership that allows you to advertise your business and USE IT. Page with highest traffic in this specific area … www.Paulding.com … business advertising membership $150/year. Every time you post with your business ID, your business name (and web page link) is put in front of potential customers. Post about your specials, sales, what have you. (Be VERY careful to remember that every post is representative of your business).

Charity Donations

Marketing Strategy For Small Business: My #1 PR tip for small businesses: Focus, Pick one or two charity organizations or causes and donate only to them for the year. Create a letter that says why you chose the organization(s) so when you get inundated with requests for large donations, you can politely and formally say NO and still send a respectful message that you are committed to the community. You'll save a ton of money on $50 year book ads and donations to the latest event that is NOT your target market.

Hand Written Follow up Cards

Marketing Strategy For Small Business: Believe it or not, I have found a lot of success with the good old fashioned handwritten follow up card. Whether it's to say thank you, that it was a pleasure meeting, or that I'm simply looking forward to a future business relationship,

I am much more likely to hear back from that lead than someone who I simply met and didn't write to follow up with. How many hand written cards do you get in the business world these days? Almost none…it's an extremely personal effort that helps you stick out and remain memorable in your clients' mind. It seems simply and old-fashioned but it works.

Buzz Marketing at Trade Shows

Marketing Strategy For Small Business: Best tip, resist the urge to look/sound like your bigger competitors. To create buzz at a trade show for a client and demonstrate how other competitors waste customers' time, we strapped a big clock to a gurney and walked it around the show floor with two EMT types. T-shirts with the URL and booth number were the only "branding." Buzz = conversation, conversation = participation.

Personalized Gifts

Marketing Strategy For Small Business: Identify a unique, personalized gift to give your target customer's customer on the target customer's behalf. Example: A small, boutique hotel recommends a restaurant. The restaurant gives the diner a free dessert, compliments of the hotel! Everyone wins.

Entrepreneurism During a Recession

When people are out of work and jobs are scarce, interest in starting your own business rises. If there are no jobs, one solution is to make one. But, what is the best one to start where you can have an income flow immediately and not be burdened with too much monetary outlay up front? For starters, don't respond to the "make executive pay at home" or similar ads. These are almost always scams that will take whatever financial resources you have and give you nothing in return. The Federal Trade Commission keeps an extensive list of scanners. If you are tempted by one, search online to see what people are saying about it or search on the keywords "work-at-home" scams. It is appalling how many people are trying to take advantage of ordinary folks who are desperate. Here are some better ways to get some cash flow during tight economic times.

Freelance at your Old Job

The most obvious choice is to become an independent contractor or consultant in an area that you have some expertise. There are numerous freelance websites that link independent contractors with job opportunities. One outcome of tight budgets is that many businesses are closing whole departments and outsourcing many of their standard needs to avoid the overhead of office space and benefits for employees.

If you do decide to go the freelance, independent contractor route, do it professionally. You are a small business owner with one employee-you. That means setting a price for your time and/or setting fees for services and expecting a formal, written contract for the work. Do your research so that you are competitive in the market and know what businesses are hiring out what types of work. Have business cards that you hand out to everyone you meet, especially folks like your banker. Try to get yourself known to a diverse community of potential contractors. That way, if one business gets hit by recession problems, you have others that are still giving you work.

Meet a need in the Marketplace

Maybe, however, you want to take this setback in the economy as an opportunity to finally dive into your dream of owning your own business. But how do you choose which one to start? The Internet abounds with endless advice about which businesses are doing well and which are not doing well in this economy. One website will tell you that you need to start with a franchise because they know what is working and what isn't. Another will tell you that franchises are exactly where you don't want to be because many are over-extended and close to folding themselves. Even the national lists from professional surveys are only generalities and not focused on your particular market.

Your best bet is using your common sense, reading your local newspaper, and searching the Internet for consumer trends.

- Addressing problems being faced in the down economy may offer opportunities for new businesses. Consider maintaining foreclosed houses for banks, debt collection, providing financial or legal advice to help people with their debt, helping write good resumes, and selling items on the Internet for folks who need money, but are not computer savvy.
- No matter what is happening in the economy people are going to need food and health care; people will still be dying, having babies, and getting married; and people still want entertainment and to travel, albeit in much more economical ways.

- Many people are looking for training in other work skills. What skills do you have that you can teach?
- Historically, some of the most successful businesses were started during a recession to meet a new challenge. Find out what businesses thrived during down times.
- In challenging times, what people choose to buy with their limited income changes. Research consumer spending habits to find out what people are buying.
- Sometimes reading lists helps spark an idea. Scan lists of Business Possibilities to learn what others are doing.

Startup Financing

Finding the right financing that fits with a business' goals is a continuing challenge for almost every small business. For startup businesses this can be one of the biggest hurdles in getting off the ground.

Some entrepreneurs can be incredibly creative in finding ways to fund their ideas. Many work another job as a way to fund their personal business. Others finance their enterprises by going back to school. Business schools often can give you the tools and connections to get a business off the ground. Your classmates may be good business partners or the school may have a business plan competition with a prize of start-up funding for the business.

Most companies, however, find their start-up funding in more conventional ways. The most common sources are:

- 72% Personal Savings.
- 45% Banks.
- 28% Friends/Relatives.
- 10% Individual Investors.
- 7% Government-guaranteed Loans.
- 1% Venture Capital Firms.

Using personal funds is very common, partly because few banks will loan to people who not risked some of their own personal funds. However, in the long run, most businesses will need external funding of some type.

The conventional wisdom in starting a business is that it is no one will loan money to a startup. With no history and no assets, one either needs to have savings, friends and family who are willing to help or an angel. While it is impossible to deny the challenges, loans do exist and with good preparation are even relatively easy to get.

Being prepared has to be first step in seeking external funding. Write a business plan, prepare financial statements, line up references, develop a clear definition of what the business enterprise is, get introductions, and look at how you rate on other factors such as your credit rating, financial history, and business planning that lenders consider in awarding loans. Learn the lingo. It can be embarrassing to misuse terms. That immediately labels you as someone who has not done their homework-and consequently is not a good investment candidate. The Small Business Glossary lists a large number of terms you should know before talking with any person you may seek funding from.

Find out which are the right banks to approach if you want to go that route. The Small Business Administration has put together a list of commercial banks that scores the banks on how aggressive they are in small business lending. You can find which banks are business friendly in your area through their search mechanism.

One of the toughest questions is how much capital is enough. A quick model for cash needs suggests determining how much capital is needed for one year of operation. That first year, keep your initial capital separate from your income. That income should then be the initial capital for the second year. Amounts you will need to finance are that initial capital and any growth you want to introduce above and beyond the initial model. Many companies that are successful today have started that simply.

Startup Checklist

Starting your business is a busy time in any entrepreneur's life. Critical steps can be easily overlooked until you are well into the process. To help budding entrepreneurs in getting their businesses set up efficiently, legally, and soundly, here is a checklist of primary steps that every business needs to include.

This checklist assumes that you already have an idea for a business and are ready to make it real. If you are still at the stage of looking for the right business, take a look at Choosing the Right Business.

Given everything else is in place, here is a checklist of the basic areas you need to cover before opening your business:

Each of these areas needs careful consideration if your business is to become a reality and prosper. You may feel comfortable with managing some of these areas, but not others. Check out the links above for any of the areas that you are unsure about to learn more about how to handle that area of operating a business. The goal is to have a solid base for your business so that it can grow and you can be freed from unexpected problems in the future.

Price of your Product

Pricing your product or service is one of the most important business decisions you will make. You must offer your products for a price your target market is willing to pay-and one that produces a profit for your company-or you won't be in business for long. There are many approaches to pricing, some scientific, some not. Here is one framework for making pricing decisions that takes into account your costs, the effects of competition and the customer's perception of value.

Definitions:

- Cost is the total of the fixed and variable expenses (costs to you) to manufacturer or offer your product or service.
- Price is the selling price per unit customers pay for your product or service.

So, the price you set is the cost to the customer. Ideally, it should be higher than the costs you incurred in producing the product.

Think of your cost as the surface of the ocean. You must set your price above the surface to cover costs or you will quickly drown. Of course, there will be times when you decide to set prices at or below cost for a temporary, specific purpose, such as gaining market entrance or clearing inventory.

How the customer perceives the value of the product determines the maximum price customers will pay. This is sometimes described as "the price the market will bear." Perceived value is created by an established reputation, marketing messages, packaging, and sales environments. An obvious and important component of perceived value is the comparison customers and prospects make between you and your competition.

Somewhere between the your cost and "the price the market will bear" is the right price for your product or service-a price that enables you to make a fair profit and seems fair to your customers. Consequently, once you understand your costs and your maximum price, you can make an informed decision about how to price your product or service.

However, while costs are important in setting your prices, don't limit your thinking only to cost-based pricing. Value-based pricing makes you think about your business from the customer's perspective. If the customer doesn't perceive value worth paying for at a price that offers you a fair profit, you need to re-think your game-plan.

The Starting Point: Calculating Break-Even

Before you can decide upon a fair price for your product, you need to know how much it's costing you. You will need to know this no matter which pricing method you use.

Once you've identified costs, you can determine your break-even point. This is the point at which you neither make nor lose money in producing a product or delivering a service. For example, you would be at the break-even point if it cost you $100 to produce a product that you sell for $100.

A break-even analysis is the process you use to uncover those break-even numbers. To begin your break-even analysis, add up all fixed costs and determine what your variable costs are at different production volumes.

- Fixed costs, sometimes referred to as overhead, are expenses that don't vary according to production amounts-such as rent for office space (and storage space if you store inventory), office equipment (telephones, faxes, computers), insurance, and utilities.
- Variable costs are expenses that do vary with the amount of service provided or goods produced. They include costs such as hourly pay for a contractor on a specific project, and raw materials. Some variable costs don't depend specifically on the number of products produced but are still variable, such as advertising or promotion expenses.

You must know the cost of your overhead (fixed costs) as well as the incremental cost-per-unit (variable costs) before you can determine your break-even points.

Next, substitute your figures into the break-even revenue and break-even units formulas.

Calculating Break-Even Revenue

To calculate break-even dollars-the amount of revenue needed to cover both fixed and variable costs so your business neither makes nor loses money-use the following formula:

(Fixed Costs) / (1-(Variable cost per unit/Selling Price per unit).

= Revenue to Break-even.

Example: Calculating Break-Even Revenue.

To determine an appropriate hourly rate (revenue) to charge for a consultant or service business, using the break-even revenue formula, plug in total fixed costs of $30,000, variable cost-per-unit of $15 (hourly pay to consultant), and unit selling price of $30 (per hour of consulting). The formula yields a break-even annual revenue of $60,000.

$30,000 / (1-($15/$30)) = $60,000

So, this company needs revenues of $60,000 just to cover costs. If it doesn't have enough business at these rates, it loses money by being in business. If it makes more than $60,000 in revenue, it's making money.

Cost-Based Pricing

After you've determined your break-even points which establish floors for your price, there are strategies for establishing pricing based upon additional financial objectives, such as:

- Establishing a high price to make high profits initially. This strategy is used to recover high research and development costs or to maximize profits before competitors enter the market. (Pharmaceutical companies often use this strategy when introducing new drugs).
- Setting a low price on one or more products to make quick sales to support another product in development. (Some companies also employ this strategy when they need to increase cash flow.)
- Setting prices to meet a desired profit goal. For example, if the desired profit per unit is 20 percent and unit costs are $10 (taking into account your fixed and variable costs), set your price at $12.

You may also determine how many units you will need to sell to meet a profit goal by using the following formula.

Break-Even Unit Volume = (Fixed Costs / Unit Contribution Margin), Unit Contribution Margin = Selling Price per Unit-Variable cost per unit.

Value-Based Pricing

How high can a price be before the product or service is priced out of the market?

To understand the customer's perception of the value of your product or service, look at more subjective criteria such as customer preferences, product benefits, convenience, product quality, company image and alternative products offered by the competition.

- How do your customers describe what they get for their money?
- Do they save a great deal of money or time by purchasing your product or service?
- Do they gain a competitive advantage from using your service?
- Is it more convenient to use your service rather than try to do it themselves?
- What are the customer's choices?
- What does the competition charge?

With this information, you can begin to understand the maximum price the customer will pay for the benefit received. Often, a customer may think it's worth paying $75 per hour for the convenience and security of dealing with a local business, rather than a paying an impersonal chain $30 per hour. If the customer, however, is only willing to pay $30 per hour, you have to ask yourself whether you can make any money in this business.

A few value-based pricing strategies are listed below that take into account the break-even point, but are heavily weighted with subjective judgments-not just the numbers.

- Price the same as competitors. This strategy is used when offering a commodity product, when prices are relatively well established (such as with professional services) or when you have no other means to set prices. Your challenge then becomes to determine how to lower your costs so you can produce a higher profit than your competitors.

- Establish a low price (compared to the competition) on a product in order to capture a large number of customers in that market. This strategy may also be used to achieve non-financial objectives such as product awareness, meeting the competition or establishing an image of being low-cost. It works if you are able to maintain profitability at the low price, or if you're able to maintain an acceptable level of sales should you later raise prices.
- If your product has a mystique and uniqueness that is valuable to customers, you might have the ability to charge a very high price relative to your cost. Also, if your target market is affluent and you are positioning your product as a "prestige" product, an especially high price could be in order. (For example, do Rolex watches cost *that* much more to make than other brands? The high cost, however, brings a "status" benefit to Rolex's affluent market.) This strategy of charging "what customers are willing to pay"-even though it's high-requires alertness and a willingness to change on your part because customers (and competitors) might decide that you're making too much of a profit.

Discounts

Your pricing strategy might include discounts to customers who offer you a business benefit.

- You may offer cash discounts to customers who pay promptly. This rewards those who help your company maintain a steady, positive cash flow and reduce credit-collection costs.
- Offering quantity discounts for large orders often makes economic sense when the cost-per-unit to sell or deliver a product declines as the quantity increases. For example, a caterer might fill an order for 12 dozen cupcakes for one customer at 10 cents each, while cupcakes sitting in the bakery display rack might be sold to several customers throughout the day for 20 cents each. This is because the possibility that some of the cupcakes won't sell has to be taken into account. There are costs associated with having the store open for random customers' convenience.

- Seasonal discounts given to buyers who purchase during a product's slow season reward customers who essentially assist a company in balancing its cash flow and in meeting production demands.
- Trade-in allowances for returned old products that you may either re-use or re-sell for a profit may benefit both a company and customers.
- Promotional allowances often make economic sense. For example, if your product is sold by a retail chain which includes your product in its ads or in promotional activities, those activities leverage your marketing efforts. If so, you might choose to discount your price to this retail chain.

4

Human Resource in Small Business

Human Resources Management

Many small businesses operate with no employees. One person handles the whole business with perhaps occasional help from family or friends. Making the leap to hiring someone to help is a big one because all of a sudden you need to worry about payroll, benefits, unemployment insurance, and what seems like a myriad of other details. And, this does not even take into consideration the host of problems that can arise from personality conflicts and loss-of-control of all the processes in running your business. Human Resources refers to the labour, physical and mental abilities that the people in your organization contribute to producing the goods and services of your business. The administration of human resources involves:

Staffing;

- Developing personnel sources.
- Recruiting potential employees.
- Equal Employment Opportunity.

Equal Employment Opportunity

One of the most confusing aspects of managing employees for small businesses is knowing what legal responsibilities they must meet under equal employment opportunity laws. There are many myths and misperceptions about what you must and must not do, and how honours it is to comply with these laws. Here are the answers to some of the most freqently answered questions that the EEOC receives.

1. What laws does the EEOC enforce and do they apply to my business?

2. How do I determine if a business of my size is covered by the EEO laws?
3. Who may file a charge of discrimination with the EEOC?
4. When can a charge of discrimination be filed?
5. Can a small business resolve a charge without undergoing an investigation or facing a lawsuit?
6. What employment records must I keep?
7. What reports must small employers file with EEOC?
8. How will I know if a charge of discrimination has been filed against my company?
9. What can I expect to happen in an EEOC investigation?
10. What records am I required to keep if I receive an EEOC charge?
11. What happens if a charge is dismissed by the EEOC?
12. What does the EEOC do if it determines that a violation of the law has occurred?
13. If my company is found to have violated the law, what could happen?
14. What should I do to prevent retaliation against and preserve relationships with current employee charging parties?
15. What are Fair Employment Practices Agencies and how do they relate to the EEOC?
16. What is the Immigration Reform and Control Act and must my business comply with it?
17. What about affirmative action?
18. Where can I find information about the Family and Medical Leave Act?
19. What is the Small Business Regulatory Enforcement Fairness Act?

Hiring Issues

Employee Registration Requirement

All U.S. employers are responsible for completion and retention of Form I-9 for each individual they hire for employment in the United States. This includes citizens and non-citizens. On the form, the employer must verify the employment eligibility and identity documents presented by the employee and record the document information on the Form I-9. I-9 Forms can be obtained by downloading from the U.S. Citizenship and Immigration Service (USCIS) Website.

Equal Employment Opportunity Commission (EEOC) Requirements

When advertising for and interviewing job candidates, it's important to focus exclusively on the skill and experience needed for the position. Under Title VII of the Civil Rights Act of 1964, the Americans with Disabilities Act (ADA), and the Age Discrimination in Employment Act (ADEA), it is illegal to discriminate in any aspect of employment, including hiring; compensation, assignment, or classification of employees; job advertisements; recruitment; testing; training and apprenticeship programs; or other terms and conditions of employment. Many states and municipalities also have enacted protections against discrimination and harassment based on sexual orientation, status as a parent, marital status and political affiliation. For information, please contact the EEOC District Office nearest you. Take a look at interviewing guidelines to learn more about what you can and cannot ask in an interview.

Union Requirements

Right to Work states secure the right of employees to decide for themselves whether or not to join or financially support a union, and makes it illegal for unions to require membership as a condition of employment. In non-Right to Work states, employees may be required to join unions in order to retain employment at some companies regardless of opposing political views or religious beliefs. If unions have or are forming in your business, find out what the law is in your state.

Reference Checks

When called for reference checks, employers are generally expected to reveal only the employees' date of hire, date of termination and job title, and are prohibited from giving confidential information. If the applicant signs a "waiver and hold harmless agreement" as a condition for applying for employment, the employer may feel more comfortable specifying additional information specified by the agreement.

Credit Checks

To obtain a credit report on an employee or prospective employee, the employer must provide clear and conspicuous written notice that a credit report may be requested, and obtain written consent from the applicant or employee.

Background Checks

Employers generally have the right to access arrest and conviction records that are public information, but whether employers can use such information for hiring decisions varies from state to state. Some states allow employers to discriminate based on criminal convictions, but not on arrests. Other states apply varying rules depending on the position or industry being applied for. Check with your State labour department to find out what laws may apply to you.

Employing Foreign Workers

If you are contemplating hiring foreign workers, be sure to review the U.S. Citizenship and Immigration Services Employment Handbook.

Minors

The Fair Labour Standards Act (FLSA) sets wage, hours worked, and safety requirements for minors (individuals under age 18) working in jobs covered by the statute. The rules vary depending upon the particular age of the minor and the particular job involved. As a general rule, the FLSA sets 14 years of age as the minimum age for employment, and limits the number of hours worked by minors under the age of 16.

General Interview Guidelines

How do you select the right person for your business? There is no perfect answer, but the interview process can be a tremendous help if you use it effectively. To do that, you must have completed all of the other steps in the hiring process in order to get the most out of the interview process.

Interviewing candidates for a position within your company is one of the final steps in the hiring process. Before you get to this step, you want to make sure that you've completed all of the preceding steps since each of these steps will have a direct impact on how effective the interview process will be. Below is a list of the steps involved in the hiring process. Note that after you have completed the interviewing process, there are still two additional key steps that you need to complete. In order to achieve the best hiring results possible, just remember that all of the steps are important. In order, the key steps to finding the right person to fill a position in your company include:

1. *Determining your need to hire a new employee:* Are you properly utilizing the skills and talents of your current employees? Do you know what needs to be done? Can your business growth support a new employee?
2. *Conducting a thorough job analysis:* What are the job's essential functions and key performance criteria?
3. Writing a job description and job specification for the position based on the job analysis.
4. *Determining the salary for the position, based on internal and external equity:* Is the salary comparable and proportional with the salaries and responsibilities of other positions inside your company as well as similar positions out in the marketplace?
5. *Deciding where and how to find qualified applicant:* What are the recruitment techniques to be used? What is the time frame for conducting your search? Remember, advertising is not the only, or necessarily the best, way to recruit.
6. Collecting and reviewing a fair amount of applications and resumes and then selecting the most qualified candidates for further consideration.
7. Interviewing the most qualified candidates for the position, based on the job's description and specification.
8. Checking references.
9. *Hiring the best person for the job:* Hopefully, after reviewing all of the resumes, you will be able to pick and choose a select number of qualified applicants to be interviewed. (If not, you may want to expand your time frame and re-write any ad copy and/or look at another recruitment technique)

Here are some pointers on conducting a successful interview:

Employee Termination

Few supervisors and managers look forward to firing people. Nevertheless, you need to know how to terminate employees in a way that preserves their dignity while meeting your organization's needs. Even the most experienced managers experience stress and anxiety when they go through the termination process. Having a clear idea of the process won't make it any more pleasant, but could prevent you from making costly mistakes. The key to a successful termination begins with hiring and continues throughout the employer/employee relationship. Having a good Employee Handbook and adequate training build a strong base for subsequent actions. Performance Reviews also play a critical role in a successful termination. However, the actual process of the termination is what stays in everyone's mind about the quality of the company, for a long time after the termination is over.

A termination impacts everyone-even the termination of someone that is not liked-will affect co-workers if it is not handled properly. In most states, employees have the right to claim unemployment benefits and drawing against your unemployment insurance often raises your tax rate. The burden of proof is almost always on the employer to prove the reason for the separation in unemployment claims cases. Make certain you are familiar with applicable federal and state laws. In some cases written notification may be required in advance of the separation.

The best you can hope for when terminating someone is to continue to have the terminated employee as a friend of the company in the future. The worst thing that can happen is a long drawn out legal process with lawyers and government agencies. And, don't forget that a former employee can be your best (or worst) salesperson.

Training and Development

- Initial Training.
- Training Needs Analysis.
- Preparation of training programs.
- Management and supervisory development.

Employee Health and Safety

Employers are responsible for providing a safe and healthful work place for their employees. The Occupational Safety and Health Administration (OSHA), an agency of the U.S. Department of Labour, has the responsibility of assuring the safety and health of America's workers by setting and enforcing standards; providing training, outreach and education; establishing partnerships; and encouraging continual improvement in work place safety and health.

Twenty-four states, Puerto Rico and the Virgin Islands operate their own OSHA-approved safety and health programs under Section 18 of the Act. While the programs in these states may differ in some respects from Federal OSHA, the standards imposed by State Plan

States must be at least as effective as Federal OSHA standards. A list of states that operate their own safety and health programs can be found on OSHA's website.

Safety and Health Add Value

Addressing safety and health issues in the work place saves the employer money and adds value to the business. Recent estimates place the business costs associated with occupational injuries at close to $170 billion-expenditures that come straight out of company profits.

When workers stay whole and healthy, the direct cost-savings to businesses include:

- lower workers' compensation insurance costs;
- reduced medical expenditures;
- smaller expenditures for return-to-work programs;
- fewer faulty products;
- lower costs for job accommodations for injured workers;
- less money spent for overtime benefits.

Safety and health also make big reductions in indirect costs, due to:

- increased productivity;
- higher quality products;
- increased morale;
- better labour/management relations;
- reduced turnover;
- better use of human resources.

Employees and their families benefit from safety and health because:

- their incomes are protected;
- their family lives are not hampered by injury;
- they have less stress.

Simply put, protecting people on the job is in everyone's best interest-our economy, our communities, our fellow workers and our families. Safety and health add value to businesses, workplaces and lives.

Developing a Profitable Strategy for Handling Occupational Safety and Health

Nobody wants accidents to happen in his or her business. A serious fire, a permanent injury, or the death of an employee or owner can cause the loss of profit or even an entire business. To prevent such losses, you don't have to turn your business upside down. You may not have to spend a lot of money, either. You do need to use good business sense and apply recognized prevention principles.

There are reasons why accidents happen. Something goes wrong somewhere. It may take some thought, and maybe the help of friends or other trained people, to figure out what went wrong, but an accident always has a cause-a reason why. Once you know why an accident happened, it is possible to prevent future incidents. You need some basic facts and perhaps some help from others who already know some of the answers. You also need a plan to prevent accidents.

Not all dangers at your worksite depend on an accident to cause harm, of course. Worker exposure to toxic chemicals or harmful levels of noise or radiation may happen in conjunction with routine work as well as by accident.

You may not realize the extent of the exposure or harm that you and your employees face. The effect may not be immediate. You need a plan that includes prevention of these health hazard exposures and accidents. You need a safety and health management system.

It is not difficult to develop such a plan. Basically, your plan should address the types of accidents and health hazard exposures that could happen in your work place. Because each work place is different, your program should address your specific needs and requirements.

There are four basic elements to all good safety and health programs. These are as follows:

Management Commitment and Employee Involvement

The manager or management team leads the way, by setting policy, assigning and supporting responsibility, setting an example and involving employees.

Worksite Analysis

The worksite is continually analysed to identify all existing and potential hazards.

Hazard Prevention and Control

Methods to prevent or control existing or potential hazards are put in place and maintained.

Training for Employees, Supervisors and Managers

Managers, supervisors and employees are trained to understand and deal with worksite hazards.

Regardless of the size of your business, you should use each of these elements to prevent work place accidents and possible injuries and illnesses.

The Four-Point Work place Program is based upon the Safety and Health Program Management Guidelines issued by OSHA in January 1989. Although voluntary, these guidelines represent OSHA's policy on what every worksite should have in place to protect workers from occupational hazards. The guidelines are based heavily on OSHA's experience with its Voluntary Protection Programs (VPP), which recognize excellence in work place safety and health management.

Privacy Issues

You should know the privacy laws that protect your employees. Here is a brief overview of some of the issues that need to be considered in managing employees.

Employee Surveillance

Employers should carefully research local employee privacy laws. While the Federal Electronic Communications Privacy Act provides some protection for workers, the types of monitoring that may be conducted vary widely from state to state. Check the law in your state before beginning telephone, camera, computer, or any other type of electronic monitoring.

Personal Appearance

Employers are generally free to set reasonable guidelines concerning neatness, dress, appearance, and hygiene. However, such codes are always in danger of legal attack, usually on the grounds that they are discriminatory or violate a person's right to privacy. In some states, employers requiring uniforms may be required to supply or compensate employees for the uniform. Check the law in your state before setting guidelines.

Off-Duty Behaviour

In most states, employers may discipline or terminate employees for off-duty behaviour that might embarrass the company or disrupt its operations, though some methods of obtaining information about off-duty conduct may infringe on privacy rights. Some states, such as Michigan and Illinois, restrict employers from gathering information regarding an employee's off-duty behaviour. Check the law in your state before taking any action against an employee.

Drug and Alcohol Testing

The Supreme Court has upheld an employer's right to test employees for drugs and alcohol. However, some state and local governments have passed laws prohibiting testing, and the subject is always bound to raise privacy law issues. Check on the laws in your state before planning a testing policy.

Lie Detector Tests

The federal Polygraph Protection Act protects most American workers from taking a lie detector test as a condition of employment or continued employment. In many states, however, the law does not apply to applicants in law enforcement agencies, persons in sensitive positions relating to national security, or applicants in drug manufacturing and distributing.

Psychological and Personality Tests

Federal law does not prohibit an employer from requiring an employee or prospective employee to take a psychological or personality test. However, check the law in your state before requiring any candidate or existing employee to take such a test.

Searches

Private employers may generally conduct on-premises searches of employer-owned vehicles, equipment, desks, lockers, briefcases, and other items. In most states, searches of an employee's personal items may be legal if the employee has a reasonable expectation of privacy. Public employees enjoy constitutional protections that guard against many kinds of searches.

Employee Handbook

Employee Handbooks are also often called Policy and Procedures Manuals. The Handbook/Manual is a statement of the policies of the business and how the business is to be conducted. The company employee handbook is one of the most important communication tools between your company and your employees. Not only does it set forth your expectations for your employees, but it also describes what they can expect from the company. It is essential that your company has one and that it be clear and as unambiguous as possible. Misunderstandings or misstatements can create legal liabilities for your business. In legal disputes courts have considered an employee handbook to be a contractual obligation, so word it carefully.

The company employee handbook and related personnel policies should be one of the first formal communications that you will have with an employee after they are hired. Make sure the first impression is a good one. Similarly, in the event of a dispute or poor performance review, this will be the first place that the employee turns.

The handbook should contain enough detail to avoid confusion, but not so much as to overwhelm. For instance, if there are other documents (i.e. group insurance handbook, and retirement plan documents) which more appropriately provide details, don't try to recreate the information in the handbook. Instead, offer a brief summary and refer to the other document in the employee handbook. Make sure that you are familiar with the myriad of laws and regulations for employment. It is always wise to consult with a lawyer on any topics that you don't understand.

The actual policies in the manual will vary from company to company, depending on its size, number of employees, and benefits offered. Regardless of the size or complexity of your business, once you hire your first employee its best to take the time to think through the policies for your company, have at least the minimum list of policies for your employees, and write them down.

Employee Work Hours

Federal laws pertaining to work hours are enforced by the Wage and Hour Division of the Department of Labour's Employment Standard Administration. The Wage and Hour Division enforces federal minimum wage, overtime pay, record keeping, and child labour requirements of the Fair Labour Standards Act (FLSA) and the labour requirements of the Davis-Bacon and Related Acts, the McNamara O'Hara Service Contract Act (SCA), the Contract Work Hours and Safety Standards Act, and the Copeland Anti-Kickback Act. The Wage and Hour Division has a variety of guidance materials available for both employees and employers on the subject of work hours.

Here are some Work Hours subtopics that are of particular interest.

Breaks and Meal Periods

Federal law does not require lunch or coffee breaks. However, when employers do offer short breaks (usually lasting about 5 to 20 minutes), federal law considers the breaks work-time that must be paid. Unauthorized extensions of authorized work breaks need not be counted as hours worked when the employer has expressly and unambiguously communicated to the employee that the authorized break may only last for a specific length of time, that any extension of the break is contrary to the employer's rules, and any extension of the break will be punished.

Bona fide meal periods (typically lasting at least 30 minutes), serve a different purpose than coffee or snack breaks and, thus, are not work time and are not compensable.

Flexible Schedules

A flexible work schedule is an alternative to the traditional 9 to 5, 40-hour work week. It allows employees to vary their arrival and/or departure times. Under some policies, employees must work a prescribed number of hours a pay period and be present during a daily "core time." The Fair Labour Standards Act (FLSA) does not address flexible work schedules. Alternative work arrangements such as flexible work schedules are a matter of agreement between the employer and the employee (or the employee's representative). The Department of Labour has conducted numerous surveys and published articles and reports on the subject.

Fulltime Employment

The Fair Labour Standards Act (FLSA) does not define full-time employment or part-time employment. This is a matter generally to be determined by the employer. Whether an employee is considered full-time or part-time does not change the application of the FLSA, nor does it affect application of the Service Contract Act or Davis-Bacon and Related Acts wage and fringe benefit requirements.

Holidays

The Fair Labour Standards Act (FLSA) does not require payment for time not worked, such as vacations or holidays (federal or otherwise). These benefits are generally a matter of agreement between an employer and an employee (or the employee's representative).

On a government contract to which the labour standards of the McNamara O'Hara Service Contract Act (SCA) apply, holiday and/or vacation fringe benefit requirements are stated in the SCA wage determinations in contracts that exceed $2,500.

On a government contract to which the labour standards of the Davis-Bacon and Related Acts apply, holiday pay and/or vacation pay is required for specific classifications of workers only if the Davis-Bacon wage determination in the covered contract specifies such requirements for workers employed in those classifications.

Job Sharing

Job sharing means that two (or more) workers share the duties of one full-time job, each working part time, or two or more workers who have unrelated part-time assignments share the same budget line. The Fair Labour Standards Act (FLSA) does not address job sharing. Job sharing is a matter of agreement between an employer and an employee (or the employee's representative).

The benefits of job sharing are said to include increased morale and productivity. Job sharing can also be an attractive way to recruit new employees and retain current ones. In order for a job sharing arrangement to be successful, however, both individuals must be able to handle the position as efficiently as one person.

Night Work and Shift Work

Extra pay for working night shifts is a matter of agreement between the employer and the employee (or the employee's representative). The Fair Labour Standards Act (FLSA) does not require extra pay for night work. However, the FLSA does require that covered, nonexempt workers be paid not less than time and one-half the employee's regular rate for time worked over 40 hours in a work week.

Overtime

For covered, nonexempt employees, the Fair Labour Standards Act (FLSA) requires overtime pay to be at least one and one-half times an employee's regular rate of pay after 40 hours of work in a work week. Some exceptions apply under special circumstances to police and firefighters and to employees of hospitals and nursing homes.

Some states have overtime laws. In cases where an employee is subject to both the state and federal overtime laws, the employee is entitled to overtime according to the higher standard (i.e., the standard that will provide the higher overtime pay).

Extra pay for working weekends or nights is a matter of agreement between the employer and the employee (or the employee's representative).

The Contract Work Hours and Safety Standards Act (CWHSSA) requires contractors and subcontractors on most federal contracts over $100,000 for services or construction to pay labourers and mechanics at least one and one-half times their basic rate of pay for all hours worked over 40 in a work week.

CWHSSA also applies to most federally assisted construction contracts.

Parttime Employment

The Fair Labour Standards Act (FLSA) does not address part-time employment. Whether an employee is considered full-time or part-time does not change the application of the FLSA.

Record keeping and Reporting

Every employer covered by the Fair Labour Standards Act (FLSA) must keep certain records for each covered, nonexempt worker. There is no required form for the records, but the records must include accurate information about the employee and data about the hours worked and the wages earned. The following is a listing of the basic records that an employer must maintain:

- Employee's full name and social security number.
- Address, including zip code.
- Birth date, if younger than 19.
- Sex and occupation.
- Time and day of week when employee's work week begins. Hours worked each day and total hours worked each work week.
- Basis on which employee's wages are paid.
- Regular hourly pay rate.
- Total daily or weekly straight-time earnings.
- Total overtime earnings for the work week.
- All additions to or deductions from the employee's wages.
- Total wages paid each pay period.
- Date of payment and the pay period covered by the payment.

Sick Leave

Federal law does not require sick leave. If you quit your job before using all of your sick leave, your employer is not obligated to pay you for that time.

The Family and Medical Leave Act (FMLA) provides for up to 12 weeks of unpaid leave for certain medical situations for either the employee or a member of the employee's immediate family; however, in many instances paid leave may be substituted for unpaid FMLA leave.

Travel Time

Time spent travelling during normal work hours is considered compensable work time. Time spent in home-to-work travel by an employee in an employer-provided vehicle, or in activities performed by an employee that are incidental to the use of the vehicle for commuting, generally is not "hours worked" and, therefore, does not have to be paid. This provision applies only if the travel is within the normal commuting area for the employer's business and the use of the vehicle is subject to an agreement between the employer and the employee or the employee's representative.

Vacation Leave

The Fair Labour Standards Act (FLSA) does not require payment for time not worked, such as vacations, sick leave or federal or other holidays. These benefits are matters of agreement between an employer and an employee (or the employee's representative).

On a government contract to which the labour standards of the McNamara O'Hara Service Contract Act (SCA) apply, holiday and/or vacation fringe benefit requirements are stated in the SCA wage determinations in contracts that exceed $2,500.

On a government contract to which the labour standards of the Davis-Bacon and Related Acts apply, holiday pay and/or vacation pay is required for specific classifications of workers only if the Davis-Bacon wage determination in the covered contract specifies such requirements for workers employed in those classifications.

Weekend Work

Extra pay for working during weekends is generally a matter of agreement between the employer and the employee (or the employee's representative). The Fair Labour Standards Act (FLSA) does not require extra pay for weekend work. However, covered, non-exempt employees must be paid at least one and one-half times their regular rates of pay for the time worked over 40 hours in a work week.

Record Keeping

- Making certain you adhere to all labour laws governing employers.
- Maintaining individual employee files.
- Maintaining all of the department records.
- Preparing departmental reports for top management.

Job Descriptions

A job description describes the major areas of an employee's job or position. A good job description begins with a careful analysis of the important facts about a job. Include information of the tasks involved, the methods used to complete the tasks, the purpose and responsibilities of the job, the relationship of the job to other jobs, and the qualifications needed for the job. It is important to make a job description practical by keeping it dynamic, functional and current. Don't get stuck with an inflexible job description. A poor job description will keep you and your employees from trying anything new and learning how to perform their job more productively. A well-written, practical job description will help you avoid having employees refuse to carry out a relevant assignments because it isn't in their job description.

Many jobs are subject to change, due either to personal growth, organizational development and/or the evolution of new technologies. Flexible job descriptions will encourage your employees to grow within their positions and learn how to make larger contributions. As an example, your office manager may be routinely ordering office supplies for the company and keeping the storage closet well stocked when they could be developing and implementing a system of ordering office supplies that promotes cost savings and efficiency within the organization.

When writing a job description, keep in mind that the job description will serve as a major basis for outlining job training or conducting future job evaluations.

A Job Description should include:

Job Title

Job Objective or Overall Purpose Statement: This statement is generally a summary designed to orient the reader to the general nature, level, purpose and objective of the job. The summary should describe the broad function and scope of the position and be no longer than three to four sentences.

List of Duties or Tasks Performed: The list contains an item by item list of principal duties, continuing responsibilities and accountability of the occupant of the position. The list should contain each and every essential job duty or responsibility that is critical to the successful performance of the job. It should begin with the most important functional and relational responsibilities and continue down in order of significance. Each duty or responsibility that comprises at least five percent of the incumbent's time should be included in the list.

Relationships and Roles: Describe the relationships and roles the person in the position holds within the company. Include any supervisory positions, subordinating roles and/or other working relationships.

When using Job Descriptions for recruiting situations, you may also want to attach the following:

Job Specifications, Standards and Requirements: The minimum qualifications needed to perform the essential functions of the job-education, experience, knowledge and skills. Any critical skills and expertise needed for the job should be included. For example, for a receptionist, critical skills may be having 1) a professional and courteous telephone manner; 2) legible hand-writing if messages are to be taken; 3) the ability to handle a multiple-lined phone system for a number of staff members; and 4) the patience and endurance to sit behind a desk all day.

Job Location: Where the work will be performed.

Equipment to be Used in the Performance of the Job: Collective Bargaining Agreements: Agreements and terms that relate to job functions, if applicable.

Non-Essential Functions: Functions which are not essential to the position or any marginal tasks that might be performed by the person in the position.

Salary Range: Range of pay for the position.

Keep each statement in the job description crisp and clear:

- Structure your sentences in classic verb/object and explanatory phrases. Since the job title is implied, it may be left out. For example, a sentence pertaining to the description of a receptionist position might read: "Greets office visitors and personnel in a friendly and sincere manner."
- Always use the present tense of verbs.
- If necessary, use explanatory phrases telling why, how, where or how often to add meaning and clarity. For example: "Collects all employee time sheets on a bi-weekly basis for payroll purposes."
- Omit any unnecessary articles such as "a", "an", "the" or other words for an easy-to-understand, to-the-point description. Using the above example, if this rule had not been followed, the statement would have read, "Greets all visitors and the office personnel to the building in a friendly and a sincere manner."
- Use unbiased terminology. Use the plural approach or construct sentences in such as way that gender pronouns are not required. For instance, use "them" instead of "he" or "she" in reference to the person in the position.
- Avoid using words which are subject to differing interpretations. Try not to use words such as "frequently," "some," "complex," "occasional," and "several" because they are ambiguous and open to interpretation.

Employee Compensation

Compensating an employee is not simply a process of settling upon a mutually agreeable salary. There are a number of regulations and reporting requirements that need to be met. Here is some information a variety of issues surrounding compensation that you need to be aware of.

Competitive Wages

When deciding pay rates for skilled workers, it may be helpful to keep tabs on the going rates for your industry and area. The U.S. Department of Labour's Bureau of Labour Statistics Web site maintains a comprehensive list of median and mean salaries across the United States by occupation, industry and area of the United States.

Minimum Wage Requirements

The Fair Labour Standards Act (FLSA) establishes current minimum wage requirements for employees.

Exceptions include lower wages for employees under 20 years of age for a defined period of time, certain full-time students, apprentices, interns and workers with disabilities. Many states also have minimum wage laws. In cases where an employee is subject to both the state and federal minimum wage laws, the employee is entitled to the higher of the two minimum wages.

Overtime Wages

The rate for all hours worked over a 40 hour work week are at least 1 1/2 times an employee's regular rate of pay. Some exceptions to overtime pay include administrative or executive employees, which fall under the "white collar exemption," as well as outside sales employees.

Child Support Enforcement

Every U.S. employer, large and small, must comply with state and federal laws pertaining to child support enforcement. The three principal requirements include:

1. You must report all newly hired employees to your State Directory of New Hires.
2. When you receive a valid Order or Notice to Withhold Income for Child Support for an employee, you must follow the terms of the Order/Notice and deduct the specified amount from each paycheck within the allowable limits. This amount must then be remitted within designated time frames.
3. You must provide information to the state or local child support enforcement agency for information about an employee, such as information about his or her earnings, current residence, and health insurance coverage, and report the termination of an employee for whom you are withholding child support (whether the employee is fired, resigns or is temporarily laid off).

Wage Garnishment

Wage garnishment occurs when an employer withholds the earnings of an individual for the payment of a debt as the result of a court order or other equitable procedure. Learn about employers' responsibilities and employees' rights.

Student Loan Garnishment Actions

Section 488A of the Higher Education Act authorizes the U.S. Department of Education and student loan guarantors to collect defaulted federally-financed student loans by means of an administrative garnishment order to the former student's employer, without the need for a court order.

Employee Benefit Plans

The Employee Retirement Income Security Act (ERISA) sets uniform minimum standards required by federal law to ensure that employee benefit plans are established and maintained in a fair and financially sound manner.

Workers' Compensation Programs

Learn the ins and outs of general federal and state workers' compensation rules, or look up specialized programs to aid coal miners, longshoremen and workers from other industries.

Employee Benefits

Not only do employee benefits play an important role in recruiting and retaining employees, but they also have a significant financial and administrative impact on a business. Most employees have come to expect a comprehensive benefits program. Indeed, the absence of a program or an inadequate program can seriously hinder a company's ability to attract and keep good personnel. Employers must be aware of what employees need and want, and be ready to make informed decisions when they select employee benefits.

Designing the right benefit plan for your employees is a complex task. There are many issues to consider, including tax and legal aspects, funding, and finding the right vendors or administrators.

A Good Employee Benefit Plan:

- Protects employees and their families from economic hardship brought about by sickness, disability, death or unemployment.
- Provides retirement income to employees and their families.
- Provides a system of leave or time off from work.

Certain benefits are mandated by law. The employer must pay in whole or in part for certain legally mandated benefits and insurance coverage. A comprehensive benefit plan should include some or all of the following elements:

- Health insurance.
- Disability insurance.
- Life insurance.
- Retirement plan.
- Flexible compensation (cafeteria plans).
- Leave.
- Perquisites.

To help you in Deciding what type of Benefits you want to offer, answer these Questions:

1. How much are you willing to pay for this coverage?
2. What kinds of benefits interest your employees?
3. Do you want employee input?
4. What do you think a benefits plan should accomplish?
5. Do you think it is more important to protect your employees from economic hardship now or in the future?
6. Is a good medical plan more important than a retirement plan?
7. Do you want to administer the benefits plan, or do you want the administration done by an insurance carrier?
8. What is your employee group like today?
9. Can you project what your employee situation might look like in the future?

Finding a benefit plan that meets your budget constraints and fills the needs of your employees is not easy. Here are some places to check for rates and availability of plans:

- Your local chamber of commerce.
- Independent insurance agents.
- Trade associations of your business.
- State departments (or commissions) of insurance.
- Community business leaders.

- Benefit consultants or actuaries.
- Service Corps of Retired Executives (Score).

To reduce risk, select insurance underwriters with top BEST ratings. HMOs and Blue Cross/Blue Shield are not rated by Best, but are regulated by state governments. Check with other users and state regulators on the history of the particular plan you are considering.

Rising costs are prompting small business owners to take a look at a form of health care coverage previously considered an option only for big business: self insurance.

Once you have Narrowed the Possibilities down to a few plans, ask each agent to Provide Information on the Following items:

1. Who is the insurance company?
2. Is it committed to small business?
3. How solvent is it? What is its rating?
4. What is the carrier's reputation for customer service?
5. What is the choice of doctors and hospitals?
6. How does the company manage health care costs?
7. Who administers the plan?
8. What information must the employer provide?
9. How are the employees enrolled?

An adequate benefit program has become essential to today's successful business, large or small. With careful planning you and your employees can enjoy good health and retirement protection at a cost your business can afford.

Advantages of Human Resource Diversity

The importance of human resource diversity in today's work place cannot be ignored. The simple reason for this is that the world is dramatically and rapidly changing and evolving all around us. More and more women and minorities are now entering the work place and the need for a diversified work environment is becoming more and more evident. Today is it estimated that in the US minorities represent over 50% of American society. This figure in itself is quite staggering considering that over two decades earlier minorities made just 25% of the population.

The reason why diversity is now such a hot topic and is given so much significance is that the world has realized how important diversification actually is.

Diversification celebrates the differences in people and is now important to a healthy and non-prejudiced society. By being able to understand and celebrate the differences between ourselves and others, we not only achieve success in our personal lives but in our professional lives as well.

At the moment many large multinational corporations and business are aggressively promoting human resource diversity in the work place as they now understand that this results in a higher employee retention rates, fewer complaints and grievances, and provides much easier access to newer markets.

Diversity initiatives not only improve the quality of an organization's work force, but are also the mechanism for a better return on investment in human capital.

So what does diversity actually mean? Well to be honest there is no one correct definition of diversity, but in the work place however a commonly agreed upon definition by many is that diversity encompasses gender, race, culture, age, family/carrer status, religion and disability.

It is very important that today's work place be diversified as it mans that a business can adopt and develop new and creative approaches to managing people to ensure a high level of work performance.

Some of the Reason why Diversity has become such a key word in human Resources is that:

- Women and minorities are now playing a significant role in society. Women are now major bread winners for the family as they takeover roles of leadership and decision making positions.
- A large majority of the working population now balances career responsibilities as well as dependent children.
- Here are an increased number of dual income families.
- There have been a number of changes made to the 'conventional' family structure with single parent families.
- The current work force is ageing.

Advantages of Human Resource Diversity

The Advantages of Human Resource Diversity Include:

- More efficient and effective personal and interpersonal communication between employees as well as with the general public.
- Improved team work performance.
- Increased creativity and innovation in the work place.
- A more enhanced problem solving capacity.
- A greater opportunity for equality in the work place.
- Overall staff well being.
- Higher staff morale.
- A wider talent pool to choose from.
- Improved customer service and satisfaction.
- A positive community image.

Besides these basic Advantages of human Resource Diversity, other Advantages Include:

- In an increasingly global market place, diversity increases cultural awareness and sensitivity, thus making it easier for a company to ease into a foreign market. If your firm does business with multilingual communities such as Hispanic, Italian or Japanese communities you are able to understand their customs, traditions, language and culture much better, therefore making it easier for you to do business with them.
- A diverse staff also helps to bridge cultural differences, so that a business can better establish itself in a foreign market.
- Diversity also helps to capitalize on new markets.
- Human resource diversity provides a more sensitive customer relationship environment where consumers from all over the world are understood and appreciated.

How to Create a Positive Relationship with Employees

Employers sometimes have a bad relationship with employees because they do not know how to create a positive atmosphere. Here are some tips for promoting a positive relationship with your employees.

Instructions

Step 1: Communication is important. Make sure employees know what you expect and don't make them guess or assume they are doing a good job when they are not. Tell them if they are doing well or poorly.

Step 2: Listening to your employees is important. Employees are of great value, since they know what is going on around them. Asking for their opinion can provide valuable information.

Step 3: Consistent behaviour is important to display to your employees. Favoritism should be avoided. The same standard should be applied to all employees. If you favour certain employees by assigning certain ones the preferred work without sharing among all, it causes resentment and they will have less respect for you.

Step 4: Follow your own policies and set the standard. Do not practice double standards.

Step 5: Treat your employees with respect. If you treat employees with dignity they will treat you the same. Leter, you have to discipline, fire or investigate them they will take the bad news much better if they feel you have treated them fairly in the past.

Step 6: Base your decisions on the job. Do not make business decisions based on race, gender, or any other reason. Base the decision on the which employee has the ability to perform the job not on your pet.

Step 7: When an employee has made a mistake, act immediately. The faster you deal with a problem the faster it stops.

Step 8: Keep good records for your business on employee performance evaluations, firings, discipline or any other employee matter.

Increasing the Bottom Line

Taking careful steps to build trust, respect and goodwill among employees doesn't just make it more fun to go to work, it can also boost your bottom line. Research by Leadership IQ shows that "the overwhelming majority of employees are not giving 100 percent at work; 72 percent admit that they're not giving their all," says Mark Murphy, CEO of Atlanta-based research firm Leadership IQ and author of *Hundred Percenters: Stop Making Your Employees Happy, Start Making Them Great*, to be released in November by McGraw-Hill. "One big reason is because their boss is not leading them in a way that encourages them to give 100 percent."

Employees of large corporations often view themselves as working for an impersonal entity, while those at small businesses conflate the organization and its owner. Quite simply, if employees like and respect you, they're more invested in your company and interested in its success. They're willing to work harder and give more. But if they don't care about you, they don't care about your company.

"Dislike and disrespect can turn into resentment," says James Harwood, CEO of Ravens Fire Group, a rental service consulting firm in Asheville, N.C. "Negative attitudes can turn into mediocre work and even theft. Those with negative attitudes can pull down other workers with them."

For many small companies, employees are the primary asset, says Stephone Darby, president and CEO of Advanced Information Technologies, Inc., in Florence, Ala. "For companies like us, if employees perform their work with expertise and timeliness and provide good customer service, the employer will retain their customers, grow their business with them and get referrals based on their relationship with them," Darby says.

When the employer provides an environment that is conducive to earning respect, employees will perform their work to these levels of expectation. But if there is not a mutual respect between an employer and employees, there is a great likelihood that one or more of these requirements will not be met. In turn, the employer will lose customers and sacrifice the growth of the company.

Employee Relationships in a Recession

While it sounds good to build and maintain positive relationships with employees, priorities often get shifted during an economic downturn—and relationships with employees may suffer. "For the majority of leaders, their leadership performance is suffering right now," Murphy says.

Some business owners are slacking simply because they can get away with it, as employees are just happy to have a job at the moment, Murphy says. Some others are dealing with such high personal stress levels that they are neglecting to give feedback or provide coaching and training. "They're so stressed and frazzled that they're forgetting some of the basics of leading a company," Murphy says.

But the recession won't last forever and those companies that survive recessions are the ones that continue to focus on developing high performers and keeping people engaged, Murphy says. "The best way to win in a recession is to keep employees' chins up."

Murphy's research shows about 70 percent of companies that make positive progress during a recession will continue those gains after the recession is over. The organizations that suffer during a recession "often maintain that suffering for a great deal of time after the recession is over," he says, frequently due to increased turnover rates when the job market improves. "A recession shakes things up in the marketplace and offers an opportunity to take market share. What if you're the one company that's able to motivate employees and keep them going while your competitors' employees are frozen in fear? This is your chance to win."

Bridge the Boss-Employee Gap

Keep your company afloat through the recession—and ensure that employees will stick around when times get better—with some of the following strategies:

1. Nix double standards. Don't expect employees to follow your instructions if you don't follow the same instructions yourself. "You can't just sit back and not have the same standard for yourself as you have for your employees," Weatherwax says.
2. Share the work. Nothing widens the gap between employer and employee like doling out the "dirty work," such as asking employees to do something unethical or simply to work an unreasonable number of hours. To earn employees' respect, business owners, "should never ask an employee to do something that they would not be willing to do themselves," Darby says.
3. Make them laugh. Humour is proven to reduce stress and take the edge off of a tense conversation. "As the boss, you can set the tempo or the mood for the business day," Weatherwax says. "If you can have fun with your employees and joke with them, they'll have more fun and they'll joke with the customers too."

4. Enforce consequences. Whether it's rewarding good work or holding employees accountable for mistakes, enforcing consistent consequences helps workers know what to expect. "Sometimes in tough times we overlook bad behaviour and don't recognize the good work being done by high performers," Murphy says.
5. Share your thought process. Especially during tough times when employees are worried about keeping their jobs, you can earn goodwill by being open about the choices you make, whether it's to cut costs or cut personnel. "The more transparent a leader becomes with his decision making process, the more likely employees are to trust those decisions," Murphy says. "Share the data, explain where you got that data, and why you decided what you did. What scares employees is the unknown, and if you're not transparent, they'll expect the worst."

5

Development of Small Scale Industries

Small Scale Industries may sound small but actually plays a very important part in the overall growth of an economy. Small Scale Industries can be characterized by the unique feature of labour intensiveness. The total number of people employed in this industry has been calculated to be near about one crore and ninety lakhs in India, the main proponents of Small scale industries.

The importance of this industry increases manifold due to the immense employment generating potential. The countries which are characterized by acute unemployment problem especially put emphasis on the model of Small Scale Industries It has been observed that India along with the countries in the Indian continent have gone long strides in this field.

Advantages Associated with Small Scale Industries

- This industry is especially specialized in the production of consumer commodities.
- Small scale industries can be characterized with the special feature of adopting the labour intensive approach for commodity production. As these industries lack capital, so they utilize the labour power for the production of goods. The main advantage of such a process lies in the absorption of the surplus amount of labour in the economy who were not being absorbed by the large and capital intensive industries. This, in turn, helps the system in scaling down the extent of unemployment as well as poverty.

- It has been empirically proved all over the world that Small Scale Industries are adept in distributing national income in more efficient and equitable manner among the various participants in the process of good production than their medium or larger counterparts.
- Small Scale Industries help the economy in promoting balanced development of industries across all the regions of the economy.
- This industry helps the various sections of the society to hone their skills required for entrepreneurship.
- Small Scale Industries act as an essential medium for the efficient utilization of the skills as well as resources available locally.

Small Scale Industries enjoy a lot of help and encouragement from the government through protecting these industries from the direct competition of the large scale ones, provision of subsidies in the form of capital, lenient tax structure for this industry and many more.

SSI in India

Overview

Since the time of independence, the small-scale sector in India has been a major contributor to country's Gross Domestic Product (GDP). This traditional sector in India is considered to have huge growth prospect with its wide range of products. With 40 percent share in total industrial output and 35 percent share in exports, the small-scale industrial sector in India is acting as Engine of Growth in the new millennium.

The definition for small-scale industrial undertakings has changed over time. Initially they were classified into two categories-those using power with less than 50 employees and those not using power with the employee strength being more than 50 but less than 100. However the capital resources invested on plant and machinery buildings have been the primary criteria to differentiate the small-scale industries from the large and medium scale industries. An industrial unit can be categorized as a small-scale unit if it fulfils the capital investment limit fixed by the Government of India for the small-scale sector.

As per the latest definition which is effective since December 21, 1999, for any industrial unit to be regarded as Small Scale Industrial unit the following condition is to be satisfied:-

Investment in fixed assets like plants and equipments either held on ownership terms on lease or on hire purchase should not be more than Rs 10 million. However the unit in no way can be owned or controlled or ancillary of any other industrial unit.

The traditional small-scale industries clearly differ from their modern counterparts in many respects. The traditional units are highly labour consuming with their age-old machineries and conventional techniques of production resulting in poor productivity rate whereas the modern small-scale units are much more productive with less manpower and more sophisticated equipments.

Khadi and handloom, sericulture, handicrafts, village industries, coir, Bell metal are some of the traditional small-scale industries in India. The modern small industries offer a wide range of products starting from simple items like hosiery products, garments, leather products, fishing hook etc. to more sophisticated items like television sets, electronics control system, various engineering products especially as ancillaries to large industrial undertakings.

Nowadays Indian small-scale industries (SSIs) are mostly modern small-scale industries. Modernization has widened the list of products offered by this industry. The items manufactured in modern Small-scale service & Business enterprises in India now include rubber products, plastic products, chemical products, glass and ceramics, mechanical engineering items, hardware, electrical items, transport equipment, electronic components and equipments, automobile parts, bicycle parts, instruments, sports goods, stationery items and clocks and watches.

Since Independence the Government of India has Nurtured this sector with Special care with the Following aims:-

- To develop this sector as a major source of employment.
- To encourage decentralized industrial expansion.
- To ensure equitable distribution of income.
- To mobilize capital investment and entrepreneurship skills.

The small scale sector has played a very important role in the socio economic development of the country during the past 50 years. It has significantly contributed to the overall growth in terms of the Gross Domestic Product (GDP), employment generation and exports. The performance of the small scale sector, therefore, has a direct impact on the growth of the overall economy.

The performance of the small scale sector in terms of parameters like number of units (both registered and unregistered). During the one year period i.e., 2000-01 over 1999-2000, the number of SSI units is estimated to have increased by 1,58,000, production at current prices by Rs. 72,609 crore and at constant prices by Rs. 33,714 crore.

Employment increased by 7,14,000 persons, while exports were higher by Rs. 5,778 crores. According to projections made by the Ministry of Small Scale Industries during 2000-01, the SSI sector recorded growth in production of 8.09 per cent over the previous year. The small scale industries sector has recorded higher growth rate than the industrial sector as a whole (4.9 per cent during 2000-01). It contributed about 40 per cent towards the industrial production as a whole and 35 per cent of direct exports from the country.

The Government has been taking various measures from time to time in order to enhance the productivity, efficiency and competitiveness of the SSI sector. In pursuance of the comprehensive policy package announced last year, the major developments that have taken place in the SSI sector during 2001-02 are briefly.

Sickness in the SSI Sector

As on March 31, 2001, there were 2,49,630 sick SSI units which had obtained loans from banks. An amount of Rs. 4,506 crore of bank credit was blocked in these units. Of these only 13,076 units were considered potentially viable by the banks with outstanding credit of Rs. 399 crore. Further, banks had identified 2,25,488 units with outstanding bank credit amounting to Rs. 3,943 crore as unviable.

Rehabilitation of sick units is a costly proposition as it involves rescheduling of past overdues with concessions on interest amount due, additional credit for modernisation and technology upgradation and provision for fresh working capital. Presently, the State Level Inter-Institutional Committee (SLIIC) of banks and financial institutions is the only forum looking into rehabilitation of potentially viable sick SSI units. However, in the absence of statutory backing, SLIICs has no power to enforce its decisions.

To tackle the problem of rehabilitation of potentially viable sick SSI units, the RBI constituted a working group on November 25, 2000 under the chairmanship of Shri S.S. Kohli, the then chairman of Indian Banks Association, to look into the issue. The Working Group submitted its report in May, 2001. All the major recommendations of the working group have been accepted by the RBI, including a change in the definition of Sick SSI units, norms for deciding on the viability of sick units, etc. The revised definition would enable banks to take action at an early stage for revival of the units.

Based on the accepted recommendations of the Working Group, the RBI has drawn up the revised guidelines for Rehabilitation of Sick SSI units, which have been circulated on January 16, 2002 to all the Banks for implementation.

In 1947 after gaining independence, India initiated a path of industrialization to achieve economic prosperity. India focused on developing the manufacturing base. Much of the countries development was done through the five year plans. Industries like iron and steel, oil refineries, cement and fertilizer were brought under the gamut of public sector enterprises. The decision makers then encouraged the development of small scale industries. They perceived that Indian small scale industries would play a vital role in the economic progress of the country and had immense potential for employment generation. Developing small scale sector would also result in decentralized industrial expansion, better distribution of wealth and to encourage investment and entrepreunial talent.

The government has initiated several policies for the growth and development of small scale industries. They included reservation of certain items to be manufactured only by the small scale sector. Other measures include credit marketing, technology, and entrepreneurship development, fiscal, financial and infrastructural support. In 1999, the government established the Ministry of Small Scale Industries and Agro and Rural industries to make policy decisions for the development and well being of the small scale industries.

Initially the small scale sector was characterized as traditional labour intensive units with outdated machineries and inefficient production techniques. But in the recent past the condition of the small scale units has improved. Today they have installed modern machines, applied better management techniques and are much more productive than before.

SSI-Location

Small Scale Industries are located throughout the country, though predominantly in the rural areas. The small scale industries in the rural areas are skill based, wherein the skill for manufacturing is passed on from one generation to another. Some of the goods manufactured in these units are textile handicrafts, woodcarving, stone carving, metal ware etc. Small scale industrial factories are also present in urban areas and usually they account for the maximum volume of production for that particular good in the country. For e.g. Ludhiana in the state of Punjab is the main centre in the country for producing woolen hosiery, sewing machine parts, bicycles and its parts, similarly Tiruppur in Tamil Nadu accounts for small scale firms that are involved in spinning, weaving and dying of cotton garments.

Post Liberalization

Post liberalization economic conditions has created immense growth prospect for the small scale industries. The government has also supported the small scale industries by the way of implementing policies like investment ceiling for the SSI sector and priority lending. The formation of WTO in 1995 resulted in a major challenge to the well being of the SSI. The protection given to the SSI in the form of reservation and quantitative restrictions has been withdrawn. More than 160 items reserved under the SSI category have been de reserved. It has been found that if the SSI upgrades the technology, adopt better management practices, reengineer the factories to improve productivity and provide qualitative product, they would be competitive in the post WTO scenario. The advancement in computer and telecommunication technology, increase in e commerce, opening up of markets due to WTO, mergers and acquisitions, improved infrastructure and outsourcing noncore area of business have all contributed to the growth of SSI.

Ministry of Small Scale Industries

The Ministry of Small Scale Industries (SSI) is a defunct Indian government ministry. It was merged with the Ministry of Agro and Rural Industries to form the Ministry of Micro, Small and Medium Enterprises. The ministry was tasked with the promotion of micro and small enterprises (MSEs).

The Ministry of Small Scale Industries and Agro and Rural Industries (SSI&ARI) was created in October 1999. In September 2001, the ministry was split into the Ministry of Small Scale Industries (SSI) and the Ministry of Agro and Rural Industries (ARI). The Ministry of Small Scale Industries merged with the Ministry of Agro and Rural Industries to form the Ministry of Micro, Small and Medium Enterprises in 2007

The Small Industries Development Organization (SIDO) was under the control of the ministry, as was the public sector undertakings National Small Industries Corporation Limited (NSIC).

The Small Industries Development Organisation

It is the Office of the Development Commissioner for Small Scale Industries. SIDO was established in 1954 on the basis of the recommendations of the Ford Foundation. It has over 60 offices and 21 autonomous bodies under its management. These autonomous bodies include Tool Rooms, Training Institutions and Project-cum-Process Development Centres.

Various Services provided by SIDO to the SMEs:-

- facilities for testing, toolmenting, training for entrepreneurship development.
- preparation of project and product profiles.
- technical and managerial consultancy.
- assistance for exports.
- pollution and energy audits.

SIDO also provides economic information services and advises Government in policy formulation for the promotion and development of SSIs. The field offices also work as effective links between the Central and the State Governments.

Small Scale Industries

A small scale industry (SSI) is an industrial undertaking in which the investment in fixed assets in plant & machinery, whether held on ownership term or on lease or hire purchase, does not exceed Rs.1 Crore. However, this investment limit is varied by the Government from time to time.

Entrepreneurs in small scale sector are normally not required to obtain a licence either from the Central Government or the State Government for setting up units in any part of the country. Registration of a small scale unit is also not compulsory. But, its registration with the State Directorate or Commissioner of Industries or DIC's makes the unit eligible for availing different types of Government assistance like financial assistance from the Department of Industries, medium and long term loans from State Financial Corporations and other commercial banks, machinery on hire-purchase basis from the National

Small Industries Corporation, etc. Registration is also an essential requirement for getting benefits of special schemes for promotion of SSI viz. Credit guarantee Scheme, Capital subsidy, Reduced custom duty on selected items, ISO-9000 Certification reimbursement & several other benefits provided by the State Government.

The Ministry of Micro, Small and Medium Enterprises acts as the nodal agency for growth and development of SSIs in the country. The ministry formulates and implements policies and programmes in order to promote small scale industries and enhance their competitiveness. It is assisted by various public sector enterprises like:-

- Small Industry Development Organisation (SIDO) is the apex body for assisting the Government in formulating and overseeing the implementation of its policies and programmes/ projects/schemes.
- National Small Industries Corporation Ltd (NSIC) was established by the Government with a view to promoting, aiding and fostering the growth of SSI in the country, with focus on commercial aspects of their operation.
- The Ministry has established three National Entrepreneurship Development Institutes which are engaged in development of training modules, undertaking research and training and providing consultancy services for entrepreneurship development in the SSI sector. These are:-
  - National Institute of Small Industry Extension Training (NISIET) at Hyderabad,
  - National Institute of Entrepreneurship and Small Business Development (NIESBUD) at Noida
  - Indian Institute of Entrepreneurship (IIE) at Guwahati
- The National Commission for Enterprises in the Unorganised Sector (NCEUS) has been constituted with the mandate to examine the problems of enterprises in the unorganised sector and suggest measures to overcome them.
- Small Industries Development Bank of India (SIDBI) acts as apex institution for financing SSIs through various credit schemes.

Provisions Relating to Taxation of Small Scale Industries

In a developing country like India, Small Scale Industries play a significant role in economic development of the country. They are a vital segment of Indian economy in terms of their contribution towards country's industrial production, exports, employment and creation of an entrepreneurial base. These industries by and large represent a stage in economic transition from traditional to modern technology. Small industry plays a very important role in widening the base of entrepreneurship. The development of small industries offers an easy and effective means of achieving broad based ownership of industry, the diffusion of enterprise and initiative in the industrial field.

Given their importance, he Government policy framework right from the First plan has highlighted the need for the development of SSI sector keeping in view its strategic importance in the overall economic development of India. Accordingly, the policy support from the Government towards Small Scale Industries has tended to be conducive and favourable to the development of small entrepreneurial class. Government accords the highest preference to development of SSI by framing and implementing suitable policies and promotional schemes.

The most important promotional policy of the Government for the SSI's is fiscal incentives in the form of tax concessions and exemptions of direct or indirect taxes leviable on production or profits.

How to Start a Small Scale Industry?

Sources of Capital to Finance your Company can be:

- Long-term loans for acquiring fixed assets like land and building, plant and machinery, other installations, fittings, fixtures and so on.
- Short-term loans to meet the day-to-day requirements of business, such as procurement of raw materials, wages for workers, transport costs, etc.
- The State Financial Corporations/State Development Corporations/commercial banks provide long-term loans.
- All small scale industrial units engaged in process activity are eligible for financial assistance except for the activities covered by the restricted list issued by DC (SSI) Office or under the special regulation list.
- State Financial Corporations provide financial assistance of up to Rs.60 lakhs to private/ public limited companies, and up to Rs.30 lakhs to proprietary/partnership firms.

- Rates of interest charged vary according to the size of the loan and the category of the entrepreneur, for example SC/ST, women, ex-servicemen, physically handicapped persons, etc.
- Composite loans of up to Rs. 50,000 are provided for meeting both long-term and short-term loans so that small entrepreneurs do not have to go to other institutions
- Under the 'single window scheme', the State Financial Corporations and the State Industrial Development Corporations provide financial assistance
- This scheme is refinanced by the Small Industries Development Bank of India (SIDBI)

Registration / Statutory Licenses And Clearances:

Provisional (Temporary) Registration

Provisional Registration Entitles you to:

- Apply for a shed or a plot in an industrial estate or a developed area.
- Apply for corporation/ Municipality and/or other licenses.
- Apply for power/water connection.
- Apply for financial assistance from banks and other institutions.
- Obtain sales tax, excise registration, etc. wherever required.
- Apply to the National Small Industries Corporation/ State Small Scale Industries corporation/ other institutions for procuring machinery on hire-purchase basis.
- Take other steps/ approvals that may be necessary to establish the industrial units, including obtaining import license for capital goods/ raw materials.

Provisional (Temporary) Registration

- You will be issued a provisional (temporary) SSI registration certificate.
- It is usually provided for a period of one year and can be subsequently renewed for four more periods of six months each.
- If the entrepreneur is not in a position to commence production on account of circumstances beyond his control, extension of the provisional registration period would be considered.

Contact

Apply on the prescribed application form to the General Manager, District Industries Centre (DIC) functioning at the respective district headquarters.

Permanent Registration

The Entrepreneur can apply for Permanent Registration After:

- The factory building is ready.
- All requisite machinery, testing equipment and pollution control equipment are installed.
- Power connection is established.

In order to bring uniformity in registration certificates, the office of the Development Commissioner (Small Scale Industries), New Delhi has prescribed a common registration form to be used by all States/ UT Governments throughout India.

Contact: Apply on the prescribed application form to the General Manager, District Industries Centre (DIC) functioning in the headquarters of the respective districts.

Statutory Licenses / Clearances

Some of the procedures or licenses applicable for the effective functioning of the small scale enterprises are listed below. Depending on the product-line chosen, the size of the unit/number of workers and so on, an entrepreneur should seek approval for specific regulations applicable in his case.

S. N.	*Type of Product, Activity or Service*	*Licensing Authority*
1.	Manufacture of drugs and cosmetics	State Drug Controller / Drug Control Administration
2.	Manufacture of fruit and vegetable-based products	Deputy Director, Food and Vegetable Preservation, Ministry of Agriculture, Govt. of India, located in the State
3.	Industries using water and involving effluent disposal/ gaseous waste, etc.	To get clearance from: 1. The District Health Officer of the particular district 2. Director of Public Health of the State Govt.

S. N.	*Type of Product, Activity or Service*	*Licensing Authority*
4.	Units employing 10 workers or more with power, or 20 workers or more without power.	To be obtained from Chief Inspector of Factories
5.	Power connection	Officer designated by the State Electricity Board concerned.
6.	SSI approval of electronic items governed under the decentralised category	State level Technical Committee under State Directorate of Industries
7.	SSI approvals/PMP (Phased Manufacturing Programme) approval of electronic items other than decentralised items	Development Commissioner, Small Scale Industries, Nirman Bhavan, New Delhi-11 through State Directorate of Industries
8.	For units functioning in places other than Industrial Estates/ approved developed plots	Licence from, Commissioner Corporation or Municipality or Panchayat Union
9.	Pollution Control	State Pollution Control Board
10.	Registration under the State Sales Tax Act	Local Joint Commercial Tax Officer.
11.	Registration under Central Excise Act	Superintendent of Central Excise of the Area or Collector of Central Excise.

Repayment of Loans

Banks and financial institutions are extremely careful in selecting prospective entrepreneurs (borrowers) and ascertaining their creditworthiness before giving them loans.

- The owner of a small scale enterprise is permitted to repay the loan amount in installments, generally spread over a period of 8 to 10 years. These are determined by taking into account the cash generation and profitability aspects of the project.
- Normally banks and financial institutions insist on repayment of the loan amount, along with interest charges.
- The interim period normally permitted for repaying the instalments of the principal amount varies from 12 months to 24 months from the date of the first release of the loan.
- Before deciding the interim period, you should impress upon the banker the actual development period involved in respect of his project and then start the repayments.

Marketing

You must know what the market for your product is.

- In order to succeed, you should always try to know both the current market, and the potential market

You could use some of the following to increase your market:

- Displays and models.
- Advertising.
- Publicity.
- Sales connected with special events.
- Personal selling tactics.
- Customer service Public relations.
- Appropriate product design/style/packaging.
- The new entrepreneur should try to win support of his wholesalers and retailers.
- Wholesalers could be encouraged to handle his product by offering financial incentives and substantial concessions.
- The National Small Industries Corporation Ltd. (NSIC) aims to provide assistance in marketing the products of Small Scale Industries sector, under the Government Stores Purchase Programme (to meet the requirements of govt. departments, railways, defense, etc.)

Recruiting Personnel

If you have chosen a business which is too large for you and your family to run, you will have to:

- Recruit skilled and unskilled workers. If you do not know enough about the business you are setting up, you can recruit an experienced person to manage it for you. You can do this either through advertisements or through the Employment Exchange.
- Ensure that the technical personnel in your unit possess the following basic skills:
- Technical knowledge relating to the job.
- Relevant knowledge and adequate experience.
- Ability to express ideas.

Installation of Machinery

You must know the different types of machinery and equipment that are needed to set up your enterprise.

- Make a listing of the leading dealers/suppliers where the machinery is available.

The Following Factors Determine the type of Machines you will need:

- Capacity of the proposed unit.
- Minimum scale of production which is economical.
- Expected performance standards.
- Productivity Waste.
- Minimization Availability of spare parts for the new machinery.

Preparing A Project Report

A project report is a document which provides you, and investors like banks, an overall picture of your proposed business.

It allows you to work out all the different areas of your plan, so that you can identify and solve problems before they happen. When you prepare your Project Report, try to think of these points:· Technical feasibility This combines all the technical areas of your business, and shows how they will work. Some points to include are the product specifications to be adopted, the availability of raw material, an outline of the manufacturing process, quality control measures, power supply, availability of water, transport facilities and communication network. These depend on the type of business you are setting up. · Economic viability Here, you have to try to plan how you business will work financially. You need to work out all the costs you will have on one side, and things like the amount of sales and demand you will get when you sell your product on the other. Be very honest in this section, because it is better to realise that your business will fail on paper than when you have put your savings into it. This section also should contain information on any bank loans you may need to take, as well as details of the repayment schedules thereof.

Selecting your Product

The Selection of the Product is Dependant on your Capital Investment Capacity: Before embarking on any business venture, it is essential that you know whether there is a need for what you intend to produce, the profit margin, production capacity and the time of return on capital investment.

Depending on your capacity to raise resources, you can start: Tiny Units located in rural or backward areas with a population not exceeding 50,000 as per 1991 census, and an investment in plant and machinery of up to Rs. 25 lakhs. Small Scale Industrial Undertaking These are units where the investment on fixed assets (plants and machinery), does not exceed Rs. 100 lakhs. Small Scale Service Establishment Service-oriented enterprises are those with an investment in plant and machinery not exceeding Rs. 5 lakhs, and which are located in rural areas and towns with a maximum population of up to 5 lakhs. Today, 820 products have been reserved for production only by businesses in the small scale sector. You should take into account the following before setting up your business:

- Any relevant experience you may have.
- Your aptitude for the specific business.
- Your education, technical qualifications, or any training you have undergone.
- Market demand for the product.
- The presence of any large enterprises nearby which might effect your choice of product.
- The potential profitability of your business.
- Availability of raw materials and other inputs.
- Availability of technical know-how and process details.
- Competition from businesses making similar products.

The office of the Development Commissioner, Small Scale Industries has brought out a publication entitled Project Profiles in three volumes, and has a monthly publication called Laghu Udyog Samachar. These can be very useful when you are selecting your product.

Contact: You can consult the technical experts available at the various Small Industries Service Institutes and Branch Institutes, or contact the nearest District Industries Centre located in the district headquarters for preliminary consultations in this regard.

Location: For some businesses, the location is very important. When you are choosing a location, remember to take into account the following: You should pick a location close to your source of raw material, and close to the market where you want to sell your product.

- The location should have a good transportation system. This will cut down your costs when getting your raw materials and when you are taking your products to market.
- In some areas, there are incentives and concessions available to help set up industries.
- Find out about the climatic, geographical and environmental factors that could affect your industry or the transport system.

Assessing Profit Generation

You should possess accurate data regarding the cost of production in order to keep a strict control on costs.

- This will also facilitate concrete decision-making.
- If your business does not make profit, you need to quickly identify the reason. Make sure you have minimised your costs and, if necessary, adjust your production volume.
- You should work out your monthly profits by calculating total sales revenue minus the total costs per month. This will allow you to see whether your business is growing successfully or not.

A Healthy and Wealthy Enterprise

If you are not able to make profits and pay the installments of principal and interest to the financiers, you are in for trouble.

6

Purchasing for Small Business Inventory and Quality Control

Purchasing

Purchasing refers to a business or organization attempting to acquire goods or services to accomplish the goals of the enterprise. Though there are several organizations that attempt to set standards in the purchasing process, processes can vary greatly between organizations. Typically the word "purchasing" is not used interchangeably with the word "procurement", since procurement typically includes Expediting, Supplier Quality, and Traffic and Logistics (T&L) in addition to Purchasing.

Overview

Purchasing managers/directors, and procurement managers/directors guide the organization's acquisition procedures and standards. Most organizations use a three-way check as the foundation of their purchasing programs. This involves three departments in the organization completing separate parts of the acquisition process. The three departments do not all report to the same senior manager to prevent unethical practices and lend credibility to the process. These departments can be purchasing, receiving; and accounts payable or engineering, purchasing and accounts payable; or a plant manager, purchasing and accounts payable. Combinations can vary significantly, but a purchasing department and accounts payable are usually two of the three departments involved.

When the receiving department is not involved, it's typically called a two-way check or two-way purchase order. In this situation, the purchasing department issues the purchase order receipt not required. When an invoice arrives against the order, the accounts payable department will then go directly to the requestor of the purchase order to verify that the goods or services were received. This is typically what is done for goods and services that will bypass the receiving department. A few examples are software delivered electronically, NRE work (non reoccuring engineering services), consulting hours, etc...

Historically, the purchasing department issued Purchase Orders for supplies, services, equipment, and raw materials. Then, in an effort to decrease the administrative costs associated with the repetitive ordering of basic consumable items, "Blanket" or "Master" Agreements were put into place. These types of agreements typically have a longer duration and increased scope to maximize the Quantities of Scale concept. When additional supplies are required, a simple release would be issued to the supplier to provide the goods or services. Another method of decreasing administrative costs associated with repetitive contracts for common material, is the use of company credit cards, also known as "Purchasing Cards" or simply "P-Cards". P-card programs vary, but all of them have internal checks and audits to ensure appropriate use. Purchasing managers realized once contracts for the low dollar value consumables are in place, procurement can take a smaller role in the operation and use of the contracts. There is still oversight in the forms of audits and monthly statement reviews, but most of their time is now available to negotiate major purchases and setting up of other long term contracts. These contracts are typically renewable annually.

This trend away from the daily procurement function (tactical purchasing) resulted in several changes in the industry. The first was the reduction of personnel. Purchasing departments were now smaller. There was no need for the army of clerks processing orders for individual parts as in the past. Another change was the focus on negotiating contracts and procurement of large capital equipment. Both of these functions permitted purchasing departments to make the biggest financial contribution to the organization. A new terms and job title emerged – Strategic sourcing and Sourcing Managers. These professionals not only focused on the bidding process and negotiating with suppliers, but the entire supply function. In these roles they were able to add value and maximize savings for organizations. This value was manifested in lower inventories, less personnel, and getting the end product to the organization's consumer quicker. Purchasing manager's success in these roles resulted in new assignments outside to the traditional purchasing function – logistics, materials management, distribution, and warehousing. More and more purchasing managers were becoming Supply Chain Managers handling additional functions of their organizations operation. Purchasing managers were not the only ones to become Supply Chain Managers. Logistic managers, material managers, distribution managers, etc. all rose the broader function and some had responsibility for the purchasing functions now.

In accounting, purchases is the amount of goods a company bought throughout this year. They are added to inventory. Purchases are offset by Purchase Discounts and Purchase Returns and Allowances. When it should be added depends on the Free On Board (FOB) policy of the trade. For the purchaser, this new inventory is added on shipment if the policy was FOB shipping point, and the seller remove this item from its inventory. On the other hand, the purchaser added this inventory on receipt if the policy was FOB destination, and the seller remove this item from its inventory when it was delivered.

Goods bought for the purpose other than direct selling, such as for Research and Development, are added to inventory and allocated to Research and Development expense as they are used. On a side note, equipments bought for Research and Development are not added to inventory, but are capitalized as assets...

Purchasing: Topics

Acquisition Process

The revised acquisition process for major systems in industry and defense. The process is defined by a series of phases during which technology is defined and matured into viable concepts, which are subsequently developed and readied for production, after which the systems produced are supported in the field.

The process allows for a given system to enter the process at any of the development phases. For example, a system using unproven technology would enter at the beginning stages of the process and would proceed through a lengthy period of technology maturation, while a system based on mature and proven technologies might enter directly into engineering development or, conceivably, even production. The process itself includes four phases of development:

- Concept and Technology Development: is intended to explore alternative concepts based on assessments of operational needs, technology readiness, risk, and affordability.
- Concept and Technology Development phase begins with concept exploration. During this stage, concept studies are undertaken to define alternative concepts and to provide information about capability and risk that would permit an objective comparison of competing concepts.
- System Development and Demonstration phase. This phase could be entered directly as a result of a technological opportunity and urgent user need, as well as having come through concept and technology development.
- The last, and longest, phase is the Sustainment and Disposal phase of the program. During this phase all necessary activities are accomplished to maintain and sustain the system in the field in the most cost-effective manner possible.

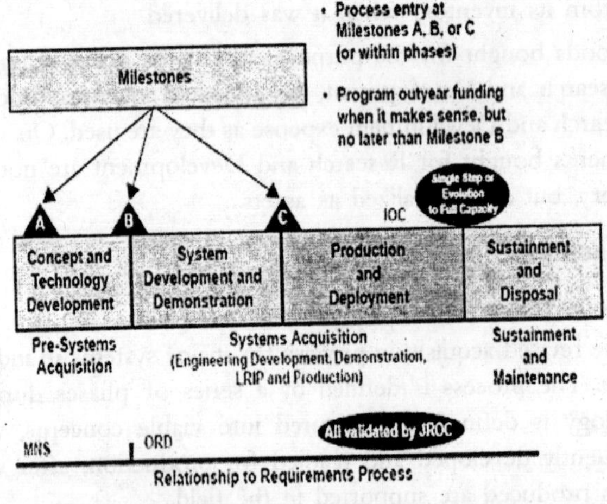

Model of the Acquisition Process

Selection of Bidders

This is the process where the organization identifies potential suppliers for specified supplies, services or equipment. These suppliers' credentials (qualifications) and history are analysed, together with the products or services they offer. The bidder selection process varies from organization to organization, but can include running credit reports, interviewing management, testing products, and touring facilities. This process is not always done in order of importance, but rather in order of expense. Often purchasing managers research potential bidders obtaining information on the organizations and products from media sources and their own industry contacts. Additionally, purchasing might send Request for Information (RFI) to potential suppliers to help gather information. Engineering would also inspect sample products to determine if the company can produce products they need. If the bidder passes both of these stages engineering may decide to do some testing on the materials to further verify quality standards. These tests can be expensive and involve significant time of multiple technicians and engineers. Engineering management must make this decision based on the cost of the products they are likely to procure, the importance of the bidders' product to production, and other factors. Credit checks, interviewing management, touring plants as well as other steps could all be utilized if engineering, manufacturing, and supply chain managers decide they could help their decision and the cost is justifiable.

Other organizations might have minority procurement goals to consider in selection of bidders. Organizations identify goals in the use of companies owned and operated by certain ethnicities or women owned business enterprises. Significant utilizing of minority suppliers may qualify the firm as a potential bidder for a contract with a company or governmental entity looking to increase their minority supplier programs.

This selection process can include or exclude international suppliers depending on organizational goals and criteria. Companies looking to increase their pacific rim supplier base may exclude suppliers from the Americas, Europe, and Australia. Other organizations may be looking to purchase domestically to ensure a quicker response to orders as well as easier collaboration on design and production.

Organizational goals will dictate the criteria for the selection process of bidders. It is also possible that the product or service being procured is so specialized that the number of bidders are limited and the criteria must be very wide to permit competition. If only one firm can meet the specifications for the product then the purchasing managers must consider utilizing a "Sole Source" option or work with engineering to broaden the specifications if the project will permit alteration in the specifications. The sole source option is the part of the selection of bidders that acknowledges there is sometimes only one reasonable supplier for some services or products. This can be because of the limited applications for the product cannot support more than one manufacturer, proximity of the service provided, or the products are newly designed or invented and competition is not yet available.

Bidding Process

This is the process an organization utilizes to procure goods, services or equipment. Processes vary significantly from the stringent to the very informal. Large corporations and governmental entities are most likely to have stringent and formal processes. These processes can utilize specialized bid forms that require specific procedures and detail. The very stringent procedures require bids to be open by several staff from various departments to ensure fairness and impartiality. Responses are usually very detailed. Bidders not responding exactly as specified and following the published procedures can be disqualified. Smaller private businesses are more likely to have less formal procedures. Bids can be in the form of an email to all of the bidders specifying products or services. Responses by bidders can be detailed or just the proposed dollar amount.

Most bid processes are multi-tiered. Acquisitions under a specified dollar amount can be "user discretion" permitting the requestor to choose who ever they want. This level can be as low as $100 or as high as $10,000 depending on the organization. The rationale is the savings realized by processing these request the same as expensive items is minimal and does not justify the time and expense. Purchasing departments watch for abuses of the user discretion privilege. Acquisitions in a mid range can be processed with a slightly more formal process. This process may involve the user providing quotes from three separate suppliers. Purchasing may be asked or required to obtain the quotes. The formal bid process starts as low as $10,000 or as high as $100,000 depending on the organization. The bid usually involves a specific form the bidder fills out and must be returned by a specified deadline. Depending of the commodity being purchased and the organization the bid may specify a weighted evaluation criterion. Other bids would be evaluated at the discretion of purchasing or the end users. Some bids could be evaluated by a cross-functional committee. Other bids may be evaluated by the end user or the buyer in Purchasing. Especially in small, private firms the bidders could be evaluated on criteria or factors that have little if anything to do with the actual bid. Examples of these factors are history of the bidder with the company, history of the bidder with the company's senior management at other firms, and bidder's breadth of products.

Technical Evaluation

Technical Evaluations, evaluations of the technical suitability of the quoted goods or services, if required, are normally performed prior to the Commercial Evaluation. During this phase of the procurement process, a technical representative of the company (usually an engineer) will review the proposal and designate each bidder as either technically acceptable or technically unacceptable. Selling is important.

Commercial Evaluation

Payment Terms

Cost of Money-Cost of Money is calculated by multiplying the applicable currency interest rate multiplied by the amount of money paid prior to the receipt of GOODS. If the money were to have remained in the Buyer's account, interest would be drawn. That interest is essentially an additional cost associated with such Progress or Milestone payments.

Manufacturing Location-The manufacturing location is taken into consideration during the evaluation stage primarily to calculate freight costs and regional issues which may be considered. For instance, in Europe it is common for factories to close during the month of August for Summer holiday. Labour agreements may also be taken into consideration and may be drawn into the evaluation if the particular region is known to frequent labour unions.

Manufacturing Lead-Time-the manufacturing lead-time is the time from the placement of the order (or time final drawings are submitted by the Buyer to the Seller) until the goods are manufactured and prepared for delivery. Lead-times vary by commodity and can range from several days to years.

Transportation Time-Transportation time is evaluated while comparing the delivery of goods to the Buyer's required use-date. If Goods are shipped from a remote port, with infrequent vessel transportation, the transportation time could exceed the schedule an adjustments would need to be made.

Delivery Charges-the charge for the Goods to be delivered to a stated point. Bid Validity Packing Bid Adjustments Terms and Conditions Seller's Services Standards Organizations Financial Review Payment Currency Risk Analysis-market volatility, financial stress within the bidders Testing.

Negotiating

Negotiating is a key skillset in the Purchasing field. One of the goals of Purchasing Agents is to acquire goods per the most advantageous terms of the buying entity (or simply, the "Buyer"). Purchasing Agents typically attempt to decrease costs while meeting the Buyer's other requirements such as an on-time delivery, compliance to the commercial terms and conditions (including the warranty, the transfer of risk, assignment, auditing rights, confidentiality, remedies, etc.).

Good negotiators, those with high levels of documented "cost savings", receive a premium within the industry relative to their compensation. Depending on the employment agreement between the Purchasing Agent (Buyer) and the employer, Buyer's cost savings can result in the creation of value to the business, and may result in a flat-rate bonus, or a percentage payout to the Purchasing Agent of the documented cost savings.

Purchasing Departments, while they can be considered as a support function of the key business, are actually revenue generating departments. For example, if the company needs to buy $30 million USD of widgets and the Purchasing Department secures the widgets for $25M USD, the Purchasing Department would have saved the company $5M USD.

That savings could exceed the annual budget of the department, which in effect would pay the department's overhead-the employee's salaries, computers, office space, etc.

Post-Award Administration

Post-award administration typically consists of making minor changes, additions or subtractions, that in some way change the terms of the agreement or the Seller's Scope of Supply. Such changes are often minor, but for auditing purposes must be documented into the existing agreement. Examples include increasing the quantity of a Line Item or changing the metallurgy of a particular component.

Purchasing for small Business

Using Your Budget to Control Costs

Your budget must be a vibrant document, one that is well considered and that is used on an ongoing basis. Use it as a historical reporting system. Don't look at how you've measured up to your goals months or even weeks after a period has closed. Check the important elements (direct costs as one example) far more frequently.

Use a Line Item Method

When you created your chart of accounts, you created a list of general categories such as office expense or repairs and maintenance. For the purposes of your profit and loss statement, those categories are all that is needed. But for the purpose of cost control, you may want to break down these items into sub categories. For example:

Utilities

- Gas.
- Electric.
- Water.
- Sewage.

Office Expense

- Supplies.
- Equipment leases.
- Postage.
- Temporary help.

Insurance

- Liability.
- Auto.
- Health.
- Life.
- Workers' compensation.

This will give you detailed information on exactly where the money is being spent so you can monitor and correct any serious excesses. Comparing your fixed expense to the budget and the amount spent a year earlier on the same items is a good way to see if you are still in line.

Monitor on a Regular Basis

Even when the trend is exactly where you want it to be, don't give up the regular habit of monitoring costs against budget. You can create a statement that looks like the one that follows:

	Budget	Actual		
	1999	Jan	YTD	+/-
Sales				
Cost of goods				
Gross profit				
etc.				

If you had anticipated sales of $600,000 for 1999 and your sales for January were $42,000, then the top line would read:

	Budget	Actual		
	1999	Jan	YTD	+/-
Sales	$50,000	42,000	42,000	(8,000)

You will know at a glance whether you are over or under in any budget category, and then you can research the line items if necessary to identify and correct any problems.

Give Budget Authority to Managers

A critical element in delegation of work and authority is assigning responsibility for expenditures and bottom line outcomes. At the beginning of each period, identify the amount of money budgeted for each department manager and ask them to create a list of priorities. Then on each reporting period, check the results of their expenditures against the amounts budgeted. Perhaps you can include an incentive program for those who come in under budget. Whether in the corporate world or the world of small business, it is human nature to spend all the money in the budget because there is always some piece of equipment to upgrade or replace, or there is some inventory that is difficult to source and creates the desire to stockpile. Put a prize on resisting that urge, and don't forget to explain all the reasonings behind budget decisions.

Be Prepared to Sacrifice

A healthy business can bring a good return, long term, to a prudent operator. Don't make the mistake of choosing short-term satisfaction at the risk of long-term stability. Keep all the expenditures within reason until the company is well on its feet and able to easily afford them.

Payroll and the Cost of Labour

For many businesses, particularly those in the service industry, such as restaurants or manufacturing companies that are labour intensive, the cost of payroll is the single largest line item on the profit and loss statement. Therefore, these are costs that must be budgeted and must be monitored for progress.

The Administration of your Payroll

The two key elements in establishing an effective payroll administration system are, first, setting company policy regarding pay and, second, determining how often payroll will be done and who will do it. These are the decisions made by the business owner, and they should be well thought out not just made on the run.

Establishing Payroll Policy

Unless you are utilizing union labour and subject to a negotiated contract, the parameters (within the law) of payroll are yours to set. You will likely negotiate vacation time with new employees and ultimately set a company wide standard such as one week after the first year, two weeks after year three, and three weeks after year five. It is best to be conservative going in; you can always loosen the policy, but it is almost impossible to take time back once it has been given. The same goes for paid holidays such as Thanksgiving, Christmas, and so on. Decide how many you can afford and be conservative. The day after Thanksgiving is appreciated because it makes a four-day weekend, but it is not necessary. The last portion of these "time off days" are sick time and personal leave. Find out what is typical in your type of business; you want to be competitive to attract the right people, but again be cautious in the beginning.

Consider this: If you give two weeks vacation, five holidays, and five sick or personal days, that is a total of 20 days. The work year is 260 days long, and that means that almost 8 percent of your labour costs is being paid for nonproductive time. As we go along and look at other benefits, you will see how expensive employees are—far beyond the wages you think you are paying. Remember this when setting budgets. The average "extra" cost of each employee is 35 percent, so a $40,000-a-year person is actually a $54,000-a-year person.

Getting the Payroll Processed

If you have a small number of employees and a good computer system, you can do your payroll processing in-house. But as your numbers grow and the type of information you want gets more complicated, sending this task out to an outside service makes far more sense. Make sure that the person who tracks and transmits your payroll keeps accurate records; the use of a time clock is one good way to be sure all hours worked are correctly maintained. Vacation days as well as paid time off should be scrutinized to be fair to both employer and employee.

Benefits can be Costly: Keep to a Budget

Without adding anything additional, your payroll is increased by approximately 24 percent by the cost of vacations, FICA (Social Security) contribution, unemployment insurance, and statutory workers' compensation insurance. But that does not end many benefit packages that may also include health (including dental) insurance as well as life insurance plus perks such as car expense, which may be required in certain circumstances. This can add up in a hurry and, if not controlled, may make the company unprofitable or uncompetitive.

Again, be cautious at the outset because adding benefits is far easier than trying to reduce them. Full health coverage for a family can easily cost $600 per month, or $7,200 per year. For an employee earning $40,000 per year, this is an 18 percent add-on and would increase the benefits to a total of 42 percent (24 percent established by vacation, tax, and other insurance), making the cost closer to $60,000. This is a fairly high place to start unless you are working in a competitive situation for specific skills or talents.

The issue of company cars as a benefit is a difficult one as well. The total cost can be substantial and remains fixed regardless of the productivity of your employees, normally sales personnel, because the cost isn't tied to any set level of sales. Why not start with a reimbursement plan (mileage and perhaps a gas card), and if the cost seems to be justified, you can consider the car as well; just remember that insurance will also be a cost, as will maintenance, parking, and all other incidentals.

For many companies, payroll for both direct and indirect labour is the largest line item. Remember that there are costs beyond the pay itself, and keep them in line by creating and sticking to a budget.

Payroll Taxes

Keep in mind that you must budget for those taxes that are add-ons to your payroll. First is the federal FICA tax, which is for Social Security and Medicare. You will also pay a tax to the Internal Revenue Service as well as your state for a contribution to the unemployment fund. The percentage on the FICA tax is fixed at 7.8 percent but the unemployment tax is variable depending on the status of your account. The more people who collect, the higher the fee. Know how much and when these payments are due and take great care that you have set aside the money to pay them.

It is a serious mistake not to pay your taxes on a timely basis. The late fees for not filing and not paying can be enormous and add up to a 50 percent penalty to the taxes you owe. Once this unobligated and unaccounted cost is added to a company's expenses, profits go out the window and cash flow is strangled. And trying to avoid payments won't work because the taxing bodies have strong powers of enforcement behind them. This is a situation to avoid at all costs.

The Lowdown on Purchasing

Purchasing may not be quite as razzle-dazzle as creating exciting marketing campaigns, but it can be just as crucial to your bottom line. If your business has a profit margin of 10 percent on sales and you cut expenses by just over 5 percent, your profit will soar by 50 percent! Without changing the profit margin, sales would have to increase by 50 percent to achieve the same result!

Spec Sheets

Before making purchases, you need to create exact specification sheets for the items you want to buy. For items such as office supplies, developing spec sheets won't be very time-consuming, especially if you purchase some items on a regular basis.

What should a spec sheet include? Let's assume that you want to purchase a computer. You may not want to specify a particular brand and model. You may, instead, want to specify a price ceiling or price range. You will need to list any special computer features or options that are necessary. And you may want to list features and options that you would like if price criteria can still be maintained. Spec sheets should also specify delivery times, warranty or service requirements, and payment terms such as COD, net thirty, or credit card use.

Vendors

For some products and most services you will want to prequalify vendors by getting testimonials from satisfied customers, reading product reviews, visiting vendor plants, meeting with key personnel, or perhaps sampling the product or service.

Quotes

Once you have developed your spec sheets and made a list of eligible vendors, you are ready to go out for quotes. For almost any purchase of $100 or more, it is recommended that you get at least two quotes. If the item or service being purchased costs considerably over $100, three quotes are recommended. When requesting quotes, ask the vendor when you might expect to receive its quotation.

Never just send out a written request for a quotation or the vendor will be unlikely to give your request serious attention. Always talk to a salesperson. If it is a significant quote, meet with the salesperson face to face. Never hesitate to ask a salesperson to come and visit you. Often a salesperson can influence the price and other terms attendant to your order. If the work involves developing a quote, the sales representative can usually push the estimator to work within a tighter margin.

Even if the company offers standard pricing, a sales representative may be able to extend higher volume pricing to you if you establish a good rapport. Especially if yours is a new business, a good word from the salesperson to the credit manager may mean the difference between cash in advance and thirty-day terms.

Purchase Orders

Once you have decided on a vendor and are ready to proceed with a purchase, it is always a good idea to use written purchase orders. If you don't use purchase orders you are going to find yourself receiving goods and services that are the wrong style, type, or colour than those you ordered. You may be charged a higher price or sent the wrong quantity. The purchase order should specify the name of the item or service being purchased, and any details specified in your spec sheet. You need to state the quantity being purchased, delivery date, delivery address, shipping method and payment, and packing and receiving requirements.

You should detail each cost you are incurring and also state the total cost of the items or services ordered to avoid misunderstanding.

It is also a good idea to use purchase orders printed with your company name. If you don't, you are more likely to be asked for a prepayment or deposit on goods or services ordered.

Acceptance

When the product is delivered, be sure that whoever signs for the package also inspects the order. When you sign for delivery from a trucking company or other shipper you are generally agreeing that the quantity is correct and that the shipment bears no obvious damage. Have your shipping and receiving department or other personnel count the quantity or number of cartons delivered. Receiving should also check for any visible damage to the outside of the shipping containers. Receiving needs to get a copy of the receipt for delivery that has been signed. This will serve as your receiving slip.

As soon as possible, the shipment should be opened and inspected. Quantity, quality, and adherence to purchase order specs should be checked. If there is any problem, you are in a much stronger position if you call the vendor and point out discrepancies immediately.

Don't hesitate to complain about problems or seek improvements. Call the salesperson you have been dealing with. Most vendors want to build long-term relationships with their customers!

Invoices

Eventually you will receive an invoice for the merchandise or service you have purchased. Compare your purchase order and receiving slip against the invoice. Don't be surprised if the invoiced payment due is higher than the purchase order total.

Many businesses are very good at adding extra charges. They may state price increases or cite some "minor" charge that they neglected to inform you about up front. Call them. Say, "Too bad!" Your purchase order specifies exactly what you intended to pay for the merchandise or service and you are not obligated to pay for any additional charges. Be firm, but be polite. You can always say that you will be happy to pay the hidden charges next time—that is, if you use the vendor next time!

Eliminate the Overhead!

"Overhead, like the government, tends to just grow and grow. To reduce overhead takes incredible discipline and a willingness to risk civil war with all affected employees."

Overhead is a Threat to your Survival!

A low-cost structure is essential for being competitive, and low overhead is crucial for this. Overhead costs don't directly make your product or deliver your service. They don't directly benefit your customer. Overhead just adds to your cost structure and makes you less competitive.

Overhead is like government bureaucracy—it just grows and grows. And the more it grows the harder it is to see its benefit. Once you add an expense to overhead it's hard to take it away.

Unfortunately, too many employees love overhead! They love nice desks; they love new computers; they love new buildings; they love deep carpet; they love nice offices! But all these trappings of success are just that—traps—and each and every overhead expense threatens every company and every person that works there.

Get Rid of the Office!

There was one move I put off making for several years that by itself chopped our overhead to shreds and gave us a huge competitive advantage. I delayed moving to a commercial office.

For four years I operated my book publishing business out of my basement apartment. This wasn't just a one-person office. I had up to seven people working there. And we also used it as a warehouse. I'd have neighbours move their cars so semitrailers could back down the driveway. I'd open the large kitchen window to load books in and out. I remember one night waking up to find that a pile of boxes with books had fallen on top of me while I slept.

My MBA friends laughed at this low-budget business setup, but today no one laughs at the 100 percent equity I hold in my $10 million business.

Don't Get Seduced by Technology!

It's incredibly easy to get seduced by the latest advances in high technology and by expensive equipment that you either don't need or could make do with a less expensive version.

Years ago when I was running a busy newspaper sales office, I was shocked to see how expensive multiline phone systems were. So by our reception desk on the first floor I installed six single-line phones for incoming calls and installed six matching extensions on our second floor, using an intercom to announce incoming calls. It looked very crude, and it was appallingly unprofessional, but it worked, and it saved us a lot of money.

Today, the backbone of our accounting system is still an ancient IBM system 36 computer. But I was a lot less embarrassed about this relic in our office when I saw one in operation at the leading wholesaler in our industry.

Try Selective Upgrading!

Personal computers and related software can be a significant expense for a small business and even for a larger one. Often a firm will decide to unilaterally upgrade all of their PCs and software. But there is very little volume savings on PCs and usually not too many savings on software—in fact, I've seen some software site licenses that are more expensive than buying multiple copies off the shelf.

So I would suggest that you look at who really needs the latest and most powerful PCs and who really needs the latest version of an expensive software package. Usually software versions are backward and forward compatible anyway.

But don't skimp by not buying the appropriate software licenses. You could be subject to massive fines and embarrassment if you don't have a software license, not just for each package, but for each PC the software is installed on.

Turning Garbage into Greenbacks

Most companies spend a lot of money getting their waste hauled away. But my company makes a lot of money getting its waste removed! I would like to tell you that this was a result of my brilliant insight, but that would simply not be true.

As we went through one of our perennial cash crunches a couple of years ago, I got everyone together and said,"Don't panic, we're not going to cut jobs—but we do need everyone's help to cut costs. And we'll give some small cash awards for the best suggestions."

Well, sure enough, most people panicked anyway and told one another we were about to go out of business. But they still liked the cash award idea, and we got lots of great suggestions—including the "money from wastepaper" plan from some of the hourly guys in the warehouse. These fellows directed us to a paper converter who would not only pick up our paper waste for no charge—but also pay us thousands of dollars for it.

Getting Rock-Bottom Costs

"A really low cost structure gives you plenty of leeway for making errors—which is particularly important if you're going to make anywhere near as many mistakes as I have!"

Low Costs Allow Room for Mistakes!

A really low cost structure is one of the most important competitive weapons a business can have at its disposal. It has certainly been important for me. For years my business was terribly undercapitalized, and I was often testing my bank's patience. On top of that, I was always making mistakes. Ad campaigns that didn't sell, products that the market spit back at us, a customer who one year returned virtually all of a half-million dollars in purchases, even entire business units that failed—you name the mistake, I probably made it and more than once! But our low cost structure gave us a lot of leeway for making errors, and it still allowed us to make money and repay our bank loans, more or less when they were due.

Narrowly Focus your Cost Reviews!

To get competitive advantage of a low cost structure, I don't mean a percentage point or two below the industry average. I mean ten or fifteen percentage points below. From time to time you should carefully examine every single cost you incur. Not all at once—it's too overwhelming. But instead, review costs in one small part of your business at a time. Don't just focus on renegotiating prices or getting more bids. Think about every way possible to reduce the cost or, ideally, eliminate it altogether. You'll find that if you focus on just one item at a time, you'll often be able to come up with some really creative solutions. Running a small company, I never had much purchasing power with vendors—but in hindsight it was probably to my advantage, since I was forced to focus on more creative, and potentially more substantial, ways to reduce costs.

Four Steps to Lower Costs

Here's a simple four-step process for lowering costs:

1. Try to redesign the product or process to eliminate the cost entirely.
2. Try to change the specs to reduce the costs to the vendor supplying the goods or service.

3. Try to standardize the specifications or change the delivery schedule to increase volume buying capability.
4. Seek bids and negotiate.

Last year in the book industry, paper prices skyrocketed. We tried to eliminate paper altogether by launching electronic products. For books, we changed our paper specifications, typically from fifty-to thirty-five-pound paper, saving 30 percent in tonnage. Finally, we began buying paper by the carload and negotiated prices aggressively.

Lower Costs is not just Negotiating!

It's hard to get other people to shift their cost-control efforts beyond price negotiation. For example, my operations manager used to perennially complain about the increasing price of cardstock, trying to get me ready to accept an increase in his box budget. I knew he was doing a great job negotiating prices, but our costs were still poised to rise, and I don't like rising costs.

So I pushed him to look for additional solutions, such as reusing more of the boxes printers used to ship books to us, changing the assortment of boxes we use, and substituting padded envelopes for boxes on smaller-sized shipments.

At the same time, my marketing department was spending more and more money on counter displays—all of which we ship inside cardboard boxes. So I encouraged my marketing and operations managers to get together and design prepacks or self-shippers in order to eliminate the cost of a separate shipping box.

Prices are always Negotiable!

Here are a few suggestions that have worked for me in negotiating lower prices:

- Get lots of competing bids for exactly the same specs.
- Set a target price. For example, when buying a year-long service that had a standard price of $25,000 per month, I told the vendor we'd pay $10,000, period. We saved $180,000.
- Change the classification. In buying advertising from a huge media corporation that is notorious for not going off their rate card, I nonetheless insisted on a special deal. They got my business by creating a whole new low-rate category for which only our firm qualified.

- Charm the people at the vendor you are buying from—get them on your side, pushing the decision makers for a lower rate.
- Demonstrate that you will definitely buy now, given a great price.
- Always be prepared to walk if you don't get exactly the deal you want.

The Importance of Being Cheap!

"It's more than a coincidence that when I entered the market for local city guidebooks, I decided to go for the low end under the brand name Mr. Cheap's."

Penny-pinch your way to Success!

One of the most important traits for business success is being cheap! In almost any business, if your cost structure is just a couple of percentage points lower than your competition's, you can have a huge competitive advantage. When you're starting a small business with no money you learn how to be cheap really quickly. But as your business gets larger and more successful, it's easy to loosen the purse strings and not watch each expense so carefully. Also, as you hire people it becomes a challenge to get them to adapt the same frugal mind set that you acquired by skimping along in the early days of your business.

Big Companies are Getting Cheaper, Too!

If you think being cheap is just for small companies, you better think again. More and more larger corporations are using cost control as a competitive weapon. For example, in New England almost every large regional discount department store chain has gone bankrupt! And who's gaining market share? Wal-Mart! Talk about cost advantages. The general and administrative costs at one of these large, troubled regional discounters was 27 percent of sales. Wal-Mart's is 15 percent. This cost difference alone can explain the difference between spectacular success and spectacular bankruptcy! Wal-Mart's costs aren't just lower because they're bigger. They're lower because Sam Walton was the cheapest CEO in America—and by no coincidence, also the richest! Even when Wal-Mart was a fraction of the size of its competitors, so were its costs!

Cut your costs with One Call!

Al Dunlop, known as "chainsaw Al" by some of his detractors for the massive layoffs he's instituted, led an incredible turnaround at Scott Paper by selling off major divisions, repositioning the remaining product lines, creating new marketing strategies, and reviewing every single cost with a fine-tooth comb. But when you read through his wonderful autobiography, Mean Business (which the armchair book reviewers did not appreciate as much as I did), he singles out one phone call that made more difference at Scott Paper than any other action. In this call, Al cut the single biggest cost dramatically—the cost of paper. He didn't just put the paper cost out to bid. Instead, he demanded an unheard-of low price and then offered to give all of his business to the vendor who would meet this price.

Save your Money And Rent a Dump!

Being cheap isn't just a method for looking at every cost... it's a mindset. I remember hearing a man talk about a business he was going to start. "I'm going to do everything right. I'm going to get the best equipment; the best location; the best furniture; the best of everything,"... and he's probably had the best bankruptcy, too! I once went to a bankruptcy auction at an incredibly lavish office complex. There were original paintings on the walls, built-in multimedia screens, skylights—the whole nine yards. I filled up a truck with beautiful furniture that I paid just about nothing for. During the auction a lot of us were wondering what kind of firm this was. It turned out that it was a consulting firm and one of my business school professors had been chairman emeritus. Lots of brains in a business can help you get ahead—but a cheap mindset can keep you out of bankruptcy!

Growth Breeds Wasteful Spending!

As my still-small company grows, I see an attitude of complacency to costs growing along with it—and I can fully appreciate how large corporations can get pulled into wasting money needlessly. For example, I hear people saying things like: "A corporation of our size needs to look like this... or ought to be doing that...." When you hear this kind of talk, you can bet that someone is trying to justify something that has no justification! Another explanation for needless expenditures that amazes me goes something like this: "Well, we spent $3,000 on company sweatshirts, so I figured $200 for a subscription to a newsletter is a drop in the bucket." One day I found my marketing people had become almost totally focused on conveying the right corporate image in our trade ads as opposed to trying to sell product! Again the explanation was that at our growing size we shouldn't be so concerned any more with directly generating sales!

Inventory

What is "Inventory"?

The word inventory simply means the goods and services that businesses hold in stock. There are, however, several different categories or types of inventory. The first is called materials and components. This usually consists of the essential items needed to create or make a finished product, such as gears for a bicycle, microchips for a computer, or screens and tubes for a television set. The second type of inventory is called WIP, or work in progress inventory. This refers to items that are partially completed, but are not the entire finished product. They are on their way to becoming whole items but are not quite their yet. The third and most common form of inventory is called finished goods. These are the final products that are ready to be purchased by customers and consumers. Finished goods can range from cakes to furniture to vehicles. Most people think of the finished goods as being part of an inventory stock, but the parts that create them are held accountable in inventory as well.

There's many different ways that companies handle their inventory. Overall it depends on what kind of business it is. For example, a food manufacturer who makes canned fruit may take into account every single piece of that can in its inventory. The materials used to make the can, the labels, the fruit, and the sugary filling could all be part of the overall analysis of inventory. Keeping track of inventory can be a complex process. The term for watching inventory is called logistics. Logistics is a detailed process by which all inventory is tracked and logged. Several different people are involved in logistics. This can include everything from the owner of the company to the transportation company that delivers the goods to the manufacturing plant. By using complex systems such as barcode integration, every piece of inventory from the smallest parts to the largest finished product can be tracked and observed. You may wonder why companies keep such a close eye on their inventory. The answer is really simple: the bottom line. Without inventory control, millions of dollars could be lost each year just because there was no accountability for everything involved in making a product. Of course, inventory is also important on the checks and balances side. Accountants keep an eye on inventory counts in order to be sure that fraud or embezzlement is not occurring. This also serves as a backup to check and be sure that everything is in its place and nothing out of the ordinary is taking place. There have actually been books written on how to reconcile inventory, keep accurate stock counts, reasons that errors occur, tools to use to help make sure inventory is on time and in its place, and much more. Once you learn about the various forms of inventory and the importance of making sure it is logged properly, the process of tracking it should be fairly streamlined and simple, giving your business a cost-effective and competitive edge.

Inventory Control System

A process for keeping track of objects or materials. In common usage, the term may also refer to just the software components.

Modern inventory control systems rely upon barcodes, and potentially RFID tags, to provide automatic identification of inventory objects. In an academic study performed at Wal-Mart, RFID reduced Out of Stocks by 30 percent for products selling between 0.1 and 15 units a day. Inventory objects could include any kind of physical asset: merchandise, consumables, fixed assets, circulating tools, library books, or capital equipment. To record an inventory transaction, the system uses a barcode scanner or RFID reader to automatically identify the inventory object, and then collects additional information from the operators via fixed terminals (work stations), or mobile computers.

Applications

An inventory control system may be used to automate a sales order fulfilment process. Such a system contains a list of order to be filled, and then prompts workers to pick the necessary items, and provides them with packaging and shipping information.

Real time inventory control systems use wireless, mobile terminals to record inventory transactions at the moment they occur. A wireless LAN transmits the transaction information to a central database.

Physical inventory counting and cycle counting are features of many inventory control systems which can enhance the organization.

Inventory Investment

The management of your inventory, for a company that sells products, is crucial to the success of your company. If you hold too much inventory on your shelves or in your warehouse, you run the risk of obsolescence and getting stuck with inventory that you can't sell. If you hold too little inventory, then you are risking stock outs and loss of customer good will. Either problem will cost your business money.

How do you best manage your investment in inventory to maximize your profits and cash flow and minimize your expenses? You have to categorize your inventory into dead inventory, slow-moving inventory, and productive inventory and deal with it appropriately.

There is an unspoken 80/20 rule in business for different situations. In the case of inventory, you usually get about 80 percent of your sales from 20 percent of your inventory. From a productivity standpoint, your inventory can be divided up into categories: dead inventory, slow inventory, and productive inventory.

Always Invest in Assets with a Positive Rate of Return

This sounds like a no-brainer, but it isn't. Money that you have invested in inventory has been invested at a negative rate of return! You actually don't know if you are going to make any money on that investment or not. The longer it sits in your warehouse or on your store shelves, the more money you lose. You make no money on inventory until it is sold. In fact, you lose money. Invest in inventory conservatively and wisely as your money is more wisely invested elsewhere unless you are sure you can sell your inventory and sell it quickly.

Don't Accumulate Excess Inventory

Perhaps the most dangerous thing you can do as a small business owner is accumulate too much inventory. Too much inventory will turn a healthy business into a sick business in a short amount of time. In an economy on the verge of emerging from recession, don't be tempted to stock up too much on the inventory you sell. You don't yet know how fast the economy is going to recover or what the demand will be for your product. Stock up slowly and track your sales to sell what is selling and what is not.

Get Rid of Dead Inventory that is not Performing

Dead inventory is inventory that has been sitting on your shelves not selling for some period of time. Some define dead inventory as stock that hasn't sold in 12 months. That's too long! I define dead inventory as stock that hasn't sold in 6 months. It is probably dragging down your inventory turnover ratio. Some businesses feel like they have to keep some level of dead inventory on the shelves because it may consist of some parts, for example, that are necessary replacement parts for products they sell in their business or have sold in the past. Those businesses might consider ordering those parts by special order when their customers need them instead of holding them on their shelves.

Instead of holding dead inventory on your shelves, mark it down for quick sale. For the dead inventory that doesn't sell, deem it "unsellable" and check with the distributor to see if they will take it back. You may have to strike a deal to try a new product they are pushing, but that is OK. If that doesn't work, donate it to charity. At least, you'll get a tax write-off.

Take a look at the Slow-Moving Inventory

Slow-moving inventory is not dead inventory because it is moving, but it may be moving toward obsolescence. In the current economic environment, slow-moving inventory may be hard to identify. Companies that sell products have experienced an unprecedented slowdown in their business due to the Great Recession. Those environmental factors have to be taken into account when analysing inventory movement.

That said, slow moving inventory ties up your cash in idle inventory. It creates a negative impact on profitability and cash flow. If you have investors in your company, it lowers their return on equity. In order to determine if some of your inventory is really slow-moving, you need to look at companies like your own, particularly in the same industry.

If you use an SKU system, you can isolate each individual product and calculate that product's inventory turnover. If you set a target inventory turnover for products that your company sells and the item you have isolated falls under that target, then you can mark it as slow-moving and take action to get it off your shelf or out of your warehouse. You can then use some of the techniques you use for getting rid of dead inventory.

Productive Inventory

This is what you want-your cash cow, your productive inventory This is the inventory that sells, adds to your profit and your cash flow During the recession, even this productive inventory may have been selling slowly, but it's still selling and as the economy picks up, you should see a nice increase in the sale of your productive inventory. You can't take it for granted. Track what you think is productive inventory and make sure it is productive. If it isn't, move it to the slow-moving or dead inventory categories.

Use the inventory turnover ratio to calculate how your productive inventory is doing. You may even want to do this by product line. Be aware that the inventory turnover ratio is dependent on the industry you are in. Some industries turn inventory fairly slowly, maybe 5 times per year. Others turn inventory rapidly, up to 20 times per year. Usually, the higher the number, the better you are doing.

Unless you manage your inventory investment actively and wisely, your active, healthy business can turn sour quickly. Don't let this happen!

Inventory control is concerned with minimizing the total cost of inventory. In the U.K. the term often used is stock control. The three main factors in inventory control decision making process are:

- The cost of holding the stock (e.g., based on the interest rate).
- The cost of placing an order (e.g., for row material stocks) or the set-up cost of production.
- The cost of shortage, i.e., what is lost if the stock is insufficient to meet all demand.

The third element is the most difficult to measure and is often handled by establishing a "service level" policy, e.g, certain percentage of demand will be met from stock without delay.

The ABC Classification The ABC classification system is to grouping items according to annual sales volume, in an attempt to identify the small number of items that will account for most of the sales volume and that are the most important ones to control for effective inventory management.

Reorder Point: The inventory level R in which an order is placed where R = D.L, D = demand rate (demand rate period (day, week, etc.), and L = lead time.

Safety Stock: Remaining inventory between the times that an order is placed and when new stock is received. If there are not enough inventories then a shortage may occur.

Safety stock is a hedge against running out of inventory. It is an extra inventory to take care on unexpected events. It is often called buffer stock. The absence of inventory is called a shortage.

Quantity Discount Model Calculation Steps:

- Compute EOQ for each quantity discount price.
- Is computed EOQ in the discount range?
- If not, use lowest cost quantity in the discount range.
- Compute Total Cost for EOQ or lowest cost quantity in discount range.
- Select quantity with the lowest Total Cost, including the cost of the items purchased.

The following This Java Script compute the optimal values for the decision variables based on currently available information about the above factors. Enter the needed information, and then click the Calculate button. In entering your data to move from cell to cell in the data-matrix use the Tab key not arrow or enter keys.

Inventory Accounting

Inventory accounting may sound like a huge undertaking but in reality, it is quite straightforward and easy to understand. You start with the inventory you have on hand. No matter when you sell product, the value of your inventory will remain constant based on accepted and rational methods of inventory accounting. Those methods include weighted average, first in/first out, and last in/first out.

Weighted Average

Weighted average measures the total cost of items in inventory that are available for sale divided by the total number of units available for sale. Typically this average is computed at the end of an accounting period.

Suppose you purchase five widgets at $10 apiece and five widgets at $20 apiece. You sell five units of product. The weighted average method is calculated as follows:

Total Cost of Goods for Sale at Cost (divided):

- Total Number of Units Available for Sale = Weighted Average Cost per Widget
- Five widgets at $10 each = $50
- Five widgets at $20 each = $100
- Total number of widgets = 10
- Weighted Average = $150 / 10 = $15
- $15 is the average cost of the 10 widgets.

First in/first out

First in, first out means exactly what it says. The first widgets you bring into inventory will be the first ones sold as product. First in, first out, or FIFO as it is commonly referred to, is based on the principle that most businesses tend to sell the first goods that come into inventory.

Suppose you buy five widgets at $10 apiece on January 3 and purchase another five widgets at $20 apiece on January 7. You then sell five widgets on January 30. Using first in, first out, the five widgets you purchased at $10 would be sold first. This would leave you with the five widgets that you purchased at $20, which would leave the value of your inventory at $100.

Last in/first out

This method, commonly referred to as LIFO, is based on the assumption that the most recent units purchased will be the first units sold. A "widget" is an imaginary item that could be just about any product. The advantage of last in, first out accounting, or LIFO, is that typically the last widgets purchased were purchased at the highest price and that by considering the highest priced items to be sold first, a business is able to reduce its short-term profit, and hence, taxes.

Suppose you purchase five widgets at $10 apiece on January 4 and five more widgets at $20 apiece on February 2. You then sell five widgets on February 20. The value of your inventory, using LIFO, would be $50, since the most recent widgets purchased, at a total value of $100 on February 2, were sold. You were left with the five widgets valued at $10 each.

LIFO and FIFO Inventory Accounting Methods

LIFO, last-in-first-out and FIFO, first-in-first-out the two most common inventory accounting methods. The choice of the method of inventory accounting by a small business can directly impact its balance sheet, income statement, and statement of cash flows. Not only do companies have to track the number of items sold, but they have to track the cost of items each item. These two methods are ways in which they can do that. Each will have a different effect on their financial statements.

How is Inventory Determined?

Inventory can be broken down into three categories: raw materials, work-in-process, and finished goods. Raw materials are inventory used to produce assets for sale. Work-in-process is assets in production for sale. Finished goods are assets intended for sale. The inventory equation is the following:

1. Beginning Inventory + Net Purchases-Cost of Goods Sold = Ending Inventory.

There are two common methods for accounting for this inventory.

LIFO-Last-In, First-Out

LIFO assumes that the last items put on the shelf are the first items sold. LIFO is a good system to use when your products are not perishable or become obsolete. Under LIFO, when prices rise, the higher priced items are sold first and the lower priced products are left in inventory. This increases a company's cost of goods sold and lowers their tax liability and, as a result, their net income.

This inventory accounting method seldom approximates replacement costs for inventory, which is one of its drawbacks. In addition, it usually does not correspond to the actual physical flow of goods.

Let's use the gasoline industry as an example. Let's say that a tanker truck delivers 2,000 gallons of gasoline to Henry's Service Station on Monday and the price at that time is \$2.35/gallon. On Tuesday, the price of gasoline has gone up and the tanker truck delivers 2,000 more gallons at a price of \$2.50/gallon. Under LIFO, the gasoline station would assign the \$2.50 gallon gasoline to Cost of Goods Sold and the remaining \$2.35 gallons of gasoline would be used to calculate the value of ending inventory at the end of the accounting period.

FIFO-First-In, First-Out

FIFO assumes that the first items put on the shelf are the first items sold, so your oldest goods are sold first. This system is generally used by companies whose inventory is perishable or subject to quick obsolescence. If prices go up, FIFO will give you a lower cost of goods sold because you are using your older, cheaper goods first. Your bottom line will look better to your investors, if you have any, but your tax liability will be higher because you have higher profit. A positive about the FIFO method is that it represents recent purchases and, as such, more accurately reflects replacement costs.

Going back to the gasoline industry example, under FIFO, the gasoline station would assign the \$2.35 gallon gasoline to Cost of

Goods Sold and the remaining $2.50 gallons of gasoline would be used to calculate the value of ending inventory at the end of the accounting period.

Financial Statement Problems with LIFO

A LIFO liquidation can result when your company experiences declines in your inventory quantities. In this case, a lot of your older inventory is sold or liquidated. This creates an inflated profit margin that isn't real and seriously distorts net income. This has across the board impacts. You should add the LIFO liquidation profits to the current ratio numerator and adjust the denominator to reflect FIFO inventory instead of LIFO inventory in order to properly state your liquidity position. You should make exactly the same adjustments to the inventory turnover ratio. Inventory accounting is only one part of a company's management of their inventory investment, but an important one.

Average Inventory Cost

Definition: Item price minus discounts, plus freight and taxes. The average is found by adding the beginning cost inventory for each month plus the ending cost inventory for the last month in the period. If calculating for a season, divide by 7. If calculating for a year, divide by 13.

Examples: For a 6-month season: Inventory at cost in Jan $52,000, Feb $35,000, March $48,000, April $65,000, May $35,000 and June $60,000 (52,000 + 35,000 + 48,000 + 65,000 + 35,000 + 60,000) ÷ 7 = $42,142.86

How much will Inventory Cost for My Retail Startup?

Evaluating startup costs can be difficult for new retailers. If several of the steps to planning a business require you to have a retail business license, how will you obtain the necessary information to determine whether or not your retailing business plan is a viable one? The bottom line is many of the figures for the business plan will need to be estimates.

Answer: Vendors and suppliers generally only send catalogs with dealer price lists to established businesses. A few may share this information if you explain to them you are planning a new business, but many will not.

Luxury items and hand-crafted merchandise generally allow for higher markups, while your basic and essential products may have a smaller profit margin. Retail markup typically runs between 30 and 40 percent, depending on the industry segment.

Let's say you plan to sell a $19.95 item to your customers. That item will probably cost between $14 and $15 wholesale. Industry research, especially reports from trade associations, can offer some insight on what markup your retail segment uses. Shipping, handling, and any other expenses related to obtaining the merchandise should be considered in determining inventory costs.

Small Business Inventory Management

Presented in this Small Business Inventory Management guide is a sampling of information that should be helpful to business owners and managers in dealing with small business inventory management problems. Included is a balanced selection in terms of emphasis on techniques, on the one hand, and general management principles on the other.

"Inventory" to many business owners is one of the more visible and tangible aspects of doing business. Raw materials, goods in process, and finished goods, all represent various forms of inventory encountered in a manufacturing organization. Each type represents money tied up until the inventory leaves the factory as a purchased product. Likewise, merchandise stocks in a retail store contribute to profits only when their sale puts money into the cash register.

In a literal sense, inventory refers to stock of anything necessary to do business. These stocks represent a large portion of the business investment and must be well managed in order to maximize profits. In fact, many small businesses cannot absorb the types of losses arising from poor inventory management. Unless inventories are controlled they are unreliable, inefficient, and costly. In attempting to control inventories, managers usually lean towards keeping inventory levels on the high side, yet this greater investment (given a constant amount of profit), yields a lower return on the dollar invested. This is one of the contradictory demands made upon the manager with respect to keeping inventory, others include:

- Maintain a good assortment of products-but not too many;
- Increase inventory turnover-but only at a good profit level;

- Keep stocks low-but not too low;
- Make volume purchases to obtain lower prices-but don't overbuy; and
- Get rid of obsolete items-but not before their replacements have taken hold in the market.

Successful Inventory Management

Successful inventory management involves simultaneously attempting to balance the costs of inventory with the benefits of inventory. Many business owners often fail to appreciate fully the true costs of carrying inventory-which include not only direct costs of storage, insurance, taxes, etc., but is also the cost of money tied up in inventory. And it is often not realized that small reductions in inventory investment may result in large percentage changes in the company's total cash position. For example, one reward of improved inventory management may be an increase in working capital without the necessity of having to borrow money.

Computation of the Inventory Turnover Rate

One commonly used, simple measure of managerial performance is the inventory turnover rate. This value gives a rough guideline by which managers can set goals and measure performance, but it must be realized that the turnover rate varies with the function of inventory, the type of business, and how the ratio is calculated (whether on sales or cost of goods sold). For example, on a cost of goods sold basis, the average inventory turnover rate for manufacturers of paper board containers ranges from 4.5 to 21.0.

Values such as these are published periodically by the trade associations and professional organizations; they can be useful in setting guidelines for one's own company, but must be used with care.

Manual Record keeping Methods

At a very basic level, business inventory records provide the information needed to make decisions about inventory management. But the number and kinds of records maintained, as well as the type of control system needed, depend upon the type and size of inventory. In very small businesses where visual control is used, records may not be needed at all or only for slowly moving or expensive items. But in a larger organization where many items from various suppliers are involved, more formal inventory records, such as kardex files, are appropriate. In such a case, regardless of the type of records maintained, the accuracy and discipline of the recording system is critical. It is important to remember, however, that in many cases attempts to improve management and reduce costs fail, not simply because of insufficient records, but rather because of inaccurate and carelessly recorded inventory data.

Many small manufacturers, wholesalers, and retailers with relatively few items in inventory use manual inventory control system. They use card records, inventory tags and accounting data to capture the information necessary to establish economic order quantities, order points, and other parameters for effective inventory control. However, as the number of item, supplies, and general importance of inventory increases, it is often desirable to consider use of a computerized system for inventory control.

Using Computers in Inventory Management

Today, the use of computer systems to control inventory is far more feasible for small business than ever before, both through the widespread existence of computer services organizations (listed in the yellow pages of many telephone directories) and the decreasing cost of micro computers. Often the justification for such a computer-based system is enhanced by the fact that company accounting and billing procedures can also be handled on the computer.

Most computer manufacturers offer free, written information on the inventory management systems available for their computers. In addition, computer service companies often have material readily available describing the use of their particular computer "software" programs for inventory management. These companies provide a good source of information on general descriptions of particular inventory management techniques, as well as help on specific inventory management problems.

Whether a manual or computerized inventory management system is used, the important thing to remember is that inventory management involves two separate, but closely related elements: the first is knowing what and how much to order, when to order and what price to pay; the second is making sure that the items, once brought into inventory, are used properly to produce a profit.

Quality Control

1. Printable Version.
2. Download PDF.
3. Cite this Page.

Quality control refers to the process, most often implemented in manufacturing, of monitoring the quality of finished products through statistical measures and an overall corporate commitment to producing defect-free products. Quality control principles can also be utilized in service industries.

Deming's Fourteen Points

The term "quality control" came into common use in the 1950s thanks to W. Edward Deming, whose "Fourteen Points" have become the bible for quality control proponents. With the post-war world returning to normal manufacturing patterns, Deming preached that inspecting products for quality after they were manufactured was unacceptable. Instead, he proposed a process known as "statistical quality control" that would use closely monitored performance measures to gauge quality as a product was being manufactured. The goal of statistical quality control was to gather data that would allow for the constant improvement of manufacturing processes, which would in turn improve quality control. Introducing such statistical controls could be expensive, but Deming argued that instituting quality measures ultimately saved companies money.

Another important tenet of Deming's beliefs was that upper management was largely to blame for quality failures. He firmly believed that, given the right tools and working environment, workers would strive to create the highest quality products possible. In Deming's own words, "the basic cause of sickness in American industry and resulting unemployment is failure of top management to manage." He believed that strong leadership led to an inspired work force that did not fear management and did not fear taking chances when seeking ways to improve quality.

If strong leadership is the buzzword for managers in a quality environment, then empowerment is the key concept for workers in Deming's system. Improved education and training are the key factors in reaching employees and making them believe that their increased participation in the work process is an essential part of improving quality. Involvement, participation, and teamwork are seen as absolute musts if a quality work place is to be created.

The Japanese were the first to adopt Deming's Fourteen Points, and with great success. As an example, Deming learned of one Japanese factory that doubled production in just one year and was expecting to gain an additional 25 percent improvement the following year, with no increase in the amount of hours worked. All this occurred as a result of simply improving quality. What is most significant about this achievement is the year it happened—1951. Many American and European companies chose to ignore these dramatic results and nearly perished as a result. Critics contend that by the time American manufacturing plants realized that quality control was a significant issue, it was the late 1970s and Japanese firms such as Honda and Sony were taking over large portions of the American consumer market.

In the 1990s, most American firms have embraced quality control practices. Analysts indicate that when firms first began adopting these principles, many went too far, becoming bogged down in quality control charts and measurements of inconsequential operating factors. In too many cases, American industry went from ignoring statistical quality control to applying it to every single facet of a business, no matter how small. This overemphasis quickly disappeared, however, and has been replaced by a commitment to overall quality control that is unprecedented in the American work place.

The Scope of Japanese Influence

Because they have been practicing quality management since the 1950s, the Japanese are still the leader in producing quality products in a number of industries and are still the role model for U.S. companies to emulate. For example, a study of the air conditioning industry in the early 1990s found that the worst Japanese air conditioning plant had an error rate that was less than one-half that of the *best* U.S. company.

This drastic difference is largely due to the Japanese adherence to one of Deming's most important ideas—that quality should be "designed in" to a product instead of "inspected out." Japanese firms treat suppliers as equals, sharing information with them as if the supplier was an internal department of the company. This ensures that quality is already a part of the product before it is even manufactured.

Another common practice in Japan that has found its way to the United States are "quality circles." Workers are brought together on a regular basis to brainstorm about quality and manufacturing processes, all with an eye towards improving quality. The circles are a success if management follows through on its end of the deal and incorporates the suggestions made in the quality circles into operations. When workers see their suggestions implemented, it increases their confidence in management and in the company as a whole, which in turn increases their commitment to the company and to producing high quality goods.

A highly trained work force is one of the keys to producing quality goods, and the training programs of many American companies reflect this recognition, for they are allocating more time and money to this area. Still, many U.S. companies lag behind in this respect. Researchers have stated that a higher commitment to training and lifelong learning are needed if the commitment to quality is to continue.

Today, the key components of quality control that were preached by Deming and practice by the Japanese—including benchmarking, supplier partnering, and continuous improvement—have found their way into American industry. Each of these components demands a closer look.

Benchmarking

Benchmarking is a continuing process of measuring products, services, and practices against your strongest competitors. More simply stated, it means using the best companies as the yardstick against which your company measures itself. If your company comes up short, than improvements must be made to ensure that your products are just as high in quality as those of your competitor.

There are two types of benchmarking. The first, competitive benchmarking, entails benchmarking against direct competitors in the marketplace. This can include comparing specific numerical or statistical measurements—return on assets used, market share, etc. The more detailed information that can be obtained about a competitor, the better.

The second method, noncompetitive benchmarking, can take two forms. The first is measuring your company against the best companies in the world, regardless of industry. Companies such as 3M, Coca-Cola, and General Electric are considered to be trendsetters and leaders in quality, so companies from nearly every industry study them and copy their best practices. Business analysts note that noncompetitive benchmarking is a broader—and sometimes more useful—instrument of quality control. By only benchmarking against competitors, a company only ensures it will be as good as that competitor. By benchmarking against the best companies in the world, a company can aspire to be as good as those companies and can surpass the competition in its own industry. Additionally, companies may find it easier to gain access to information about companies they do not compete with because they are not seen as a threat to the well being of the company.

The second type of noncompetitive benchmarking is internal benchmarking, which involves comparing functions or processes in different departments within the same organization. Internal benchmarking is often seen as a logical starting point for a business that is attempting to use benchmarking for the first time.

To successfully benchmark, a company must first look closely at its own practices and conduct a rigorous self-assessment. Once that self-assessment is completed, the company has a good idea of where it stands on each quality issue and can successfully compare itself to other companies. The self-assessment must be honest and thorough. It should identify weaknesses, but should also highlight strengths. Improving weaknesses that are identified should be tied to stated company strategic aims.

Supplier Partnering

Supplier partnering is an increasingly common practice in the United States. Simply put, it means that manufacturers work directly with their parts and components suppliers to improve quality at the supplier's location. This can involve direct participation in the supplier's operations—that is, staff from the manufacturer might work on-site at the supplier's office or provide technical assistance and equipment—or simply a very close working relationship that more resembles a partnership rather than a simple business transaction between two unrelated companies.

One of the biggest methods of partnering with suppliers involves sharing the use of statistical controls. This is an underdeveloped area in the United States that should grow in the coming years. Most manufacturers have switched to outsourcing as a means of cutting the costs of production. This increased emphasis on outsourcing means that the companies that supply the parts or components must place just as much emphasis on quality as the manufacturer if the finished product is to be high quality. Among the quality issues that still need to be addressed in the manufacturer-supplier relationship are:

- Inconsistent quality levels from suppliers, even from different plants of the same supplier.
- While most first-level, or Tier 1, suppliers have made a commitment to quality control, that commitment has yet to be made by Tier 2 suppliers (those companies that supply smaller parts or raw material to the Tier 1 supplier). The importance of quality must trickle all the way down the supply chain to be meaningful.
- In many industries, mergers are occurring at a record pace. Whenever a merger of two suppliers occurs, there is the chance that quality will suffer while the details of the merger are hammered out.

In many industries, especially the auto industry, manufacturers are overcoming these supplier problems by helping the suppliers meet quality standards.

The other facet of supplier partnering means that the manufacturer also actively seeks out feedback from the supplier on how the former's operations can be improved. Suppliers often have a unique perspective on the industry they work in and on the companies they supply and can provide valuable advice on how to make changes for the better. When this happens, it is important that the two companies have a framework in place to manage the partnering system. This can mean that the manufacturer's purchasing department would be deemed as the intermediary between the two companies, passing information from the supplier back to the appropriate internal customers.

Continuous Improvement

Continuous improvement (CI) is a method for improving every facet of a company's operations and increasing competitiveness by developing a company's resources. The improvement can involve many goals—producing products with zero defects or achieving 100 percent customer satisfaction—but CI has the same basic principles no matter what the goal:

- Involve the entire company at all levels.
- Find savings by improving existing processes, not by investing more money.

- Gather data about company operations and quantify that data, which becomes the baseline against which improvements will be measured.
- Do not forget that common sense is perhaps the most important component of CI.
- Do not just give lip service to improvement—implement or practice ideas.

Continuous improvement most often involves creating a team that includes representatives from all areas of the company. The team first spends time learning—about the company they work for (looking at it in new ways) and about other companies (benchmarking is common during this phase). The necessary quantitative data is created. The team then proposes solutions to management and begins to implement those solutions. Once that is achieved, follow-up mechanisms must be put in place that seek additional improvements as time goes by. The team might change members with the passage of time, but hopefully it will become an established and accepted part of the company even as its roster changes. If the endeavor works as planned, the team will have improved quality to show as a result of its initial efforts. This can make even skeptical employees buy into the concept, which in turn leads to the continued search for even more improvements—hence the term continuous improvement. Follow-up mechanisms can include regular audits or regularly scheduled meetings to evaluate progress.

Other Quality Buzzwords

Quality control and literature about it have become a huge cottage industry in the business world. In addition to the terms outlined in this article, there are several other popular concepts and terms associated with quality control that are actually offshoots of the larger issue, or separate issues altogether. Among the most popular are:

ISO 9000—This is a series of international standards that set out requirements and recommendations that specify how management operations are to be conducted at a company to ensure that quality is the end result. ISO 9000 is part of the "conformance to specifications" school of quality control that believes that, by setting standards for companies to follow that the consumer is aware of, and ensuring that those standards are never deviated from, then quality is achieved. Essentially, its goal is to prevent nonconformity. Companies must undergo a comprehensive program to apply for ISO 9000 certification, reviewing and documenting management procedures, creating job descriptions from the ground up, preparing a quality manual, and submitting to periodic standards checks by an external body. The process is not cheap, but it does give a company that qualifies for the certification a badge to demonstrate its commitment to quality.

Six Sigma—This defect-reduction program was pioneered by General Electric's Jack Welch. A sigma is a mark on a bell curve that measures standard deviation. In American industry today, most companies average between 35,000 and 50,000 defects per million operations; GE followed this trend by averaging 35,000, or 3.5 sigma. Welch determined that this was unacceptable—he wanted the error rate reduced to an almost nonexistent 3.4 errors per million operations, or "Six Sigma," a concept first introduced by Motorola in the early 1990s. Motorola was able to achieve six sigma quality, but it took eight years to go from three to six. Welch mandated that GE reach the mark in five years. More and more companies are expected to follow the lead of GE and Motorola, since both companies are considered world leaders.

Quality awards—As quality control grows in popularity, companies strive to prove to customers that quality is their most important concern. One way they do this is to compete for the plethora of quality awards that are now available. The most famous of these is the Malcolm Baldridge National Quality Award, but others such as the European Quality Award and the Deming Award also exist. Additionally, there are hundreds of state, regional, and local quality awards. The awards, which are given to both large and small companies, carry a rigorous set of quality standards that a company must meet or exceed before it can even be considered for an award. Some companies coincide the launch of new quality control programs with announcements that they will be seeking one of the awards as a means of giving employees an incentive to improve quality and as a means of demonstrating to customers their commitment to quality.

Mistake-prooing, or poka-yoke—"Poka-yoke" is a Japanese term that comes from two words that mean "avoid error." The concept was created by a Toyota engineer who felt that workers should always strive to avoid making any mistakes. The concept most often refers to "designing in" methods of avoiding mistakes—for example, putting guards on drill presses that prevent the machine from drilling a hole too deep and ruining a part. As a result, poka-yoke has come to have a second meaning. In addition to referring to the broad concept, it refers to any tool or process used to prevent a mistakes. Mistake-proofing is one of the easiest ways for small companies to reduce errors. It is easy and relatively inexpensive to perform an audit of existing poka-yokes and to draw up a flow chart of a production process to identify where other poka-yokes might be installed. Once the initial work is done, adding new poka-yokes can be an ongoing and continuous process. One warning to business owners—using the terms "mistake-proofing" or "fool-proofing" can anger workers, who may view the terms as being disparaging.

Finally, there is one term associated with the quality control movement that is too broad and too important to cover here. Total quality management, or TQM, has become an important quality movement in its own right and is fully explained in a separate entry in this book.

The Future of Quality Control

Despite the growing importance of quality control in the United States, there is still room for improvement in many areas. One of the most important is the attitude towards teams, especially cross-functional ones. Teams are recognized by quality experts as one of the best ways to increase speed to market and improve quality. Slowly, as American firms adopt other quality measures, they are also adopting the team philosophy. Still, improvements must be made. Too many firms still rely on the old styles of product development and production, handing off responsibility for a product from one department to the next with no interaction between the departments. Another problem to be overcome in the future is downsizing. One of the key business principles of the 1990s, downsizing means improving technology and work processes so that the same amount of work can be done with fewer employees. While the move to downsize has improved the bottom line at many companies, it has also raised quality concerns. Some believe that there has been a marked reduction in the quality of some products because too many firms engaged in downsizing without making sure that their internal processes and infrastructure was adequately equipped to handle the loss of employees.

Traditional Way of Quality Control and its Drawbacks

Quality control is the more traditional way that businesses have used to manage quality. Quality control is concerned with checking and reviewing work that has been done. But is this the best way for a business to manage quality?

Under traditional quality control, inspection of products and services (checking to make sure that what's being produced is meeting the required standard) takes place during and at the end of the operations process.

There are three main points during the production process when inspection is performed:

1. When raw materials are received prior to entering production.
2. Whilst products are going through the production process.
3. When products are finished-inspection or testing takes place before products are despatched to customers.

The problem with this sort of inspection is that it doesn't work very well!

There are several problems with inspection under traditional quality control:

1. The inspection process does not add any "value". If there were any guarantees that no defective output would be produced, then there would be no need for an inspection process in the first place!
2. Inspection is costly, in terms of both tangible and intangible costs. For example, materials, labour, time, employee morale, customer goodwill, lost sales.
3. It is sometimes done too late in the production process. This often results in defective or non-acceptable goods actually being received by the customer.
4. It is usually done by the wrong people-e.g. by a separate "quality control inspection team" rather than by the workers themselves.
5. Inspection is often not compatible with more modern production techniques (e.g. "Just in Time Manufacturing") which do not allow time for much (if any) inspection.
6. Working capital is tied up in stocks which cannot be sold.
7. There is often disagreement as to what constitutes a "quality product". For example, to meet quotas, inspectors may approve

goods that don't meet 100% conformance, giving the message to workers that it doesn't matter if their work is a bit sloppy. Or one quality control inspector may follow different procedures from another, or use different measurements.

As a result of the above problems, many businesses have focused their efforts on improving quality by implementing quality management techniques-which emphasise the role of quality assurance. As Deming (a "quality guru") wrote:

"Inspection with the aim of finding the bad ones and throwing them out is too late, ineffective, costly. Quality comes not from inspection but from improvement of the process."

Quality Control

In engineering and manufacturing, quality control and quality engineering are used in developing systems to ensure products or services are designed and produced to meet or exceed customer requirements.

Quality control is the branch of engineering and manufacturing which deals with assurance and failure testing in design and production of products or services, to meet or exceed customer requirements.

Quality Assurance

One of the most widely used paradigms for quality assurance management is the PDCA (plan-do-check-act) approach, also known as the Shewhart cycle.

PDCA (plan-do-check-act) is an iterative four-step problem-solving process typically used in business process improvement. It is also known as the Deming cycle, Shewhart cycle, Deming wheel, or plan-do-study-act.

Meaning

Plan: Establish the objectives and processes necessary to deliver results in accordance with the expected output. By making the expected output the focus, it differs from other techniques in that the completeness and accuracy of the specification is also part of the improvement.

Do: Implement the new processes. Often on a small scale if possible.

Chec: Measure the new processes and compare the results against the expected results to ascertain any differences.

Act: Analyse the differences to determine their cause. Each will be part of either one or more of the P-D-C-A steps. Determine where to apply changes that will include improvement. When a pass through these four steps does not result in the need to improve, refine the scope to which PDCA is applied until there is a plan that involves improvement.

About: PDCA was made popular by Dr. W. Edwards Deming, who is considered by many to be the father of modern quality control; however it was always referred to by him as the "Shewhart cycle." Later in Deming's career, he modified PDCA to "Plan, Do, Study, Act" (PDSA) so as to better describe his recommendations.

The concept of PDCA is based on the scientific method, as developed from the work of Francis Bacon. The scientific method can be written as "hypothesis"-"experiment"-"evaluation" or plan, do, and check. Shewhart described manufacture under "control"-under statistical control-as a three step process of specification, production, and inspection. He also specifically related this to the scientific method of hypothesis, experiment, and evaluation. Shewhart says that the statistician "must help to change the demand [for goods] by showing...how to close up the tolerance range and to improve the quality of goods." Clearly, Shewhart intended the analyst to take action based on the conclusions of the evaluation. According to Deming during his lectures in Japan in the early 1950's the Japanese participants shortened the steps to the now traditional *plan, do, check, act.* Deming preferred *plan, do, study, act* because "study" has connotations in English closer to Shewhart's intent than "check."

A fundamental principle of the scientific method and PDSA is iteration-once a hypothesis is confirmed (or negated), executing the cycle again will extend the knowledge further. Repeating the PDSA cycle can bring us closer to the goal, usually a perfect operation and output. In Six Sigma programs, the PDSA cycle is called "define, measure, analyse, improve, control" (DMAIC). The iterative nature of the cycle must be explicitly added to the DMAIC procedure.

PDSA should be repeatedly implemented in spirals of increasing knowledge of the system that converge on the ultimate goal, each cycle closer than the previous. One can envision an open coil spring, with each loop being one cycle of the Scientific Method-PDSA, and each complete cycle indicating an increase in our knowledge of the system under study. This approach is based on the belief that our knowledge and skills are limited, but improving. Especially at the start of a project, key information may not be known; the PDSA-scientific method-provides feedback to justify our guesses (hypotheses) and increase our knowledge. Rather than enter "analysis paralysis" to get it perfect the first time, it is better to be approximately right than exactly wrong. With the improved knowledge, we may choose to refine or alter the goal (ideal state). Certainly, the PDSA approach can bring us closer to whatever goal we choose.

Rate of change, that is, rate of improvement, is a key competitive factor in today's world. PDSA allows for major 'jumps' in performance ('break throughs' often desired in a Western approach), as well as Kaizen (frequent small improvements associated with an Eastern approach). In the United States a PDSA approach is usually associated with a sizable project involving numerous people's time, and thus managers want to see large 'breakthrough' improvements to justify the effort expended. However, the Scientific Method and PDSA apply to all sorts of projects and improvement activities.

The power of Deming's concept lies in its apparent simplicity. The concept of feedback in the Scientific Method, in the abstract sense, is today firmly rooted in education. While apparently easy to understand, it is often difficult to accomplish on an on-going basis due to the intellectual difficulty of judging one's proposals (hypotheses) on the basis of measured results. Many people have an emotional fear of being shown "wrong," even by objective measurements. To avoid such comparisons, we may instead cite complacency, distractions, loss of focus, lack of commitment, re-assigned priorities, lack of resources, etc.

Failure Testing

A valuable process to perform on a whole consumer product is *failure testing* (also known as stress testing), the operation of a product until it fails, often under stresses such as increasing vibration, temperature and humidity. This exposes many unanticipated weaknesses in a product, and the data is used to drive engineering and manufacturing process improvements.

Stress testing is a form of testing that is used to determine the stability of a given system or entity. It involves testing beyond normal operational capacity, often to a breaking point, in order to observe the results. Stress testing may have a more specific meaning in certain industries, such as fatigue testing for materials.

IT Industry

In software testing, stress test refers to tests that put a greater emphasis on robustness, availability, and error handling under a heavy load, rather than on what would be considered correct behaviour under normal circumstances.

In particular, the goals of such tests may be to ensure the software doesn't crash in conditions of insufficient computational resources (such as memory or disk space), unusually high concurrency, or denial of service attacks.

Examples:

- A web server may be stress tested using scripts, bots, and various denial of service tools to observe the performance of a web site during peak loads.

Hardware

When modifying the operating parameters of a CPU, such as in overclocking, under clocking, over volting, and undervolting, it may be necessary to verify if the new parameters (usually CPU core voltage and frequency) are suitable for heavy CPU loads. This is done by running a CPU-intensive program (usually Prime 95) for a long time, to see if the computer hangs or crashes. CPU stress testing is also referred to as torture testing. Software that is suitable for torture testing should typically run instructions that utilise the entire chip rather than only a few of its units.

Medicine

- A cardiac stress test is used most commonly to detect marked imbalances in blood flow to the heart muscle.
- In obstetrics, both a stress test and a nonstress test are forms of cardiotocography.

Financial Sector

Instead of doing financial projection on a "best estimate" basis, a company may do stress testing where they look at how robust a financial instrument is in certain crashes, a form of scenario analysis. They may test the instrument under, for example, the following stresses:

- What happens if the market crashes by more than x% this year?
- What happens if interest rates go up by at least y%?

- What if half the instruments in the portfolio terminate their contacts in the fifth year?
- What happens if oil prices rise by 200%?

This type of analysis has become increasingly widespread, and has been taken up by various governmental bodies (such as the FSA in the UK) as a regulatory requirement on certain financial institutions to ensure adequate capital allocation levels to cover potential losses incurred during extreme, but plausible, events. This emphasis on adequate, risk adjusted determination of capital has been further enhanced by modifications to banking regulations such as Basel II. Stress testing models typically allow not only the testing of individual stressors, but also combinations of different events. There is also usually the ability to test the current exposure to a known historical scenario (such as the Russian debt default in 1998 or 9/11 attacks) to ensure the liquidity of the institution. Stress testing reveals how well a portfolio is positioned in the event forecasts prove true. Stress testing also lends insight into a portfolio's vulnerabilities. Though extreme events are never certain, studying their performance implications strengthens understanding.

Defining Stress Tests

Stress testing defines a scenario and uses a specific algorithm to determine the expected impact on a portfolio's return should such a scenario occur. There are three types of scenarios:

- *Extreme event:* hypothesize the portfolio's return given the recurrence of a historical event. Current positions and risk exposures are combined with the historical factor returns.
- *Risk factor shock:* shock any factor in the chosen risk model by a user-specified amount. The factor exposures remain unchanged, while the covariance matrix is used to adjust the factor returns based on their correlation with the shocked factor.
- *External factor shock:* instead of a risk factor, shock any index, macro-economic series (e.g., oil prices), or custom series (e.g., exchange rates). Using regression analysis, new factor returns are estimated as a result of the shock.

In an exponentially weighted stress test, historical periods more like the defined scenario receive a more significant weighting in the predicted outcome. The defined decay rate lets the tester manipulate the relative importance of the most similar periods. In the standard stress test, each period is equally weighted.

Statistical Control

Many organizations use statistical process control to bring the organization to Six Sigma levels of quality, in other words, so that the likelihood of an unexpected failure is confined to six standard deviations on the normal distribution. This probability is 3.4 one-millionths. Items controlled often include clerical tasks such as order-entry as well as conventional manufacturing tasks. Traditional statistical process controls in manufacturing operations usually proceed by randomly sampling and testing a fraction of the output. Variances of critical tolerances are continuously tracked, and manufacturing processes are corrected before bad parts can be produced.

Statistical Process Control

Statistical process control (SPC) is an effective method of monitoring a process through the use of control charts. Control charts enable the use of objective criteria for distinguishing background variation from events of significance based on statistical techniques. Much of its power lies in the ability to monitor both process centre and its variation about that centre, by collecting data from samples at various points within the process. Variations in the process that may affect the quality of the end product or service can be detected and corrected, thus reducing waste as well as the likelihood that problems will be passed on to the customer. With its emphasis on early detection and prevention of problems, SPC has a distinct advantage over quality methods, such as inspection, that apply resources to detecting and correcting problems in the end product or service. In addition to reducing waste, SPC can lead to a reduction in the time required to produce the product or service from end to end. This is partially due to a diminished likelihood that the final product will have to be reworked, but it may also result from using SPC data to identify bottlenecks, wait times, and other sources of delays within the process. Process cycle time reductions coupled with improvements in yield have made SPC a valuable tool from both a cost reduction and a customer satisfaction standpoint.

History

Statistical process control was pioneered by Walter A. Shewhart in the early 1920s. W. Edwards Deming later applied SPC methods in the

United States during World War II, thereby successfully improving quality in the manufacture of munitions and other strategically important products. Deming was also instrumental in introducing SPC methods to Japanese industry after the war had ended.

Shewhart created the basis for the control chart and the concept of a state of statistical control by carefully designed experiments. While Dr. Shewhart drew from pure mathematical statistical theories, he understood that data from physical processes seldom produces a "normal distribution curve" (a Gaussian distribution, also commonly referred to as a "bell curve"). He discovered that observed variation in manufacturing data did not always behave the same way as data in nature (for example, Brownian motion of particles). Dr. Shewhart concluded that while every process displays variation, some processes display controlled variation that is natural to the process (common causes of variation), while others display uncontrolled variation that is not present in the process causal system at all times (special causes of variation). In 1989, the Software Engineering Institute introduced the notion that SPC can be usefully applied to non-manufacturing processes, such as software engineering processes, in the Capability Maturity Model (CMM). This idea exists today within the Level 4 and Level 5 practices of the Capability Maturity Model Integrated (CMMI). This notion that SPC is a useful tool when applied to non-repetitive, knowledge-intensive processes such as engineering processes has encountered much skepticism, and remains controversial today.

General

The following description relates to manufacturing rather than to the service industry, although the principles of SPC can be successfully applied to either. For a description and example of how SPC applies to a service environment, refer to Roberts (2005). SPC has also been successfully applied to detecting changes in organizational behaviour with Social Network Change Detection introduced by McCulloh (2007). Selden describes how to use SPC in the fields of sales, marketing, and customer service, using Deming's famous Red Bead Experiment as an easy to follow demonstration.

In mass-manufacturing, the quality of the finished article was traditionally achieved through post-manufacturing inspection of the product; accepting or rejecting each article (or samples from a production lot) based on how well it met its design specifications. In contrast,

Statistical Process Control uses statistical tools to observe the performance of the production process in order to predict significant deviations that may later result in rejected product.

Two kinds of variation occur in all manufacturing processes: both these types of process variation cause subsequent variation in the final product. The first is known as natural or common cause variation and may be variation in temperature, properties of raw materials, strength of an electrical current etc. This variation is small, the observed values generally being quite close to the average value. The pattern of variation will be similar to those found in nature, and the distribution forms the bell-shaped normal distribution curve. The second kind of variation is known as special cause variation, and happens less frequently than the first.

For example, a breakfast cereal packaging line may be designed to fill each cereal box with 500 grams of product, but some boxes will have slightly more than 500 grams, and some will have slightly less, in accordance with a distribution of net weights. If the production process, its inputs, or its environment changes (for example, the machines doing the manufacture begin to wear) this distribution can change. For example, as its cams and pulleys wear out, the cereal filling machine may start putting more cereal into each box than specified. If this change is allowed to continue unchecked, more and more product will be produced that fall outside the tolerances of the manufacturer or consumer, resulting in waste. While in this case, the waste is in the form of "free" product for the consumer, typically waste consists of rework or scrap.

By observing at the right time what happened in the process that led to a change, the quality engineer or any member of the team responsible for the production line can trouble shoot the root cause of the variation that has crept in to the process and correct the problem.

SPC indicates when an action should be taken in a process, but it also indicates when NO action should be taken. An example is a person who would like to maintain a constant body weight and takes weight measurements weekly. A person who does not understand SPC concepts might start dieting every time his or her weight increased, or eat more every time his or her weight decreased. This type of action could be harmful and possibly generate even more variation in body weight. SPC would account for normal weight variation and better indicate when the person is in fact gaining or losing weight.

How to use SPC

Initially, one starts with an amount of data from a manufacturing process with a specific metric, i.e. mass, length, surface energy of a widget. One example may be a manufacturing process of a nanoparticle type and two parameters are key to the process; particle mean-diameter and surface area. So, with the exiting data one would calculate the sample mean and sample standard deviation. The upper control limits of the process would be set to mean plus three standard deviations and the lower control limit would be set to mean minus three standard deviations. The action taken depends on statistic and where each run lands on the SPC chart in order to control but not tamper with the process. The criticalness of the process can be defined by the Westing house rules used. The only way to reduce natural variation is through improvement to the process technology, see Nelson funnel experiment.

Company Quality

During the 1980s, the concept of "company quality" with the focus on management and people came to the fore. It was realized that, if all departments approached quality with an open mind, success was possible if the management led the quality improvement process. The company-wide quality approach places an emphasis on three aspects :-

1. Elements such as çontrols, job management, defined and well managed processes, performance and integrity criteria and identification of records.
2. Competence such as knowledge, skills, experience, qualifications.
3. Soft elements, such as personnel integrity, confidence, organizational culture, motivation, team spirit and quality relationships.

The quality of the outputs is at risk if any of these three aspects is deficient in any way.

Total Quality Control

Total Quality Control is the most necessary inspection control of all in cases where, despite statistical quality control techniques or quality improvements implemented, sales decrease.

If the original specification does not reflect the correct quality requirements, quality cannot be inspected or manufactured into the product.

For instance, all parameters for a pressure vessel should include not only the material and dimensions but operating, environmental, safety, reliability and maintainability requirements.

Quality Control Management

Quality control does not get as much attention as it should with small businesses. The level of quality embedded in your system greatly determines how you are perceived in the market and how well your profit margins are doing. By embracing quality control as a primary issue, small businesses can gain significant improvements in these areas. To those unfamiliar with total quality management, quality control may seem like a secondary factor in growing a successful business.

Companies, especially small businesses, often pour their resources into sales, marketing and distribution. Quality control tends to take a backseat. Many large corporations have embraced quality control as a primary issue and have reaped the benefits. In truth, small businesses need top-notch quality control as much, if not more, than big businesses. The tangible and intangible costs associated with poor quality leave little room for argument.

Minor changes in the way a small business operates can vastly affect its product, its customers, and its mission. Adopting some simple principles of quality management can help a business gain significant competitive advantages over their competition. Is every product or service you provide guaranteed to reach the customer without any flaws or defects? If you cannot guarantee every product or service you provide is without defect, then you have a lot of room to improve. The first concept of quality control is the difference between internal and external customers.

Internal customers involve the different subdivisions of your company that pass on product or information. For example, if your sales team prints sales invoices and delivers the information to production, is an internal customer of sales. Thus, the sales department should be challenged to flawlessly deliver each sales invoice to the production team. Mistakes may snowball down the supply chain, resulting in reworking costs, scrap costs, and potentially a loss of customers.

External customers involve those who receive the products or services outside your company. Any defect or flaw that reaches your external customer is the most expensive, and potentially most devastating, of all quality problems. No defective product or service should ever reach the customer, and this needs to be a major part of your company's culture. After all, would you be willing to go back to a restaurant that served you a cold or under-cooked meal? An unsatisfied customer will very likely share his experience with others, thus leading to future lost business. A small business cannot grow or succeed if they are not delivering their best to their customers each and every time.

Identifying and Fixing Problems

In each step of your product or service production, you need to seek and destroy each and every problem that leads to defects and errors. This begins with ensuring that internal customers receive the same level of quality that external customers receive. As problems arise, employees must come together in a discussion. Although this may result in temporary line stoppages, the costs of these stoppages are insignificant when compared to the costs of future errors. If a defect occurs, chances are it will repeat itself.

Planning for Quality

When designing a new product or process, build quality control into the design. By addressing quality issues early in the development process, you can avoid many headaches down the road. Whether you're launching a new product, purchasing a new piece of software or starting a new process, make sure quality control is built into your design.

Delivering a quality product is a crucial element of customer service and internal cost control. By reducing and ultimately eliminating defects, you maintain happier customers while keeping your inspection/rework/return costs to a minimum. When it comes time to alter your operation with a new product or new piece of equipment, make sure quality control is factored into the decision.

When you're designing a new product, it's important that the product can be put together without major defects. This means the materials used and the assembly process need to be carefully thought through. By designing a product that can be produced defect free, you'll save yourself a lot of headaches. While this may not be entirely feasible, you should still aim to create a product that can be produced and assembled with as little problems as possible.

When it comes time to purchase new software, there's a great opportunity to eliminate internal defects. Before purchasing the software, you should have a strong understanding of the implications of the new computer program. For example, you should know who is most affected by the software, are you're your outside customers or internal operations? In either case, you should be aware of quality problems with the existing software and seek to eliminate these with the new software.

Due to changes in demand, you may be compelled to alter the layout of your operation. This is another great opportunity to increase your quality. You should identify all of the areas where quality problems occur with your current layout.

This could include everything from dropped products to faulty equipment. Once you've identified the quality problem areas, you should try and eliminate the causes. By altering your production layout you can create safety systems to help reduce defects in the problem areas.

It's important when purchasing a new piece of equipment that quality control is at the forefront of the decision. Often time's new equipment is purchased to increase capacity or throughput. Make sure you base this decision on expected quality as well. I witnessed a decorative baking operation, which was done completely by hand. It was a laborious process but very high in quality control. The company sought to purchase a new piece of equipment to handle the decorating process. During a trial run, it was obvious that throughput would drastically increase but with the amount of quality issues, more time would be spent fixing the defective products. When you factored in the cost of defective products and the cost to rework the product, the new machine was not worth the investment. When you're starting a new process, new product or new piece of software or equipment, you have a great opportunity to improve your quality control. Take the opportunity to build quality control into your design at the ground level. The cost of poor quality can be astronomical and by being proactive, you can greatly reduce your defects and costs while increasing your customer satisfaction.

Improving Product Quality

Companies that use a number of suppliers for the same material may be jeopardizing their quality. Whether multiple suppliers are used because of planning issues or a low-cost approach, the negative ramifications can be tremendous. Consistent materials are a necessary component of good quality control.

There are two lines of thinking when it comes to supplier-customer relationships that I often see in my consulting experience.

The first is the low-cost approach. In this scenario, the customer shops around and picks the lowest of several quoted prices. This often results in multiple suppliers being used for the same product over the course of time. The second approach is the choice of one reliable supplier and the development of a good supplier-customer relationship. While both approaches have their costs and benefits, using too many suppliers for the same material can spoil your quality and cripple your company. While the low-cost approach makes sense from a purchasing point of view, we need to be certain that we're comparing apples to apples. While two suppliers may offer the same product, the quality of the two products can be vastly different. There are a myriad of reasons for this, but the most general one is that both suppliers have different production and distribution operations. The product does not go through the same factory in both instances, so the quality is going to differ.

When you create you product, you want to be as consistent as possible. Consistency will help you deliver the highest quality product possible. Quality is of the utmost importance when it comes to delivering a product to the customer. Low-quality products are likely to be returned and the customer is not likely to repeat their business. As a result, we want to make sure we do everything we can to improve the quality of our product. When you have inconsistent materials, you're going to have an inconsistent final product. This will result in varying degrees of product being delivered to the customer. Imagine if your house painted and one half was one shade of red and the other side was another shade. I consulted for a company that manufactured liquid vitamins. When I came on board, their purchasing department had been instructed to use the low-cost approach. Typically they quoted three to four vendors and chose the lowest price. With vitamin production, there are a myriad of ingredients and a whole host of suppliers. When reviewing the product quality records and customer complaints, it was clear that their quality was out of control.

When I reviewed the production process, it was pleasantly surprising that their operation was very consistent and clean. This meant the reason for the quality issues was in the ingredients.

By ordering one ingredient for a batch from one supplier and another supplier for the next batch, the quality of each batch was vastly different. Customers often called to complain that the taste of the bottle they had last month was different than the way this month's bottle tasted. Not only does this look bad for the company, but it can raise serious issues about the safety of your product. It took some time to change the purchasing department's approach and show them the light. Eventually, the ship got turned around and they started using suppliers based on price, performance and conformance.

The consistency paid off. The product was of a much higher quality and the customers could get what they were expecting when they bought the product.

Mistake-Proof your Operation

By mistake-proofing your Operation you can make it difficult for defects to get passed on to the customer. With reduced defects you'll find your quality and customer service levels both increasing. The concept of mistake-proofing operations is common in the field of Operations Management. Mistake-proofing is generally defined as a process, where certain defects have been defined and prevented.

Once a process is mistake-proofed for a certain defect, it is impossible for that defect to occur and move on to the next station. For example, if you had an assembly line of hamburgers, and you had buns that were too small (defect) small cut out circles on the conveyor belt could be a mistake-proof spot. As buns that were too small in size passed over the hole, they would fall through. The holes effectively mistake-proof your operation and prevent small buns from passing on to the next stage of your operation. There are many advantages to mistake-proofing your operation. Defects will be greatly reduced, your process will become more efficient and quality control is made easier.

Think about the aforementioned hamburger example. Instead of having inspectors taking time to inspect the buns, the process is self-sustaining and the quality control is completed automatically. In addition, inspections and sample sizes are not fool-proof; therefore defective buns can slip past them and make it to next station or ultimately the final customer. Finding areas to mistake-proof your operation can be challenging. The process starts with the identification of a recurring defect.

Once the defect has been located, you can take measures to start improving the process. If you know an area where a defect is occurring, you should starting taking action immediately. That area should be red flagged and you and your employees should begin brainstorming possible solutions and prevention techniques.

It is crucial that you involve your employees in this process. They are the ones working on the front lines and they will have invaluable ideas regarding the process. Any idea that will start immediately helping the problem should be put into place. This may mean additional inspection time or measuring techniques (scales, rulers etc.). These methods are costly and time –consuming.

From this point you will want to develop a fool-proof system that can be incorporated into your process without much time or leg work. This can be difficult and may take time. Again, the more people you have involved in the brainstorming session the better.

Mistake-proofing techniques can be used to solve problems anywhere in your business. If you've identified a problem where customer service reps are continually missing information on sales invoices, try and find mistake proof techniques to solve the problem. Maybe the sales invoice won't save on the computer until all of the necessary data is complete. Or, a less expensive option of reorganizing the sales' invoice, so all of the pertinent information is in the same section.

You should develop a company culture that targets problem areas throughout your company. You'll find certain problems repeat themselves, and these are great areas to implement mistake-proofing techniques.

Get creative and involve all of your employees. By solving problems and putting the solution into the process, you'll find quality and productivity both increasing dramatically.

The Importance of Quality Control

Successful businesses inevitably place great emphasis on managing quality control-carefully planned steps taken to ensure that the products and services offered to their customers are consistent and reliable and truly meet their customers' needs. Multinational corporations have entire departments of highly trained specialists to design and implement their quality assurance programs. For a custom countertop fabricator, as for other small businesses that make unique, handcrafted products, quality control is also essential. Such companies cannot rely on a staff of trained experts or the standardization inherent in mass production to take care of quality control. One or a handful of managers must handle it themselves, along with every other management function. That is part of being a small business person. It is all too often true, though, that fabricators fail to institute their own carefully planned quality control procedures. I would like to suggest a few simple steps that can help a countertop fabricator or any similar small business improve the quality of its products and services. It is said that when the Japanese business that later became Sony Corporation was founded, the co-founder Mr. Ibuka established the company philosophy by stating that "If it were possible to establish conditions where persons could become united with a firm spirit of teamwork and exercise to their hearts' desire their technological capacity, then such an organization could bring untold pleasure and untold benefits." For decades, Japanese businesses have pioneered management techniques intended to improve quality continuously. American and European companies have spent years catching up.

Modern computer communication gives even the smallest business the means to rapidly access information and advice through the Internet. For those interested in developing or improving a quality control program, I recommend "Welcome to Quality Management Principles" on the Worldwide Web at http://wineasy.se/qmp/. This informative web page is maintained by Krister Forsberg of Ericsson, the Swedish telecommunications equipment manufacturer. Forsberg's brief summary of quality management principles follows:

Principle 1-Customer-Focused Organization. Organizations depend on their customers and therefore should understand current and future customer needs, meet customer requirements, and strive to exceed customer expectations.

Principle 2-Leadership. Leaders establish unity of purpose, direction, and the internal environment of an organization. They create that environment in which people can become fully involved in achieving the organization's.

Principle 3-Involvement of People. People at all levels are the essence of an organization and their full involvement enables their abilities to be used for the organization's benefit.

Principle 4-Process Approach. A desired result is achieved more efficiently when related resources and activities are managed as a process.

Principle 5-System Approach to Management. Identifying, understanding, and managing a system of interrelated processes for a given objective contributes to the effectiveness and efficiency of the organization.

Principle 6-Continual Improvement. Continual improvement is a permanent objective of the organization.

***Principle** 7*-Factual Approach to Decision Making. Effective decisions and actions are based on the logical and intuitive analysis of data and information.

***Principle** 8*-Mutually Beneficial Supplier Relationships.

Mutually beneficial relationships between the organization and its supplier enhance the ability of both organizations to create value. Let me suggest a few programs that countertop fabricators can implement, guided by these principles, to improve quality and customer satisfaction:

Call each and every customer a few days after completion of an installation to ask whether the customer is fully satisfied. Act promptly to resolve customer concerns. Enclose a brief survey form with the final invoice requesting information on the customer's opinions and expectations. Listen with great care to every one of your customer's ideas and suggestions, and thank them for their input.

All management personnel, starting with the owner, must understand and agree that quality management is essential to the success of the business. Once that agreement has been reached, every employee must be involved in the process. All too often, employees are reluctant to report quality problems, feeling that they would be "rocking the boat" or seen as criticizing co-workers to management. Every effort must be made to convince each employee that jobs and prosperity depend on quality products and services, and that teamwork and cooperation are essential in ensuring quality.

Every process required to satisfy a customer needs to be analysed with the goal of improving customer satisfaction. Profitability will inevitably follow. Functions such as sales, extending credit, ordering materials, measuring and templating, shop fabrication, delivery, installation, billing and collection can't be seen as separate, unrelated functions. Problems resulting in customer dissatisfaction or financial losses most often occur when information is being passed from one such process to another. Special care must be taken to ensure that every process connects reliably to the adjacent processes.

Most thoughtful analysis should be lavished on any chronic problem areas. For example, if several customers have recently complained about visible seams, then the whole process of assembling seams needs to be analysed in detail, with absolutely nothing taken for granted. An itemized checklist identifying every conceivable factor that could affect seam quality should be developed, with actual observations being made every step along the way. This sort of systematic approach will help develop effective solutions much more quickly and reliably than more haphazard methods.

The attitude that says, "We've always done it that way" is the enemy of continuous quality improvement. Instead, every employee should be encouraged to think, "There is no aspect of how we do our jobs that can't be improved in some way. Together, let's figure out how to do it."

Keep accurate records, and more importantly, analyse that data. Again, in this era of sophisticated $2,000 computers, not even the smallest business has any excuse to avoid analysing factual information that can be used to improve the quality of its products and services. Job costing is the basic function that is still ignored by many fabricators who bid based on what they think their competitors will bid, rather than on their actual history of costs in completing similar projects. When you can quickly quote an accurate, competitive price on custom work, you are providing an important aspect of quality to your customer-and an assurance that you will remain in business as a profit-making venture able to meet their needs in years to come.

Rely on the training and technical support offered by the manufacturers of your materials and machinery. Read the technical bulletins and manuals, attend and stay awake during the seminars, view the videos, and listen carefully to what their sales representatives have to tell you. Your suppliers are part of the team that enables you to satisfy the needs of your customers.

It seems that I'm describing very basic principles here. I can assure you that the level of quality analysis used in the product development departments of large high-tech companies is difficult for a layman to comprehend. In our small business settings, though, much of it simply seems like common sense. Unfortunately, many well meaning fabricators all too often disregard these principles. As a result, they produce poor quality work, lose customers, perhaps get sued and then go out of business. Don't be among them. Be a survivor. Put quality first.

7

Basic Financial Planning and Control

Basic Financial Planning for Small Business Owners

Who hasn't thought of owning their own business at some point in their lives? Being your own boss, not adhering to someone else's time clock, and pursuing your passion can sound very appealing. Yet the reality often falls short of the fantasy. In fact, over 80 percent of all small businesses fold within the first year. There are numerous reasons for the daunting failure rate, but high among them is lack of initial financial preparation.

Start smart. Complete the following basic, yet vital, tasks. Doing so can improve the odds that your dream business will remain open for years rather than months.

Know your Business's Start-up Requirements

There is a lot you will need to do before opening day, but first among them will be to know precisely what and how much you will need to get your company up and running. Because each venture is different, there is no exact item and cost template.

On a sheet of paper or computer spreadsheet, list what you think your company will require just to open your doors. Research the price of each line item. If you are unable to obtain the exact price, use a conservative estimate. These expenditures may include:

- Fixtures.
- Equipment.
- Decorating.

- Remodeling.
- Inventory.
- Deposits with public utilities.
- Legal fees.
- Professional fees.
- Licenses and permits.
- Advertising and promotion.
- Consulting.
- Computer expenses.
- Stationery, logos, letterhead.
- Rent before start-up.
- Insurance before start-up.

After totaling your expenses, you may come up with a figure that seems frighteningly large. If so, revisit the list and decide which are absolutely necessary and which are more discretionary. Eliminate those you can do without and obtain at a later date.

Even after trimming expenses, the amount of money you may need may be beyond the scope of mere savings. That's where loans come in. But the key is to borrow just the right amount-you do not want to be deep in debt before you are able to recoup enough to repay what you owe, or budget yourself so tightly that you are operating on a restrictive shoestring. Which is why getting the most accurate picture of what your business's start-up requirements are is so important.

Know your Overhead Costs

Many small business owners greatly underestimate how much it will cost just to pay for overhead. Think about how much the company's day-to-day operations will likely be. As you did with the first step, list all the expenses you feel will be necessary to keep your doors open. These often include:

- Your salary.
- All other salaries and wages.
- Rent.
- Advertising.
- Delivery expense.
- Supplies.

- Telephone.
- Utilities.
- Insurance.
- Taxes (inc. social security).
- Interest.
- Maintenance.
- Legal fees.
- Professional fees.

Once you have a good idea of how much money it will take to keep your business running, you will be able to gauge how much revenue you will need to cover these costs-and still make a profit.

Obtain your Credit Reports and Make Necessary Improvements

Long before you fill out the loan applications, obtain copies of your credit report from the three major credit-reporting agencies (Trans Union, Experian, and Equifax). Lenders will look to your credit history (as well as the projected profitability of your venture) to determine whether or not you are a good credit risk. Since many reports contain errors or have damage that needs fixing, the sooner you get them, the sooner you can make the necessary corrections.

If there is evidence that you have not paid your bills on time, or that you are already overextended, allow yourself plenty of time to make changes. Work to decrease your debt and make sure all of your subsequent payments are made in a timely fashion. A significant, positive difference can be made in as little as a year.

If there is erroneous information on your reports, such as accounts that are not yours or negative information that should have "aged off," you will need to start the dispute process as soon as possible. It can take months to correct errors.

Get the best and most Appropriate Financing

There is not one way to finance your business. It is important to explore all of your options before making a decision.

- Personal savings, assets, and gifts: Many people use what they have saved to finance their business. Assets such as property and investments may be sold to fund it. You may even be gifted cash that can go towards the venture. Of course this is money you don't have to repay, so interest and payments won't be a consideration (though losing it all if the business fails to thrive may be).

- Personal loans: Family members or friends may be willing to lend you money, often with low (or even no) interest expected in return. Be forewarned though-many a personal relationship has suffered irreparable damage because of such arrangements.
- You may consider borrowing against your home or your employer sponsored retirement plan. However by doing so you would be putting your home and retirement savings in danger, making these very risky decisions. Some people have even financed their business using credit cards, though interest rates are usually too high for this to be a wise choice.
- Financial Institutions: The most common way people finance their small business is by obtaining loans from their bank or credit union. These financial institutions offer loans with comparatively low interest rates and generous repayment terms. And if your credit meets their criteria and your business proposal is sound, you could be eligible for substantial capital.
- Angel Investors and Venture Capital Firms: Angel investors and venture capital firms specialize in helping new and existing companies financially. In exchange for lending you money, they usually ask for equity or partial ownership in the business. However, if your greatest desire is to be your company's sole decision maker, this will probably not be the most desirable option.
- The Small Business Administration: The Small Business Administration has special loan arrangements with private investment firms. These loans are licensed and regulated by the SBA. Not only are the terms for such loans very good, the SBA is an excellent source of support for most small business owners.

As you can see, starting your dream business takes a tremendous amount of work and effort. But with careful planning, you will gain a clear vision of how much money it will take to start your venture. Doing so can save you not just dollars, but anxiety and time in the future. Business financial management in the small firm is characterized, in many different cases, by the need to confront a somewhat different set of problems and opportunities than those confronted by a large corporation. One immediate and obvious difference is that a majority of smaller firms do not normally have the opportunity to publicly sell issues of stocks or bonds in order to raise funds. The owner-manager of a smaller firm must rely primarily on trade credit, bank financing, lease financing, and personal equity to finance the business. One, therefore faces a much more severely restricted set of financing alternatives than those faced by the financial vice president or treasurer of a large corporation.

On the other hand, when small business financial management is concern, many financial problems facing the small firm are very similar to those of larger corporations. For example, the analysis required for a long-term investment decision such as the purchase of heavy machinery or the evaluation of lease-buy alternatives, is essentially the same regardless of the size of the firm. Once the decision is made, the financing alternatives available to the firm may be radically different, but the decision process will be generally similar.

One area of particular concern for the smaller business owner lies in the effective management of working capital. Net working capital is defined as the difference between current assets and current liabilities and is often thought of as the "circulating capital" of the business. Lack of control in this crucial area is a primary cause of business failure in both small and large firms.

The business manager must continually be alert to changes in working capital accounts, the cause of these changes and the implications of these changes for the financial health of the company. One convenient and effective method to highlight the key managerial requirements in this area is to view working capital in terms of its major components:

Cash and Equivalents

This most liquid form of current assets, cash and cash equivalents (usually marketable securities or short-term certificate of deposit) requires constant supervision. A well planned and maintained cash budgeting system is essential to answer key questions such as: Is the cash level adequate to meet current expenses as they come due? What are the timing relationships between cash inflows and outflows? When will peak cash needs occur? What will be the magnitude of bank borrowing required to meet any cash shortfalls? When will this borrowing be necessary and when may repayment be expected?

Accounts Receivable

Almost all businesses are required to extend credit to their customers. Key issues in this area include: Is the amount of accounts receivable reasonable in relation to sales? On the average, how rapidly are accounts receivable being collected? Which customers are "slow payers?" What action should be taken to speed collections where needed?

Inventories

Inventories often make up 50 percent or more of a firm's current assets and therefore, are deserving of close scrutiny. Key questions which must be considered in this area include: Is the level of inventory reasonable in relation to sales and the operating characteristics of the business? How rapidly is inventory turned over in relation to other companies in the same industry? Is any capital invested in dead or slow moving stock? Are sales being lost due to inadequate inventory levels? If appropriate, what action should be taken to increase or decrease inventory?

Accounts Payable and Trade Notes Payable

In a business, trade credit often provides a major source of financing for the firm. Key issues to investigate in this category include:

- Is the amount of money owed to suppliers reasonable in relation to purchases?
- Is the firm's payment policy such that it will enhance or detract from the firm's credit rating?
- If available, are discounts being taken?
- What are the timing relationships between payments on accounts payable and collection on accounts receivable?

Notes Payable

Notes payable to banks or other lenders are a second major source of financing for the business. Important questions in this class include: What is the amount of bank borrowing employed? Is this debt amount reasonable in relation to the equity financing of the firm? When will principal and interest payments fall due? Will funds be available to meet these payments on time?

Accrued Expenses and Taxes Payable

Accrued expenses and taxes payable represent obligations of the firm as of the date of balance sheet preparation. Accrued expenses represent such items as salaries payable, interest payable on bank notes, insurance premiums payable, and similar items. Of primary concern in this area, particularly with regard to taxes payable, is the magnitude, timing, and availability of funds for payment. Careful planning is required to insure that these obligations are met on time.

As a final note, it is important to recognize that although the working capital accounts above are listed separately, they must also be viewed in total and from the point of view of their relationship to one another: What is the overall trend in net working capital? Is this a healthy trend? Which individual accounts are responsible for the trend? How does the firm's working capital position relate to similar sized firms in the industry? What can be done to correct the trend, if necessary?

Of course, the questions posed are much easier to ask than to answer and there are few "general" answers to the issues raised. The guides which follow provide suggestions, techniques, and guidelines for successful management which, when tempered with the experience of the individual owner-manager and the unique requirements of the particular industry, may be expected to enhance one's ability to manage effectively the financial resources of a business enterprise.

Business Financial Planning

There is one simple reason to understand and observe business financial planning in your business-to avoid failure. Eight of ten new businesses fail primarily because of the lack of good financial planning.

Business financial planning affects how and on what terms you will be able to attract the funding required to establish, maintain, and expand your business. Financial planning determines the raw materials you can afford to buy, the products you will be able to produce, and whether or not you will be able to market them efficiently. It affects the human and physical resources you will be able to acquire to operate your business. It will be a major determinant of whether or not you will be able to make your hard work profitable.

This section provides an overview of the essential components of financial planning and management. Used wisely, it will make the reader-the small business owner/manager-familiar enough with the fundamentals to have a fighting chance of success in today's highly competitive business environment.

A clearly conceived, well documented financial plan, establishing goals and including the use of Pro Forma Statements and Budgets to ensure financial control, will demonstrate not only that you know what you want to do, but that you know how to accomplish it. This demonstration is essential to attract the capital required by your business from creditors and investors.

What Is Financial Management?

Very simply stated, financial management is the use of financial statements that reflect the financial condition of a business to identify its relative strengths and weaknesses. It enables you to plan, using projections, future financial performance for capital, asset, and personnel requirements to maximize the return on shareholders' investment.

Tools of Financial Planning

This section introduces the tools required to prepare a financial plan for your business's development, including the following:

- Basic Financial Statements-the Balance Sheet and Statement of Income.
- Ratio Analysis-a means by which individual business performance is compared to similar businesses in the same category.
- The Pro Forma Statement of Income-a method used to forecast future profitability.
- Break-Even Analysis-a method allowing the small business person to calculate the sales level at which a business recovers all its costs or expenses.
- The Cash Flow Statement-also known as the Budget identifies the flow of cash into and out of the business.
- Pricing formulas and policies-used to calculate profitable selling prices for products and services.
- Types and sources of capital available to finance business operations.
- Short-and long-term planning considerations necessary to maximize profits.

The business owner/manager who understands these concepts and uses them effectively to control the evolution of the business is practicing sound financial management thereby increasing the likelihood of success.

Understanding Financial Statements

Financial Statements anlysis record the performance of your business and allow you to diagnose its strengths and weaknesses by providing a written summary of financial activities. There are two primary financial statements: the Balance Sheet and the Statement of Income.

The Balance Sheet

Financial statement analysis looks first at the balance sheet. The Balance Sheet provides a picture of the financial health of a business at a given moment, usually at the close of an accounting period. It lists in detail those material and intangible items the business owns (known as its assets) and what money the business owes, either to its creditors (liabilities) or to its owners (shareholders' equity or net worth of the business).

Assets include not only cash, merchandise inventory, land, buildings, equipment, machinery, furniture, patents, trademarks, and the like, but also money due from individuals or other businesses (known as accounts or notes receivable).

Liabilities are funds acquired for a business through loans or the sale of property or services to the business on credit. Creditors do not acquire business ownership, but promissory notes to be paid at a designated future date.

Shareholders' equity (or net worth or capital) is money put into a business by its owners for use by the business in acquiring assets.

At any given time, a business's assets equal the total contributions by the creditors and owners, as illustrated by the following formula for the Balance Sheet:

- Assets = Liabilities + Net worth.

This formula is a basic premise of accounting. If a business owes more money to creditors than it possesses in value of assets owned, the net worth or owner's equity of the business will be a negative number.

The Balance Sheet is designed to show how the assets, liabilities, and net worth of a business are distributed at any given time. It is usually prepared at regular intervals; e.g., at each month's end, but especially at the end of each fiscal (accounting) year.

By regularly preparing this summary of what the business owns and owes (the Balance Sheet), the business owner/manager can identify and analyse trends in the financial strength of the business. It permits timely modifications, such as gradually decreasing the amount of money the business owes to creditors and increasing the amount the business owes its owners.

All Balance Sheets contain the same categories of assets, liabilities, and net worth. Assets are arranged in decreasing order of how quickly they can be turned into cash (liquidity). Liabilities are listed in order of how soon they must be repaid, followed by retained earnings (net worth or owner's equity).

The categories and format of the Balance Sheet are established by a system known as Generally Accepted Accounting Principles (GAAP). The system is applied to all companies, large or small, so anyone reading the Balance Sheet can readily understand the story it tells.

Balance Sheet Categories

Assets and liabilities are broken down into categories as described as follows:

Assets: An asset is anything the business owns that has monetary value.

- Current Assets include cash, government securities, marketable securities, accounts receivable, notes receivable (other than from officers or employees), inventories, prepaid expenses, and any other item that could be converted into cash within one year in the normal course of business.
- Fixed Assets are those acquired for long-term use in a business such as land, plant, equipment, machinery, leasehold improvements, furniture, fixtures, and any other items with an expected useful business life measured in years (as opposed to items that will wear out or be used up in less than one year and are usually expensed when they are purchased). These assets are typically not for resale and are recorded in the Balance Sheet at their net cost less accumulated depreciation.
- Other Assets include intangible assets, such as patents, royalty arrangements, copyrights, exclusive use contracts, and notes receivable from officers and employees.

Liabilities: Liabilities are the claims of creditors against the assets of the business (debts owed by the business).

- Current Liabilities are accounts payable, notes payable to banks, accrued expenses (wages, salaries), taxes payable, the current portion (due within one year) of long-term debt, and other obligations to creditors due within one year.
- Long-Term Liabilities are mortgages, intermediate and long-term bank loans, equipment loans, and any other obligation for money due to a creditor with a maturity longer than one year.

Net Worth is the assets of the business minus its liabilities. Net worth equals the owner's equity. This equity is the investment by the owner plus any profits or minus any losses that have accumulated in the business.

The Statement of Income

The second primary report included in a business's Financial Statement is the Statement of Income. The Statement of Income is a measurement of a company's sales and expenses over a specific period of time. It is also prepared at regular intervals (again, each month and fiscal year end) to show the results of operating during those accounting periods. It too follows Generally Accepted Accounting Principles (GAAP) and contains specific revenue and expense categories regardless of the nature of the business.

Statement of Income Categories

The Statement of Income Categories are Calculated as Described Below:

- Net Sales (gross sales less returns and allowances).
- Less Cost of Goods Sold (cost of inventories).
- Equals Gross Margin (gross profit on sales before operating expenses).
- Less Selling and Administrative Expenses (salaries, wages, payroll taxes and benefits, rent, utilities, maintenance expenses, office supplies, postage, automobile/vehicle expenses, insurance, legal and accounting expenses, depreciation).
- Equals Operating Profit (profit before other non-operating income or expense).
- Plus Other Income (income from discounts, investments, customer charge accounts).

- Less Other Expenses (interest expense).
- Equals Net Profit (or Loss) before Tax (the figure on which your tax is calculated).
- Less Income Taxes (if any are due).
- Equals Net Profit (or Loss) After Tax.

Calculating the Cost of Goods Sold

Calculation of the Cost of Goods Sold category in the Statement of Income (or Profit-and-Loss Statement as it is sometimes called) varies depending on whether the business is retail, wholesale, or manufacturing. In retailing and wholesaling, computing the cost of goods sold during the accounting period involves beginning and ending inventories. This, of course, includes purchases made during the accounting period. In manufacturing it involves not only finished-goods inventories, but also raw materials inventories, goods-in-process inventories, direct labour, and direct factory overhead costs. Regardless of the calculation for Cost of Goods Sold, deduct the Cost of Goods Sold from Net Sales to get Gross Margin or Gross Profit. From Gross Profit, deduct general or indirect overhead, such as selling expenses, office expenses, and interest expenses. To calculate your Net Profit. This is the final profit after all costs and expenses for the accounting period have been deducted.

Financial Ratio Analysis

The Balance Sheet and the Statement of Income are essential, but they are only the starting point for successful financial management. Apply Ratio Analysis to Financial Statements to analyse the success, failure, and progress of your business. Ratio Analysis enables the business owner/manager to spot trends in a business and to compare its performance and condition with the average performance of similar businesses in the same industry. To do this compare your ratios with the average of businesses similar to yours and compare your own ratios for several successive years, watching especially for any unfavorable trends that may be starting. Ratio analysis may provide the all-important early warning indications that allow you to solve your business problems before your business is destroyed by them.

Balance Sheet Ratio Analysis

Important Balance Sheet Ratios measure liquidity and solvency (a business's ability to pay its bills as they come due) and leverage (the extent to which the business is dependent on creditors' funding). They include the following ratios:

Liquidity Ratios

These ratios indicate the ease of turning assets into cash. They include the Current Ratio, Quick Ratio, and Working Capital.

Current Ratios: The Current Ratio is one of the best known measures of financial strength. It is figured as shown below:

$$\text{Current Ratio} = \frac{\text{Total Current Assets}}{\text{Total Current Liabilities}}$$

The main question this ratio addresses is: "Does your business have enough current assets to meet the payment schedule of its current debts with a margin of safety for possible losses in current assets, such as inventory shrinkage or collectable accounts?" A generally acceptable current ratio is 2 to 1. But whether or not a specific ratio is satisfactory depends on the nature of the business and the characteristics of its current assets and liabilities. The minimum acceptable current ratio is obviously 1:1, but that relationship is usually playing it too close for comfort.

If you decide your business's current ratio is too low, you may be able to raise it by:

- Paying some debts.
- Increasing your current assets from loans or other borrowings with a maturity of more than one year.
- Converting non-current assets into current assets.
- Increasing your current assets from new equity contributions.
- Putting profits back into the business.

Quick Ratios. The Quick Ratio is sometimes called the "acid-test" ratio and is one of the best measures of liquidity. It is figured as shown below:

$$\text{Quick Ratio} = \frac{\text{Cash + Government Securities + Receivables}}{\text{Total Current Liabilities}}$$

The Quick Ratio is a much more exacting measure than the Current Ratio. By excluding inventories, it concentrates on the really liquid assets, with value that is fairly certain. It helps answer the question: "If all sales revenues should disappear, could my business meet its current obligations with the readily convertible `quick' funds on hand?"

An acid-test of 1:1 is considered satisfactory unless the majority of your "quick assets" are in accounts receivable, and the pattern of accounts receivable collection lags behind the schedule for paying current liabilities.

Working Capital. Working Capital is more a measure of cash flow than a ratio. The result of this calculation must be a positive number. It is calculated as shown below:

Working Capital = Total Current Assets-Total Current Liabilities.

Bankers look at Net Working Capital over time to determine a company's ability to weather financial crises. Loans are often tied to minimum working capital requirements.

A general observation about these three Liquidity Ratios is that the higher they are the better, especially if you are relying to any significant extent on creditor money to finance assets.

Leverage Ratio

This Debt/Worth or Leverage Ratio indicates the extent to which the business is reliant on debt financing (creditor money versus owner's equity):

$$\text{Debt/Worth Ratio} = \frac{\text{Total Liabilities}}{\text{Net Worth}}$$

Generally, the higher this ratio, the more risky a creditor will perceive its exposure in your business, making it correspondingly harder to obtain credit.

Income Statement Ratio Analysis

The following important State of Income Ratios measure profitability:

Gross Margin Ratio

This ratio is the percentage of sales dollars left after subtracting the cost of goods sold from net sales. It measures the percentage of sales dollars remaining (after obtaining or manufacturing the goods sold) available to pay the overhead expenses of the company.

Comparison of your business ratios to those of similar businesses will reveal the relative strengths or weaknesses in your business. The Gross Margin Ratio is calculated as follows:

$$\text{Gross Margin Ratio} = \frac{\text{Gross Profit}}{\text{Net Sales}}$$

(Gross Profit = Net Sales-Cost of Goods Sold).

Net Profit Margin Ratio

This ratio is the percentage of sales dollars left after subtracting the Cost of Goods sold and all expenses, except income taxes. It provides a good opportunity to compare your company's "return on sales" with the performance of other companies in your industry. It is calculated before income tax because tax rates and tax liabilities vary from company to company for a wide variety of reasons, making comparisons after taxes much more difficult. The Net Profit Margin Ratio is calculated as follows:

$$\text{Net Profit Margin Ratio} = \frac{\text{Net Profit Before Tax}}{\text{Net Sales}}$$

Management Ratios

Other important ratios, often referred to as Management Ratios, are also derived from Balance Sheet and Statement of Income information.

Inventory Turnover Ratio

This ratio reveals how well inventory is being managed. It is important because the more times inventory can be turned in a given operating cycle, the greater the profit. The Inventory Turnover Ratio is calculated as follows:

$$\text{Inventory Turnover Ratio} = \frac{\text{Net Sales}}{\text{Average Inventory at Cost}}$$

Accounts Receivable Turnover Ratio

This ratio indicates how well accounts receivable are being collected. If receivables are not collected reasonably in accordance with their terms, management should rethink its collection policy. If receivables are excessively slow in being converted to cash, liquidity could be severely impaired. The Accounts Receivable Turnover Ratio is calculated as follows:

$$\frac{\text{Net Credit Sales/Year}}{\text{365 Days/Year}} = \text{Daily Credit Sales}$$

$$\text{Accounts Receivable Turnover (in days)} = \frac{\text{Accounts Receivable}}{\text{Daily Credit Sales}}$$

Return on Assets Ratio

This measures how efficiently profits are being generated from the assets employed in the business when compared with the ratios of firms in a similar business. A low ratio in comparison with industry averages indicates an inefficient use of business assets. The Return on Assets Ratio is calculated as follows:

$$\text{Return on Assets} = \frac{\text{Net Profit Before Tax}}{\text{Total Assets}}$$

Return on Investment (ROI) Ratio

The ROI is perhaps the most important ratio of all. It is the percentage of return on funds invested in the business by its owners. In short, this ratio tells the owner whether or not all the effort put into the business has been worthwhile. If the ROI is less than the rate of return on an alternative, risk-free investment such as a bank savings account, the owner may be wiser to sell the company, put the money in such a savings instrument, and avoid the daily struggles of small business management. The ROI is calculated as follows:

$$\text{Return on Investment} = \frac{\text{Net Profit Before Tax}}{\text{Net Worth}}$$

These Liquidity, Leverage, Profitability, and Management Ratios allow the business owner to identify trends in a business and to compare its progress with the performance of others through data published by various sources. The owner may thus determine the business's relative strengths and weaknesses.

Forecasting Sales and Profits

Forecasting sales and profits, particularly on a short-term basis (one year to three years), is essential to planning for business success. This process, estimating future business performance based on the actual results from prior periods, enables the business owner/manager to modify the operation of the business on a timely basis. This allows the business to avoid losses or major financial problems should some future results from operations not conform with reasonable expectations. Forecasts-or Pro Forma Income Statements and Cash Flow Statements as they are usually called-also provide the most persuasive management tools to apply for loans or attract investor money. As a business expands, there will inevitably be a need for more money than can be internally generated from profits. Next, let's examine some facts affecting Forecasting sales and profits.

Facts Affecting Pro Forma Statements

Preparation of Forecasts (Pro Forma Statements) requires assembling a wide array of pertinent, verifiable facts affecting your business and its past performance. These include:

Data from prior financial statements, particularly:

a. Previous sales levels and trends.
b. Past gross percentages.
c. Average past general, administrative, and selling expenses necessary to generate your former sales volumes.
d. Trends in the company's need to borrow (supplier, trade credit, and bank credit) to support various levels of inventory and trends in accounts receivable required to achieve previous sales volumes.

Unique company data, particularly:

a. Plant capacity.
b. Competition.
c. Financial constraints.
d. Personnel availability.

Industry-wide factors, including:

a. Overall state of the economy.
b. Economic status of your industry within the economy.
c. Population growth.
d. Elasticity of demand for the product or service your business provides (Demand is said to be "elastic" if it decreases as prices increase, a demonstration that consumers can do without or with less of the goods or service. If demand for something is relatively steady as prices increase, it is "inelastic").

e. Availability of raw materials.

Once these factors are identified, they may be used in Pro Formas, which estimate the level of sales, expense, and profitability that seem possible in a future period of operations.

The Pro Forma Income Statement

In preparing the Pro Forma Income Statement, the estimate of total sales during a selected period is the most critical "guesstimate:" Employ business experience from past financial statements. Get help from management and sales people in developing this all-important number.

Then assume, for example, that a 10 percent increase in sales volume is a realistic and attainable goal. Multiply last year's net sales by 1.10 to get this year's estimate of total net sales. Next, break down this total, month by month, by looking at the historical monthly sales volume. From this you can determine what percentage of total annual sales fell on the average in each of those months over a minimum of the past three years. You may find that 75 percent of total annual sales volume was realized during the six months from July through December in each of those years and that the remaining 25 percent of sales was spread fairly evenly over the first six months of the year.

Next, estimate the cost of goods sold by analysing operating data to determine on a monthly basis what percentage of sales has gone into cost of goods sold in the past. This percentage can then be adjusted for expected variations in costs, price trends, and efficiency of operations.

Operating expenses (sales, general and administrative expenses, depreciation, and interest), other expenses, other income, and taxes can then be estimated through detailed analysis and adjustment of what they were in the past and what you expect them to be in the future.

Comparison with Actual Monthly Performance

Putting together this information month by month for a year into the future will result in your business's Pro Forma Statement of Income. Use it to compare with the actual monthly results from operations. Preparation of the information is summarized below:

Revenue (Sales)

- List the departments within the business. For example, if your business is appliance sales and service, the departments would include new appliances, used appliances, parts, in-shop service, on-site service.

- In the "Estimate" columns, enter a reasonable projection of monthly sales for each department of the business. Include cash and on-account sales. In the "Actual" columns, enter the actual sales for the month as they become available.
- Exclude from the Revenue section any revenue not strictly related to the business.

Cost of Sales

- Cite costs by department of the business, as above.
- In the "Estimate" columns, enter the cost of sales estimated for each month for each department. For product inventory, calculate the cost of the goods sold for each department (beginning inventory plus purchases and transportation costs during the month minus the inventory). Enter "Actual" costs each month as they accrue.

Gross Profit

Subtract the total cost of sales from the total revenue.

Expenses

- *Salary Expenses:* Basc pay plus overtime.
- *Payroll Expenses:* Include paid vacations, sick leave, health insurance, unemployment insurance, Social Security taxes.
- *Outside Services:* Include costs of subcontracts, overflow work farmed-out, special or one-time services.
- *Supplies:* Services and items purchased for use in the business, not for resale.
- *Repairs and Maintenance:* Regular maintenance and repair, including periodic large expenditures, such as painting or decorating.
- *Advertising:* Include desired sales volume, classified directory listing expense, etc.
- *Car, Delivery and Travel:* Include charges if personal car is used in the business. Include parking, tolls, mileage on buying trips, repairs, etc.

- *Accounting and Legal:* Outside professional services.
- *Rent:* List only real estate used in the business.
- Telephone.
- *Utilities:* Water, heat, light, etc.
- *Insurance:* Fire or liability on property or products, worker's compensation.
- *Taxes:* Inventory, sales, excise, real estate, others.
- Interest.
- *Depreciation:* Amortization of capital assets.
- *Other Expenses (specify each):* Tools, leased equipment, etc.
- *Miscellaneous (unspecified):* Small expenditures without separate accounts.

Net Profit

- To find net profit, subtract total expenses from gross profit.

The Pro Forma Statement of Income, prepared on a monthly basis and culminating in an annual projection for the next business fiscal year, should be revised not less than quarterly. It must reflect the actual performance achieved in the immediately preceding three months to ensure its continuing usefulness as one of the two most valuable planning tools available to management.

Should the Pro Forma reveal that the business will likely not generate a profit from operations, plans must immediately be developed to identify what to do to at least break even-increase volume, decrease expenses, or put more owner capital in to pay some debts and reduce interest expenses.

Break-Even Analysis

"Break-Even" means a level of operations at which a business neither makes a profit nor sustains a loss. At this point, revenue is just enough to cover expenses. Break-Even Analysis enables you to study the relationship of volume, costs, and revenue.

Break-Even requires the business owner/manager to define a sales level-either in terms of revenue dollars to be earned or in units to be sold within a given accounting period-at which the business would earn a before tax net profit of zero. This may be done by employing one of various formula calculations to the business estimated sales volume, estimated fixed costs, and estimated variable costs.

Generally, the volume and cost estimates assume the following conditions:

- A change in sales volume will not affect the selling price per unit;
- Fixed expenses (rent, salaries, administrative and office expenses, interest, and depreciation) will remain the same at all volume levels; and
- Variable expenses (cost of goods sold, variable labour costs, including overtime wages and sales commissions) will increase or decrease in direct proportion to any increase or decrease in sales volume.

Two methods are generally employed in Break-Even Analysis, depending on whether the break-even point is calculated in terms of sales dollar volume or in number of units that must be sold.

Break-Even Point in Sales Dollars

The steps for calculating the first method are shown below:

- Obtain a list of expenses incurred by the company during its past fiscal year.
- Separate the expenses listed in Step 1 into either a variable or a fixed expense classification.
- Express the variable expenses as a percentage of sales. In the condensed income statement of the Small Business Specialities Co. (below), net sales were $1,200,000. In Step 2, variable expenses were found to amount to $720,000. Therefore, variable expenses are 60 percent of net sales ($720,000 divided by $1,200,000). This means that 60 cents of every sales dollar is required to cover variable expenses. Only the remainder, 40 cents of every dollar, is available for fixed expenses and profit.
- Substitute the information gathered in the preceding steps in the following basic break-even formula to calculate the break-even point.

Remember: Increased sales do not necessarily mean increased profits. If you know your company's break-even point, you will know how to price your product to make a profit. If you cannot make an acceptable profit, alter or sell your business before you lose your retained earnings.

Cash Flow Management-Pro Forma Cash Flow Budget

If there is anything more important to the successful financial management of a business than the thorough, thoughtful preparation of Pro Forma Income Statements, it is the preparation of the Cash Flow Statement, sometimes called the Cash Flow Budget.

The Cash Flow Statement

The cash flow management and cash flow statement identifies when cash is expected to be received and when it must be spent to pay bills and debts. It shows how much cash will be needed to pay expenses and when it will be needed. It also allows the manager to identify where the necessary cash will come from. For example, will it be internally generated from sales and the collection of accounts receivable-or must it be borrowed? (The Cash Flow Projection deals only with actual cash transactions; depreciation and amortization of goodwill or other non-cash expense items are not considered in this Pro Forma.)

The Cash Flow Statement, based on management estimates of sales and obligations, identifies when money will be flowing into and out of the business. It enables management to plan for shortfalls in cash resources so short term working capital loans may be arranged in advance. It allows management to schedule purchases and payments in a way that enables the business to borrow as little as possible. Because all sales are not cash sales, management must be able to forecast when accounts receivable will become "cash in the bank" and when expenses-whether regular or seasonal-must be paid so cash shortfalls will not interrupt normal business operations.

The Pro Forma Cash Flow Statement may also be used as a Budget. Permitting the manager increased control of the business through continuous comparison of actual receipts and disbursements against forecast amounts. This comparison helps the small business owner identify areas for timely improvement in financial management.

By closely watching the timing of cash receipts and disbursements, cash balance on hand, and loan balances, management can readily identify such things as deficiencies in collecting receivables, unrealistic trade credit or loan repayment schedules. Surplus cash that may be invested on a short-term basis or used to reduce debt and interest expenses temporarily can be recognized. In short, it is the most valuable tool management has at its disposal to refine the day-to-day operation of a business. It is an important financial tool bank lenders evaluate when a business needs a loan, for it demonstrates not only how large a loan is required but also when and how it can be repaid.

A Cash Flow Statement or Budget can be prepared for any period of time. However, a one-year budget matching the fiscal year of your business is recommended. As in the preparation and use of the Pro Forma Statement of Income, the projected Cash Flow Statement should be prepared on a monthly basis for the next year. It should be revised not less than quarterly to reflect actual performance in the preceding three months of operations to check its projections.

In preparing the Cash Flow Statement or Budget start with the sales budget. Other budgets are related directly or indirectly to this budget.

Later on, before a cash budget can be compiled, you will need to know the estimated cash requirements for selling expenses. Therefore, you prepare a budget for selling expenses and another for cash expenditures for selling expenses (total selling expenses less depreciation):

> *Basic information for an estimate of administrative expenses for the coming year is easily compiled. Again, from that budget you can estimate cash requirements for those expenses to be used subsequently in preparing the cash budget.*

Now, from the information budgeted so far, you can proceed to prepare the budget income statement. Assume you plan to borrow $10,000 at the end of the first quarter. Although payable at maturity of the note, the interest appears in the last three quarters of the year. The statement will resemble the following:

Estimating that 90 percent of your account sales is collected in the quarter in which they are made, that 9 percent is collected in the quarter following the quarter in which the sales were made, and that 1 percent of account sales is uncollectible, your accounts receivable budget of collections would look like this:

> *Going back to the sales budget in units, now prepare a production budget in units. Assume you have 2,000 units in the opening inventory and want to have on hand at the end of each quarter the following quantities: 1st quarter, 3,000 units; 2nd quarter, 3,500 units; 3rd quarter, 4,000 units; and 4th quarter, 4,500 units.*

Next, based on the production budget, prepare a budget to show the purchases needed during each of the four quarters. Expressed in terms of dollars, you do this by taking the production and inventory figures and multiplying them by the cost of material (previously estimated at $1.50 per unit). You could prepare a similar budget expressed in units.

Now suppose you pay 50 percent of your accounts in the quarter of the purchase and 50 percent in the following quarter. Carry over payables from last year were $5,000. Further, you always take the purchase discounts as a matter of good business policy. Since net purchases (less discount) were figured into the $1.50 cost estimate, purchase discounts do not appear in the budgets.

Taking the data for quantities produced from the production budget in units, calculate the direct labour requirements on the basis of units to be produced. (The number and cost of labour hours necessary to produce a given quantity can be set forth in supplemental schedules).

Figure the cash payments for manufacturing overhead by subtracting depreciation, which requires no cash outlay, from the totals above, and you will have the following breakdown.

Now comes the all important cash budget. You put it together by using the Collection of Accounts Receivable Budget; Selling Expenses Budget-Cash Requirements; Administrative Expenses Budget-Cash Requirements; Payment of Purchases Budget; Direct Labour Budget-Cash Requirements: and Manufacturing Budget Cash Requirements. Take $15,000 as the beginning balance, and assume that dividends of $20,000 are to be paid in the fourth quarter.

In order to make the most effective use of your budgets to plan profits, you will want to establish reporting devices. Throughout the time span you have set, you need periodic reports and reviews on both efforts and accomplishments. These let you know whether your budget plan is being attained and help you keep control throughout the process. It is through comparing actual performance with budgeted projections that you maintain control of the operations.

Your company should be structured along functional lines, with well identified areas of responsibility and authority. Then, depending upon the size of your company, the budget reports can be prepared to correspond with the organizational structure of the company.

Remember, the Cash Flow Statement used as the business's Budget allows the owner/manager to anticipate problems rather than react to them after they occur. It permits comparison of actual receipts and disbursements against projections to identify errors in the forecast. If cash flow is analysed monthly, the manager can correct the cause of the error before it harms profitability.

Capital Management and Capital Budgeting

Types and Sources of Capital

Capital management and capital budgeting to finance a business has two major forms: debt and equity. Creditor money (debt) comes from trade credit, loans made by financial institutions, leasing companies, and customers who have made pre-payments on larger-frequently manufactured orders. Equity is money received by the company in exchange for some portion of ownership. Sources include the entrepreneur's own money; money from family, friends, or other non-professional investors; or money from venture capitalists.

Debt capital, depending upon its sources (e.g., trade, bank, leasing company, mortgage company) comes into the business for short or intermediate periods. Owner or equity capital remains in the company for the life of the business (unless replaced by other equity) and is repaid only when and if there is a surplus at liquidation of the business-after all creditors are repaid.

Acquiring such funds depends entirely on the business's ability to repay with interest (debt) or appreciation (equity). Financial performance (reflected in the Financial Statements) and realistic, thorough management planning and control (shown by Pro Formas and Cash Flow Budgets), are the determining factors in whether or not a business can attract the debt and equity funding it needs to operate and expand.

Business capital can be further classified as equity capital, working capital, and growth capital. Equity capital is the cornerstone of the financial structure of any company.

Equity is technically the part of the Balance Sheet reflecting the ownership of the company. It represents the total value of the business, all other financing being debt that must be repaid. Usually, you cannot get equity capital at least not during the early stages of business growth.

Working capital is required to meet the continuing operational needs of the business, such as "carrying" accounts receivable, purchasing inventory, and meeting the payroll. In most businesses, these needs vary during the year, depending on activities (inventory build-up, seasonal hiring or layoffs, etc.) during the business cycle.

Growth capital is not directly related to cyclical aspects of the business. Growth capital is required when the business is expanding or being altered in some significant and costly way that is expected to result in higher and increased cash flow. Lenders of growth capital frequently depend on anticipated increased profit for repayment over an extended period of time, rather than expecting to be repaid from seasonal increases in liquidity as is the case of working capital lenders.

Every growing business needs all three types: equity, working, and growth capital. You should not expect a single financing program maintained for a short period of time to eliminate future needs for additional capital. As lenders and investors analyse the requirements of your business, they will distinguish between the three types of capital in the following way:

(1) fluctuating needs (working capital);

(2) needs to be repaid with profits over a period of a few years (growth capital); and

(3) permanent needs (equity capital).

If you are asking for a working capital loan, you will be expected to show how the loan can be repaid through cash (liquidity) during the business's next full operating cycle, generally a one year cycle. If you seek growth capital, you will be expected to show how the capital will be used to increase your business enough to be able to repay the loan within several years (usually not more than seven). If you seek equity capital, it must be raised from investors who will take the risk for dividend returns or capital gains, or a specific share of the business.

Borrowing Working Capital

Working capital is defined as the difference between current assets and current liabilities. To the extent that a business does not generate enough money to pay trade debt as it comes due, this cash must be borrowed. Commercial banks obviously are the largest source of such loans, which have the following characteristics:

- The loans are short-term but renewable;
- they may fluctuate according to seasonal needs or follow a fixed schedule of repayment (amortization);
- they require periodic full repayment ("clean up");
- they are granted primarily only when the ratio of net current assets comfortably exceeds net current liabilities; and

- they are sometimes unsecured but more often secured by current assets (e.g., accounts receivable and inventory).

Advances can usually be obtained for as much as 70 to 80 percent of quality (likely to be paid) receivables and to 40 to 50 percent of inventory. Banks grant unsecured credit only when they feel the general liquidity and overall financial strength of a business provide assurance for repayment of the loan.

You may be able to predict a specific interval, say three to five months, for which you need financing. A bank may then agree to issue credit for a specific term. Most likely, you will need working capital to finance outflow peaks in your business cycle. Working capital then supplements equity. Most working capital credits are established on a one-year basis.

Although most unsecured loans fall into the one-year line of credit category, another frequently used type, the amortizing loan, calls for a fixed program of reduction, usually on a monthly or quarterly basis. For such loans your bank is likely to agree to terms longer than a year, as long as you continue to meet the principal reduction schedule.

It is important to note that while a loan from a bank for working capital can be negotiated only for a relatively short term, satisfactory performance can allow the arrangement to be continued indefinitely.

Most banks will expect you to pay off your loans once a year (particularly if they are unsecured) in perhaps 30 or 60 days. This is known as "the annual clean up," and it should occur when the business has the greatest liquidity. This debt reduction normally follows a seasonal sales peak when inventories have been reduced and most receivables have been collected.

You may discover that it becomes progressively more difficult to repay debt or "clean up" within the specified time. This difficulty usually occurs because:

- Your business is growing and its current activity represents a considerable increase over the corresponding period of the previous year;
- you have increased your short-term capital requirement because of new promotional programs or additional operations; or you are experiencing a temporary reduction in profitability and cash flow.

Frequently, such a condition justifies obtaining both working capital and amortizing loans. For example, you might try to arrange a combination of a $ 15,000 open line of credit to handle peak financial requirements during the business cycle and $20,000 in amortizing loans to be repaid at, say $4,000 per quarter. In appraising such a request, a commercial bank will insist on justification based on past experience and future projections. The bank will want to know: How the $15,000 line of credit will be self-liquidating during the year (with ample room for the annual clean up); and how your business will produce increased profits and resulting cash flow to meet the schedule of amortization on the $20,000 portion in spite of increasing your business's interest expense.

Borrowing Growth Capital

Lenders expect working capital loans to be repaid through cash generated in the short-term operations of the business, such as, selling goods or services and collecting receivables. Liquidity rather than overall profitability supports such borrowing programs. Growth capital loans are usually scheduled to be repaid over longer periods with profits from business activities extending several years into the future. Growth capital loans are, therefore, secured by collateral such as machinery and equipment, fixed assets which guarantee that lenders will recover their money should the business be unable to make repayment.

For a growth capital loan you will need to demonstrate that the growth capital will be used to increase your cash flow through increased sales, cost savings, and/or more efficient production. Although your building, equipment, or machinery will probably be your collateral for growth capital funds, you will also be able to use them for general business purposes, so long as the activity you use them for promises success. Even if you borrow only to acquire a single piece of new equipment, the lender is likely to insist that all your machinery and equipment be pledged.

Instead of bank financing a particular piece of new equipment, it may be possible to arrange a lease. You will not actually own the equipment, but you will have exclusive use of it over a specified period. Such an arrangement usually has tax advantages. It lets you use funds that would be tied up in the equipment, if you had purchased it. It also affords the opportunity to make sure the equipment meets your needs before you purchase it.

Major equipment may also be purchased on a time payment plan, sometimes called a Conditional Sales Purchase. Ownership of the property is retained by the seller until the buyer has made all the payments required by the contract. (Remember, however, that time payment purchases usually require substantial down payments and even leases require cash advances for several months of lease payments.)

Long-term growth capital loans for more than five but less than fifteen years are also obtainable. Real estate financing with repayment over many years on an established schedule is the best example. The loan is secured by the land and/or buildings the money was used to buy. Most businesses are best financed by a combination of these various credit arrangements.

When you go to a bank to request a loan, you must be prepared to present your company's case persuasively. You should bring your financial plan consisting of a Cash Budget for the next twelve months, Pro Forma Balance Sheets, and Income Statements for the next three to five years. You should be able to explain and amplify these statements and the underlying assumptions on which the figures are based. Obviously, your assumptions must be convincing and your projections supportable. Finally, many banks prefer statements audited by an outside accountant with the accountant's signed opinion that the statements were prepared in accordance with generally accepted accounting principles and that they fairly present the financial condition of your business.

Borrowing Permanent Equity Capital

Permanent capital sometimes comes from sources other than the business owner/manager.

Venture capital, another source of equity capital, is extremely difficult to define; however, it is high risk capital offered with the principal objective of earning capital gains for the investor. While venture capitalists are usually prepared to wait longer than the average investor for a profitable return, they usually expect in excess of 15 percent return on their investment Often they expect to take an active part in determining the objectives of the business.

These investors may also assist the small business owner/manager by providing experienced guidance in marketing, product ideas, and additional financing alternatives as the business develops. Even though turning to venture capital may create more bosses, their advice could be as valuable as the money they lend. Be aware, however, that venture capitalists are looking for businesses with real potential for growth and for future sales in the millions of dollars.

Applying for Capital

Below is the minimum information you must make available to lenders and investors:

1. Discussion of the Business:
   - Name, address, and telephone number.
   - Type of business you are in now or want to expand or start.
2. Amount of Money You Need to Borrow:
   - Ask for all you will need. Don't ask for a part of the total and think you can come back for more later. This could indicate to the lender that you are a poor planner.
3. How You Will Use the Money:
   - List each way the borrowed money will be used.
   - Itemize the amount of money required for each purpose.
4. Proposed Terms of the Loan:
   - Include a payback schedule. Even though the lender has the final say in setting the terms of the loan, if you suggest terms, you will retain a negotiating position.
5. Financial Support Documents:
   - Show where the money will come from to repay the loan through the following projected statements.
   - Profit and Loss Statements (one year for working capital loan requests and three to five years for growth capital requests).
   - Cash Flow Statements (one year for working capital loan requests and three to five years for growth capital requests).
6. Financial History of the Business:
   - Include the following financial statements for the last three years.
   - Balance Sheet.
   - Profit and Loss Statement.
   - Accounts Receivable and Accounts Payable Listings and Agings.

7. Personal Financial Statement of the Owner(s):
   - Personal Assets and Liabilities.
   - Resume(s).
8. Other Useful Information Includes:
   - Letters of Intent from Prospective Customers.
   - Leases or Buy/Sell Agreements Affecting Your Business.
   - Reference Letters.

Although it is not required, it is useful to calculate the ratios described earlier in this section for your business over the past three years. Use this information to prove the strong financial health and good trends in your business's development and to demonstrate that you use such management tools to plan and control your business's growth.

Understanding Capital Sources

Never enough money: How many times have you said that. You need capital to get sales, buy inventory, pay your employees, purchase assets, pay taxes, you name it you need money for it. Your need for capital is a continuing one. To just stay in business or to expand, the small business owner needs capital, but where do you get it?

Expansion opportunities or a chance to purchase cost-saving equipment can also create a need for extra capital.

Available Capital Sources

In order to secure the capital sources they need, small business owners must understand the various sources of money that are available to them such as the following:

- Capital generated internally.
- Capital available from trade creditors.
- Borrowed money.
- Sale of an ownership interest in the business to equity investors.

Each of these capital sources has unique characteristics. These characteristics must be fully understood by the small business owner so that he or she will know what sources are available and which source is best suited to the needs of the business.

This section has been designed to help the small business owner in the following ways:

- Recognize those situations that create a need for additional capital.
- Identify the capital sources that are available to the small business owner.
- Manage the business judiciously to take full advantage of the capital that can be generated internally.
- Establish a plan to permit the client to take full advantage of trade capital without jeopardizing credit status.
- Identify various specific sources of debt and equity capital.
- Identify collateral that can be used to secure loans.
- Identify potential compensation to equity investors such as opportunities for dividends, capital gains, or a future public offering that could attract equity capital.

How the need for Capital Arises

There is more than one way to skin a cat. You'd better remember this old adage when your business needs more inventory, personnel, and facilities. As your business grows, so does your need for more and more capital. Remember there is more than one way and more than one place to raise the money you need.

Causes of Additional Capital Needs

There are many factors that can create a need for additional capital. Some of the more common are as follows:

- Sales growth requires inventories to be built to support the higher sales level.
- Sales growth creates a larger volume of accounts receivable.
- Growth requires the business to carry larger cash balances in order to meet its current obligations to employees, trade creditors, and others.
- Expansion opportunities such as a decision to open a new branch, add a new product, or increase capacity.
- Cost savings opportunities such as equipment purchases that will lower production costs or reduce operating expenses.
- Opportunities to realize substantial savings by taking advantage of quantity discounts on purchases for inventory, or building inventories prior to a supplier's price increase.

- Seasonal factors, where inventories must be built before the selling season begins and receivables may not be collected until 30 to 60 days after the selling season ends.
- Current repayment of obligations or debts may require more cash than is immediately available.
- Local or national economic conditions which cause sales and profit to decline temporarily.
- Economic difficulties of customers that can cause them to pay more slowly than expected.
- Failure to retain sufficient earnings in the business.
- Inattention to asset management may have allowed inventories or accounts receivable to get out of hand.

Combination: Frequently, the cause cannot be entirely attributed to any one of these factors, but results from a combination. For example, a growing, apparently successful business may find that it does not have sufficient cash on hand to meet a current debt installment or to expand to a new location because customers have been slow in paying.

Short-and Long-Term Capital

Capital needs can be classified as either short-or long-term. Short-term needs are generally those of less than one year. Long-term needs are those of more than one year.

Short-term Financing: Short-term financing is most common for assets that turn over quickly such as accounts receivable or inventories. Seasonal businesses that must build inventories in anticipation of selling requirements and will not collect receivables until after the selling season often need short-term financing for the interim. Contractors with substantial work-in-process inventories often need short-term financing until payment is received. Wholesalers and manufacturers with a major portion of their assets tied up in inventories and/or receivables also require short-term financing in anticipation of payments from customers.

Long-term Financing: Long-term financing is more often associated with the need for fixed assets such as property, plant, and equipment where the assets will be used in the business for several years. It is also a practical alternative in many situations where short-term financing requirements recur on a regular basis.

Recurring Needs

A series of short-term needs could often be more realistically viewed as a long-term need. The addition of long-term should eliminate the short-term needs and the crises that could occur if capital were not available to meet a short-term need.

Steady Growth

Whenever the need for additional capital grows continually without any significant pattern, as in the case of a company with steady sales and profit from year to year, long-term financing is probably more appropriate.

Internal Financing Sources

Internal sources of capital are those generated within the business. External sources of capital are those outside the business such as suppliers, lenders, and investors.

For example, a business can generate capital internally by accelerating collection of receivables, disposing of surplus inventories, retaining profit in the business, or cutting costs.

Capital can be generated externally by borrowing or locating investors who might be interested in buying a portion of the business.

Internal Financing Sources

Before seeking external sources of capital from investors or lenders, a business should thoroughly explore all reasonable sources for meeting its capital needs internally. Even if this effort fails to generate all of the needed capital, it can sharply reduce the external financing requirement, resulting in less interest expense, lower repayment obligations, and less sacrifice of control. With a lower requirement, the business' ability to secure external financing will be improved. Further, the ability to generate maximum capital internally and to control operations will enhance the confidence of outside investors and lenders. With more confidence in the business and its management, lenders and investors will be more willing to commit their capital.

Basic Sources

Basically, there are three principal sources of internal capital. These are as follows:

- Increasing the amount of earnings kept in the business.

- Prudent asset management.
- Cost control.

Increased Earnings Retention

Many businesses are able to meet all of their capital needs through earnings retention. Each year, shareholders' dividends or partners' drawings are restricted so that the largest reasonable share of earnings is retained in the business to finance its growth.

As with other internal capital sources, earnings retention not only reduces any external capital requirement, but also affects the business' ability to secure external capital. Lenders are particularly concerned with the rate of earnings retention, since the ability to repay debt obligations normally depends upon the amount of cash generated through operations. If this cash is used excessively to pay dividends or to permit withdrawals by investors, the company's ability to meet its debt obligations will be threatened.

Asset Management

Many businesses have non-productive assets that can be liquidated (sold or collected) to provide capital for short-term needs. A vigorous campaign of collecting outstanding receivables, with particular emphasis on amounts long outstanding, can often produce significant amounts of capital. Similarly, inventories can be analysed and those goods with relatively slow sales activity or with little hope for future fast movement can be liquidated. The liquidation can occur through sales to customers or through sales to wholesale outlets, as required.

Fixed assets can be sold to free cash immediately. For example, a company automobile might be sold and provide cash of $5,000 or $8,000. Owners and employees can be compensated on an actual mileage basis for use of their personal cars on company business. Or if an automobile is needed on a full-time basis, a lease can be arranged so that a vehicle will be available. Other assets such as loans made by the business to officers or employees, investments in non-related businesses, or prepaid expenses should be analysed closely. If they are nonproductive, they can often be liquidated so that cash is available to meet the immediate needs of the business.

Any of the above steps can be taken to alleviate short-term cash shortages. On a long-term basis, the business can minimize its external capital needs by establishing policies and procedures that will reduce the possibility of cash shortages caused by ineffective asset management. These policies could include the establishment of more rigorous credit standards, systematic review of outstanding receivables, periodic analysis of slow-moving inventories, and establishment of profitability criteria so that fixed asset investments are more closely controlled.

Cost Reduction

Careful analysis of costs, both before and after the fact, can improve profitability and therefore the amount of earnings available for retention. At the same time, cost control minimizes the need for cash to meet obligations to trade creditors and others. Before the fact, a business can establish buying controls that require a written purchase order and competitive bids on all purchases above a specified amount. Decisions to hire extra personnel, lease additional space, or incur other additional costs can be reviewed closely before commitments are made.

After the fact, management should review all actual costs carefully. Expenses can be compared with objectives, experience in previous periods, or with other companies in the industry. Whenever an apparent excess is identified, the cause of the excess should be closely explored and corrective action taken to prevent its recurrence.

Trade Credit

Trade credit is credit extended by suppliers. Ordinarily, it is the first source of extra capital that the small business owner turns to when the need arises.

Informal Extensions

Frequently, this is done with no formal planning by the business. Suppliers' invoices are simply allowed to "ride" for another 30 to 60 days. Unfortunately, this can lead to a number of problems. Suppliers may promptly terminate credit and refuse to deliver until the account is settled, thus denying the business access to sorely needed supplies, materials, or inventory. Or, suppliers might put the business on a C.O.D. basis, requiring that all shipments be fully paid in cash immediately upon receipt. At a time when a business is obviously strapped for cash, this requirement could have the same effect as cutting off deliveries altogether.

Planning Advantages

A planned program of trade credit extensions can often help the business secure extra capital that it needs without recourse to lenders or equity investors. This is particularly true whenever the capital need is relatively small or short in duration.

A Planned Approach should Involve the Following:

- Take full advantage of available payment terms. If no cash discount is offered and payment is due on the 30th day, do not make any payments before the 30th day.
- Whenever possible, negotiate extended payment terms with suppliers. For example, if a supplier's normal payment terms are net 30 days from the receipt of goods, these could be extended to net 30 days from the end of the month. This effectively "buys" an average of 15 extra days.
- If the business feels that it needs a substantial increase in time, say 60 to 90 days, it should advise suppliers of this need. They will often be willing to accept it, provided that the business is faithful in its adherence to payment at the later date.
- Consider the effect of cash discounts and delinquency penalties for late payment. Frequently, the added cost of trade credit may be far more expensive than the cost of alternate financing such as a short-term bank loan.
- Consider the possibility signing a note for each shipment promising payment at a specific later date. Such a note, which may or may not be interest-bearing, would give the supplier evidence of your intent to pay and increase the supplier's confidence in your business.

Ready Availability

Trade credit is often available to businesses on a relatively informal basis without the requirements for application, negotiation, auditing, and legal assistance often necessary with other capital sources.

Usage

Trade credit must be used judiciously. Its easy availability is particularly welcome in brief periods of limited needs. Used imprudently, however, it can lead to curtailment of relations with key suppliers and jeopardize your ability to locate other, competitive suppliers who are willing to extend credit to your business.

Debt Capital

Debt capital is an amount of money borrowed from a creditor. The amount borrowed is usually evidenced by a note, signed by the borrower, agreeing to repay the principal amount borrowed plus interest on some predetermined basis.

Borrowing Term

The terms under which money is borrowed may vary widely. Short-term notes can be issued for periods as brief as 10 days to fill an immediate need. Long-term notes can be issued for a period of several years.

Payment Schedule

When the terms of a debt are negotiated, a payment schedule is established for both interest obligations and principal repayment.

Discounted Notes

In some cases, particularly in short-term borrowing, the total amount of interest due over the term of the note is deducted from the principal before the proceeds are issued to the borrower. Such a note is called a discounted note.

Short-term Borrowing

Short-term borrowing usually requires repayment within 60 to 90 days. Notes are often renewed, in whole or in part, on the due date, provided that the borrower has lived up to the obligations of the original agreement and the business continues to be a favourable lending risk.

Availability

Commercial banks are the ordinary source of short-term loans for small businesses.

Credit Lines

When a business has established itself as being worthy of short-term credit, and the amount needed fluctuates from time to time, banks will often establish a line of credit with the business. The line of credit is the maximum amount that the business can borrow at any one time. The exact amount borrowed can vary according to the needs of the business but cannot exceed its established credit line.

These arrangements give the business access to its requirements up to the credit limit, or line. However, it pays interest only on the actual amount borrowed, not the entire line of credit available to it.

Long-term Debt

Long-term debt is borrowing for a period greater than one year. This general classification includes "intermediate debt" which is borrowing for periods of one to 10 years.

Small Business Applications

For small businesses, borrowed capital for periods greater than 10 years is usually available only on real estate mortgages. Other long-term borrowing usually falls into the "intermediate" classification and is available for periods up to 10 years. Such loans are called "term loans."

Mortgage Payment Schedules

Principal and interest payments on mortgages usually involve uniform monthly payments that include both principal and interest.

Each successive monthly payment reduces the amount of principal outstanding. Therefore, the amount of interest owed decreases and the portion of the monthly payment applicable to principal increases. In the early years of a mortgage, the portion of the monthly payment applied against the principal is relatively small, but grows with each payment.

Term Loan Payment Schedules

For term loans, payment of principal and interest is ordinarily scheduled on an annual, semiannual, or quarterly basis.

Repayment Schedules

The dates on which principal and interest payments are due should be scheduled carefully. For example, a manufacturer with heavy sales just before Christmas and receivables collections through January might best be able to schedule repayments in February. If a payment were due in October or November, when inventories were high and receivables were climbing, the payment could be crippling.

Collateral

Loans may be secured or unsecured. In a secured loan, the borrower pledges certain assets as collateral (security) to protect the lender in case of default on the loan or failure of the business. If the business defaults on the loan through failure to meet interest obligations or principal repayments, the note-holder (lender) assumes ownership of the collateral. If the business fails, the note-holder claims ownership of those specific assets pledged as collateral before the claims of other creditors are settled.

Typical Collateral

In long-term borrowing, fixed assets such as real estate or equipment are usually pledged as collateral. For short-term borrowing, inventories or accounts receivable are the usual collateral.

Inventory Financing

Inventory financing is most commonly used in automobile and appliance retailing. As each unit is purchased by the retailer, the manufacturer is paid by the lender. The lender is repaid by the retailer when the unit is sold. Interest is determined separately for each unit, based upon the actual amount originally paid by the lender and the period between the time the money is paid and the lender is reimbursed by the retailer.

Accounts Receivable Financing

Basically, Accounts receivable Financing falls into two Categories as Follows:

- Assignments. The business pledges, or "assigns," its receivables as collateral for a loan.
- Factoring. The borrower sells its accounts receivable to a lender ("factor").

Although these arrangements are not loans, in a pure sense, the effect is the same.

Receivables Assignments

When receivables are assigned, the amount of the loan varies according to the volume of receivables outstanding. Normally, the lender will advance some specified percentage of the outstanding accounts receivable up to a specific credit limit. For example, look at the schedule below. The company can borrow up to 80% of assigned receivables, up to a maximum of $100,000.

Accounts Receivable	*Amount Borrowed*
100,000	$80,000
125,000	100,000
150,000	100,000

On the first line, accounts receivable are $100,000 and the amount loaned is 80% of $100,000, or $80,000.

On the second line, outstanding receivables are $125,000. The amount loaned increases to $100,000 ($125,000 x 0.80).

On the third line, accounts receivable are $150,000. Eighty percent of this amount would be $120,000. However, this exceeds the established limit of $100,000. Therefore, borrowing is restricted to the $100,000 limit.

In many industries, accounts receivable financing is considered a sign of weakness. However, it is quite common in others. This is particularly true in the garment industry and in personal finance companies.

When customers must pay invoices directly to a factor, it may create doubts about the company's financial stability and, therefore, its ability to deliver.

When accounts receivable are assigned, the borrower is still responsible for collection. Upon collection of any receivable, the amount borrowed should be repaid. Interest is based upon the amount borrowed and the time between receipt of proceeds by the borrower and repayment.

Factoring Accounts Receivable

When accounts receivable are factored, they are sold to the factor and the borrower has no responsibility for collection. The borrower pays the factor a service charge based upon the amount of each receivable sold. In addition, the borrower pays interest for the period between the sale of the receivable and the date the customer pays the factor. Since the factor is responsible for collection, it will only purchase those receivables for which it has approved credit.

Unsecured Debt

The secured creditor's risk is reduced by the claim against specific assets of the business. In default or liquidation, the secured creditor can take possession of these assets to recover any unpaid amounts due from the business.

Holders of unsecured notes do not enjoy the same protection. If the company defaults on a payment, the unsecured creditor under normal circumstances, can only re-negotiate the amount due, perhaps by seeking collateral, or force the company to liquidate. In liquidation, the holder of an unsecured note would normally have no rights that are superior to those of any other creditors.

Restriction on Business

Therefore, when accepting an unsecured note, the lender will often place certain restrictions on the business. A typical restriction might be to prevent the company from incurring any debt with a prior claim on the assets of the business in the event of default or failure. For example, a term note agreement might prevent a company from financing its receivables or inventories since this would result in a prior claim against the assets of the business in liquidation.

Such restrictions may have no effect on the business' ability to operate. However, in other cases, such restrictions could be severe. For example, a business may have a chance to sell to a major new customer. The new customer may insist upon 60-day credit terms which will require the business to seek additional external financing. Normally, this financing might be readily available on realistic terms from a factor. However, the restriction of the unsecured note could prevent the business from taking advantage of this significant opportunity for sales and profit improvement.

Personal Guarantees

The liability of a corporation's shareholders is generally limited to the assets of the business. Creditors have no normal claim against the personal assets of the stockholders if the business should fail. Therefore, many lenders, when issuing credit to small corporations, seek the added protection of a personal guarantee by the owner (or owners). This protects the creditors if the business fails, since they retain a claim against the personal assets of the owners to fulfil the debt obligation.

Interest Rates

The interest rates at which small businesses borrow are relatively high. Banks and other commercial lending institutions normally reserve their lowest available interest rate the so-called prime rate, for those low-risk situations such as short-term loans for major corporations and public agencies where the chances of default are slim and the costs for collection, credit search, and other administrative tasks are minimal. Because of the higher risks involved in loaning to small businesses, lenders often seek greater collateral while charging higher interest rates to offset their added costs of credit search and loan administration.

Equity Capital

Unlike debt capital, equity capital is permanently invested in the business. The business has no legal obligation for repayment of the amount invested or for payment of interest for the use of the funds.

Share of Ownership

The equity investor shares in the ownership of the business and is entitled to participate in any distribution of earnings through dividends, in the case of corporations, or drawings, in the case of partnerships.

The extent of the equity investor's participation in the distribution of earnings of a corporation depends upon the number of shares held. In a partnership, the equity investor's participation will depend upon the ownership percentage specified in the partnership agreement.

Voting Rights

The equity investor's ownership interest also carries the right to participate in certain decisions affecting the business.

Legal Liability

The personal liability of equity investors for debts of the business depends upon the legal form of the organization. Basically, the investor who acquires equity in a partnership could be personally liable for debts of the business if the business should fail. In a corporation, the liability of equity investors (shareholders) is limited to the amount of their investment. In other words, if a partnership should fail, creditors could have a claim against the personal assets of the individual partners. If a corporation should fail, the only claims of creditors would be against any remaining assets of the corporation, not against any personal assets of the shareholders.

Equity Investor's Compensation

The purchaser of an equity interest in a business expects to be compensated for the investment in any of the three following ways:

- Income from earnings distribution of the business, either as dividends paid to corporate shareholders or as drawings in a partnership.
- Capital gain realized upon sale of the business.
- Capital gain realized from selling his or her interest to other partners.

Capital Gains

Capital gain is the term used to describe any excess of the selling price of an investment over the initial purchase price. For example, if you purchased an equity interest in a business for $5,000 and later sold it for $8,000, you would realize a capital gain of $3,000.

Earnings Distribution

The equity investor in a partnership is entitled to a share of all drawings paid out to partners at a percentage established when the interest was purchased. For example, assume an investor acquired a 20% interest in a partnership. The distribution of earnings to all partners in a given year is $20,000. The holder of the 20% interest would receive $4,000.

The dividends received by the equity investor in a corporation depend upon the number of shares held. For example, if a corporation voted a dividend of $1.50 per share in a given year, the owner of 1,000 shares would receive a dividend of $1,500 (1,000 x $1.50).

Sale (or Liquidation) of Business

If a business is sold or liquidated, the equity investor shares in the distribution of the proceeds. As with an earnings distribution, the share of the proceeds in a corporation sale depends upon the number of shares held. In a partnership, each partner's share of the proceeds is based upon the percentages specified in the partnership agreement.

If the proceeds received by the equity investor exceed the original purchase price, this excess is considered a capital gain and taxed accordingly.

If the business were liquidated, the assets would be sold and the proceeds would first be used to discharge any outstanding obligations to creditors. The balance of the proceeds, after these obligations had been fulfilled, would be distributed to the equity investors in accordance with their share-holdings or percentages of interest.

Sale of Equity Interest

As a business prospers and grows, the value of an equity interest grows with it. Therefore, the equity investor may be able to sell his or her interest at a price higher than the initial acquisition cost.

For example, an equity investor in a corporation may have purchased his or her interest at $10.00 per share. As the business grows, he or she is able to sell the shares at $15.00 per share, realizing a capital gain of $5.00 on each share sold.

Capital Gains vs. Dividends

In many cases, the equity investor in a small business is primarily interested in capital gains. Aside from the tax advantages, the equity investor usually realizes that the earnings of the small business are better retained in the business than distributed as dividends or drawings. Retention of earnings permits the business to grow so that the value of the equity interest increases. The investor can realize a return on the investment through a capital gain derived from selling his or her shares or upon sale of the business.

Public Stock Offerings

When businesses are first organized, equity capital is usually secured from a combination of sources such as the original owners' personal savings and through solicitations from friends, relatives, or other persons known to have financial capability for such investments.

As the need for equity capital becomes greater, say $200,000 to $1,000,000, it is customary to seek capital through the services of professional finders, who receive a fee for securing the capital needed. These finders normally have access to wealthy individuals, capital management companies, estates, trusts, and others with sufficient capital to make such an investment.

At higher levels of capital need, shares are sold through public offerings. The public offering seeks to attract a large number of investors to purchase stock, in large or small amounts. A market is then created for the stock. Shares purchased by the public, as well as the shares held by the original owners, and any subsequent equity investors can also be sold at the going market price. These transactions do not have a direct effect on the business' capital position since it does not receive the proceeds from the sale.

The equity investor can realize a capital gain by selling shares at prices higher than the original purchase price.

Risks of Equity Investment

The equity investor assumes substantial risk. Unlike the secured creditor, the equity investor has no specific claim against any assets of the business. In liquidation, all claims of all creditors must be satisfied before any remaining assets become available for distribution to the owners. Even then, the equity investor's participation in the proceeds is restricted to a share that is proportionate to the number of shares held or the partnership interest.

Since the risks of equity investment are so substantial, particularly in the case of small businesses, equity investors expect a considerably higher return than the lender. A lender might be willing to loan money to a business at an interest rate of 10% or 12% since it has certain legal protections in the event of default or liquidation. The investor of equity capital in the same business might seek a far higher return, perhaps 20%, 50%, or even more in order to compensate for the added risk of equity investment.

Summary

This section was developed to teach you about the various sources of capital that are available to the small business owner. The need for additional capital occurs frequently in many small businesses. The ability of the owners to anticipate the need and to know the various money sources available to them will help them secure needed capital on favourable terms.

Internal Sources of Money

Those businesses that are alert to opportunities for internal capital generation will often find that this effort not only minimizes the need for external capital, but also opens the doors of the outside money market to them.

This section has explored both internal and external capital sources, showing you how you can minimize your need for external financing through proper asset management and retention of earnings.

External Sources of Money

You have seen how the availability of trade credit can be utilized intelligently in order to maintain favourable supplier relations while taking full advantage of the credit that is available to you from this vital and convenient source.

Various types of loan arrangements were also explored, considering both short-and long-term needs as well as typical requirements for security through pledging of specific assets or the owners' personal guarantees. Finally, the equity capital market was studied so that you understand what the equity investor expects in return for a commitment of capital and the effect that the equity investor's interest can have on your business.

Accounting Bookkeeping: Effective Bookkeeping Factors

Accounting bookkeeping is often viewed with disdain. It is not uncommon to hear people refer to the process of records keeping as a "necessary evil." More and more, people in business, industry and government speak of reducing the burden of maintaining detailed records, and simplifying complicated governmental records.

Importance of Accounting Bookkeeping-Why keep Records

While such concerns are important, they should not mislead you into believing that the fewer records you keep, the less paperwork will burden you. Whether these records are burdensome or not, a well run business needs to maintain them. Inadequate records may well be detrimental to the health of a business.

In our economic system, one of the primary reasons for starting and operating a business is profit. Profits from a successful business may be used for expansion of business activity, thereby creating more jobs; to increase future profitability; and to reward owners for the financial risks they take in running a business. Bookkeeping provides the basic information needed to determine the business's profit (or loss).

Decision-making: Profit/loss information comes from the bookkeeping of a business and is an important aid in decision-making. Information gathered from a review of the bookkeeping system can indicate past trends in a company's operating effectiveness. This historical data can be used to answer specific questions about the change in profitability over time, the volume of sales at different times of year, the level of employee turnover, etc. This historical perspective can be especially useful to the owner/manager in decisions about future courses of action. Information generated from the records keeping system can provide a baseline for setting future goals and directions.

Another aid to owner/manager decision-making derived from a good bookkeeping system is the ability to compare the business with similar businesses in the same industry; for instance, to determine how many times a year the inventory turned over and compare that performance to an industry average. Or a bookkeeping system could be used to determine a business's net profit as a percentage of sales which, again, could be compared to an industry average to tell the owner/manager if he or she is doing well or needs to make improvements.

The value of a good records keeping system is immeasurable. Accurate and timely information can be used by the owner/manager to make decisions that give an edge in maintaining or gaining a competitive advantage-more specifically, a good bookkeeping system can make the difference between success and failure.

Governmental Regulations

Another purpose for maintaining records-the reason complained about the most-is to satisfy governmental regulations. A well designed records keeping system will simplify the process of complying with regulations, provide an audit trail for verifying that specific transactions have occurred and serve the information needs of the owner/manager as well.

A Record for Others: Yet another purpose for maintaining records is to provide information for other people. Many small businesses are essentially one-person enterprises-a single individual is the catalyst for most activity. It is imperative that this type of business maintain complete and detailed records. If something happens to the key individual, often no one else knows what has gone on in the past. With no records system to provide continuity, the business may be forced to close or be sold for less than it is worth.

Effective Accounting Bookkeeping Factors

Records keeping, as presented in this section, can be defined as the process of identifying what records need to be kept, how they are entered and maintained, and how they can be used effectively. A record is defined as basic information which documents financial, personnel, inventory, supply, or customer activities. This information is normally recorded as the result of a transaction or event in the course of conducting the business.

A good records keeping system should be designed and used with the following factors in mind:

- Simplicity.
- Understandability.
- Reliability.

- Accuracy.
- Consistency.
- Timeliness.

Simplicity

The records keeping system should be simple to use. One of the major reasons for the dramatic acceptance of personal computers today is the fact that they are very easy to use. A records keeping system should be designed with consideration for the employee(s) who will be recording the information. Complicated forms may be only partially completed and complicated processes avoided in favour of shortcuts that result in incomplete data. A good records keeping system should be designed to gather appropriate information as simply as possible.

Understandability

Ease of understanding is another important attribute of a good records keeping system. The system itself, the way to record information, and what the recorded information means must all be easily understood. Confusion, error, and, obviously, misunderstanding can result if records that are not clear and concise.

Reliability

"Reliable" has a specific meaning in accounting. The term generally means that a particular type of transaction is recorded in the same manner each time it occurs, in keeping with accounting guidelines.

Accuracy

The necessity for maintaining accurate records seems obvious, but cannot be overemphasized. A common error, for example, when people record numbers is that they inadvertently transpose them.

Care should be taken to ensure the accuracy of all records. A good bookkeeping system will stress accuracy through built-in procedures for checking and rechecking entries. Methods for improving accuracy include double checking all entries, taking frequent trial balances, requesting client/customer verification, and stressing the need for accuracy to all employees.

Consistency

Sometimes there are several ways to record a particular piece of information. Inventory records, for example, can be maintained on an item-by-item basis, on the basis that the last item is in the first item sold (LIFO), or on the basis that the first item is in the first item sold (FIFO). Consistent records keeping means choosing one method for recording inventory, using it consistently, and not changing it arbitrarily. This does not mean that you cannot change your approach, but it does mean that changes should only be made for good reasons and that the changes in the records keeping process should be clearly identified. Keep in mind that consistent records keeping is essential for comparing records over time.

Timeliness

Timeliness is an important element in a good records keeping system. Consider the statement, "I made $5,000." Without the element of time, this statement has little meaning. Add "in one year" and the statement has more meaning. Or add "in one week" and the meaning changes dramatically. One consideration of bookkeeping, then, is time.

The more obvious reason for timeliness is the need of the owner/manager to receive information as early as possible in order to make decisions affecting the business.

Minimum Records Required

There are four basic records that a business must maintain:

(1) Sales Records,

(2) Cash Receipts,

(3) Cash Disbursements, and

(4) Accounts Receivable.

Sales Records

A record of all sales must be kept. If you use a cash register, a combined Sales and Cash Receipts record may be kept. Sales may result from a single primary activity or may result from different types of activity and be recorded in sub-categories. For example, a business might record three kinds of sales: wholesale, retail, and services.It is important to record all sales as they occur. Remember that a sale may result in cash or arrangements may be made to receive payment at a later time. In either case, the sales records should reflect that the sale has occurred.

Cash Receipts

Cash is received by a business at the time of the sale or as payment on account for a credit sale. In any case, all cash should be recorded as it is received. A small business without a cash register can enter each transaction in a Sales and Cash Receipts Journal showing the date, name, invoice number, and the amount of the sale.

Deposit all cash receipts for the day in the bank. Do not pay out small amounts directly from cash receipts. Instead, establish a petty cash fund to pay small amounts not covered by invoices. By depositing all cash receipts daily, you have a basis on which to verify the daily balance in the cash receipts book.

Cash Disbursements

Just as all cash receipts should be deposited, nearly all disbursements should be made by check. The petty cash fund, as stated earlier, should be used to make payments only on small items.

When writing a check, use an invoice or bill to support the check. In the check book, record the purpose of the check, the date, name, check number, and the amount of the check. Bank charges should be recorded in the same manner as a check except, of course, they would not have a check number.

Accounts Receivable

The fourth basic record to be maintained is for credit sales. If a business provides a product or service to a customer and agrees to accept payment at a later time, it has created an account receivable. An account receivable record normally contains information pertinent to billing and receiving payment from a customer.

Every effort should be made to ensure that accounts receivable are kept current. Bills should be prepared promptly and mailed to correct addresses. At the end of each month, accounts receivable should be "aged." Aging means listing all accounts unpaid for 30 days, 60 days, and over 6o days. Special action should be taken to collect older overdue accounts. Extraordinarily large accounts should be watched carefully.

For delinquent accounts, try to get the customer to promise payment on a specific date. Then, if payment is not made on that date, contact the customer to find out why payment was not made. Be persistent, it's your money.

Records Keeping Process

A small business involved in ordering and selling merchandise should have a records keeping process that reflects the flow of that merchandise through the business.

Ordering and Receiving

The process begins when a business orders merchandise. An order can be written or oral. Oral orders should be documented with a written record. Copies of all orders should be retained.

When merchandise is received, it should be checked for quantity and condition, checked against the packing slip, and checked against the original order. Any discrepancies should be noted and the supplier notified as soon as possible.

The merchandise is then recorded on a Receipt Log listing quantity, description, and source. The Receipt Log serves as the basis for additions to the Inventory List, which is a complete record of all goods available for sale.

When an invoice (bill) is received from a supplier requesting payment, the invoice is checked for accuracy and verified against the Receipt Log and the original purchase order. A check should then be written to the supplier for the appropriate amount.

Sales

As sales of merchandise are made, goods are removed from inventory. If the merchandise consists of large, expensive items (e.g., automobiles, refrigerators, etc.), the inventory list may be maintained on an item-by-item basis with a sale resulting in the immediate removal from the inventory list of the item sold. On the other hand, many businesses sell a large number of inexpensive items; a small grocery store, for instance, might sell 200 boxes of cereal. For these businesses a periodic physical count of merchandise available for sale is the only realistic way to keep track of inventory.

Sales can be cash or credit. In either case, the sale is recorded at the point of sale. The sales slip serves two primary purposes. First, it is the original record of the sale used to record that transaction in a journal. When a cash register is used, the cash register tape and total at the end of the day serves as the sales slip. Second, sales slips are used to reduce the inventory listed, at least when a perpetual inventory (item by item) method is used.

Sales for cash are recorded as Sales and as Cash Receipts. Sales on credit are recorded as Sales and Accounts Receivable. Credit sales require that a customer credit account be established and maintained.

Completing the Cycle

The reduced inventory resulting from sales signals the need to order more merchandise. Purchase orders are written and sent to suppliers and the cycle of merchandise flowing through the business continues.

Much of the process of recording and tracking inventory today is done by computers and or computerized cash registers. However, these systems are only as accurate as the information which is entered into them and checks and balances for human error still exist. By utilizing a computerized system it is possible to know on a daily basis what the inventory and sales for each item are and to plan for re-orders of merchandise in a more effective manner. They also provide an efficient method for determining loss by "shrinkage and theft."

Record Keeping: Maintaining Non-Financial Records

This guide deals with record keeping about people and things. The temptation is to refer to these as "non-financial" records, but they do relate to financial considerations either directly or indirectly.

Personnel Record keeping

There are many reasons to maintain accurate, reliable personnel records. Of obvious importance is the maintenance of payroll-related records to use in computation of employees' pay and withholding and employer obligations (when required), and various income tax and other withholding deductions. Personnel records are also needed for potential workers' compensation or unemployment claims; employee appraisal, promotion, or dismissal actions; and insurance information.

Classification

Personnel records can be classified in four ways: present, recent past, past, and future. Categories commonly used for personnel records are: pay related, performance related, developmental, other personnel actions, and non-confidential medical records.

There are several ways that personnel files can be maintained and stored, but the simplest is in individual employee records which are divided by the five main categories and kept in alphabetical order by employees' names. All present employees' files would be stored in a present section and past employees' files in a recent past section. This allows easy access for answering questions which often arise during the first several months following termination of employment. A past file would be maintained in storage in order to provide information that may be needed less frequently. A future section can be maintained in one of two ways: 1) a separate section in the rear of each current employee's file, or 2) a separate file for each employee for future required action.

Personnel record policies must be established and administered fairly and in compliance with the law. Check with an attorney to be sure that your policies are in compliance with all regulations.

It is important to note that when personnel records are maintained correctly, the chances of becoming involved in legal actions relating to hiring, supervision, or dismissal of employees decrease. Employee management decisions can be made based on accurate information that reduces both conflict and costs.

Job Description

As a small business grows and the need for additional employees becomes evident, the first step in the personnel process is the development of a job description. A job description clarifies the duties and responsibilities of the person employed in a particular position and aids in identifying the skills an individual needs to perform the job, serves as a basis for evaluation of an employee's performance, and clarifies organizational interaction by specifying reporting relationships. Here is a sample job description:

Sample Job Description Accounts Receivable Bookkeeper

Function of Job

Under general supervision of a designated supervisor, but with some independence, to perform duties as an accounts receivable bookkeeper.

Responsibilities

1. Responsible for all cash receipts and deposits:
   a. Prepare bank deposits daily.
   b. Maintain cash receipts ledger.
2. Responsible for the maintenance of records on all memberships:
   a. Issue billings and notices to members.

   b. Post all receipts to permanent membership records.
   c. Inform membership office of payments and balance membership records to cash receipts monthly.
3. Reconcile all bank accounts except payroll.
4. Prepare payroll bi-weekly through all phases.
5. Responsible for maintaining employee annual and sick leave records.
6. Assist in the pre-registration for the annual convention.
7. Issue, balance, and be responsible for petty cash.
8. Balance subsidiary ledger monthly.
9. Proofread budgets.
10. Perform other duties as assigned.

Employment Application

An application for employment serves several purposes. First, it provides data on job applicants in a standard format that aids in identifying individual strengths and weaknesses. A well designed employment application is also valuable in insuring that laws governing fair employment practices are observed. And, when an individual is hired, the employment application becomes the basic document for creating a personnel file for that person.

Personal information is normally the first category of information listed on an employment application. The applicant's name (and maiden name, if applicable), present and past addresses, and telephone number are needed. Also, the applicant's Social Security number should be included under personal information because it would be needed in the permanent file of an employee.

The application should also include a category identifying the educational background of the person. In addition to traditional degree and diploma information, it is valuable to know if the applicant has any specialized training that relates to present or future job responsibilities.

The next category to be included on an Employment Application is the applicant's work history.

Information regarding references is also useful in the employment process. It is advisable to request both personal and professional references. The information provided should be sufficient to allow you to contact the references.

The final category of information includes general information: *military service, foreign language proficiency, health related questions (especially the name and telephone number of a person to contact in any emergency), and any other information appropriate for the particular job being applied for. Once an applicant has been hired, the Employment Application becomes a part of the personnel file.*

Pay-Related Records

Records relating to employee pay need to be maintained. At the minimum, a copy of an Employee Tax Withholding Form, needs to be completed and maintained on each employee. This form can be used to determine federal income tax withholding required. In addition, any state or local withholding requirements should also be included in the pay-related records.

Compensation to employees for services performed can be handled in a number of ways. The most common are: salary, hourly, commission and a combination of commission plus salary/hourly. Most management positions are based on a salary and do not provide for overtime (over 40 hours weekly) payment. Many lower mid-level administrative and clerical are based on a salary classified as non-exempt. This classification of employee is paid overtime for all work performed that exceeds 40 hours per week. Therefore, that weekly/annual salary must be computed to equal an hourly rate, and accurate rates must be maintained for each work week. When compensation is based on commission, the sales records for the employee must be transferred to the personnel/payroll office. There are many different types of agreements for commission-based pay and can require several types of records. It is important to make a complete study of commission pay systems and to access the recordskeeping involved in each if you are using such a plan.

There are consulting firms that specialize in compensation plans and provide payroll servicing. You may wish to consult with one or both types of services. They can be helpful and often times more cost effective then providing the work internally.

Personnel Benefits Records

This category includes information relating to employee benefits. Complete up-to-date records should be maintained regarding vacations, military leave, sick leave, compensatory time, etc. This information can be recorded on the time card on a daily basis.

Performance Related Records

The employee appraisal process may also be used as documentation for firing an unproductive worker. It is very important to maintain and use employee performance appraisal records consistently. Using performance appraisals only on a problem employee may backfire if litigation follows. An important consideration to the successful operation of any business is the job performance of its employees. Below is a sample Employee Performance Appraisal form. All employees should be evaluated on a regular basis using consistent criteria to measure their performance. Every effort should be made to keep the appraisal job-related, avoiding personality differences as much as possible. The primary objective of an employee performance appraisal process should be a continuing effort to improve performance. Positive, constructive suggestions for improvement should be identified and discussed with the employee.

Sample Employee Performance Appraisal

Name __________ Date of Hire ________ Date of Review _________

Department _________________ Job Title/Grade _______________

Instructions: Use this form to evaluate the performance of all employees on their regular review as scheduled by personnel policy. Part I should be completed by the employee and Part II by the immediate supervisor. Be sure that the current job description has been reviewed prior to completing this evaluation to ensure accuracy of the description and a complete understanding of the job. Performance evaluation and subsequent counselling are an important part of a supervisor's responsibilities and merit serious thought and prompt attention. Upon completion of this form, the employee and supervisor should discuss and sign the evaluation.

Part I: Employee

1. Briefly describe your duties and responsibilities during the period covered by this evaluation.

   ____

   ____

2. Evaluate your performance of these activities. Where can improvements be made

   ____

   ____

by you? What have you accomplished since your last review?

____

____

3. In order to improve your performance in your present position and/or to prepare yourself for the future, what help, training, assistance, or materials do you need?

____

____

4. List the specific job related goals you have set for yourself. State your plans for accomplishing them prior to your next review.

____

____

5. Name areas you would like to be considered for as your abilities develop:

____

____

6. Additional Comments:

____

____

Part II: Supervisor

1. Has the employee stated current duties and responsibilities correctly? If not, explain.

____

____

2. Comment on the employee's acceptance of responsibility, the ability to learn and follow directions, judgment and dependability. How many months in the present position?

____

____

3. Comment on the employee's job performance with emphasis on technical knowledge and competency, quality and quantity of work, and accuracy.

____

____

4. Discuss the employee's accomplishments of previously established goals or discussion items requiring attention.

   ____

   ____

5. Describe this employee's best area of performance.

   ____

   ____

6. Describe those areas of job performance that need more attention to achieve greater effectiveness.

   ____

   ____

7. What are you doing to help the employee become more effective?

   ____

   ____

8. Comment on the nature of the employee's ability to work and get along with supervisor(s), co-workers, and customers.

   ____

   ____

9. Do you consider this employee well placed in this particular job? Why? If not, what alternatives would you suggest?

   ____

   ____

10. If this employee has shown the capacity for increased responsibilities, reassignment, or promotional consideration, what specific position(s) or general areas should be considered?

    Position/General Area:

    ____

    ____

    Readiness (In Months):

    ____

    ____

    Salary Grade Level:

    ____

    ____

11. Considering the employee's personal habits, relationships with others, technical competency on specific assignments and with proper consideration for the period of time covered by this review, provide an overall rating of job performance for this employee. Check the appropriate rating box below. Explain your response.

____ Inadequate ____Commendable ____Competent

____acceptable ____Marginal ____Distinguished.

The above evaluation has been reviewed with my supervisor

Signature of Supervisor/Date: ________________ Signature of Employee/Date: ____________

____

____

Development Records

Records relating to continuing employee development should be maintained. Employees who participate in specialized training programs or who continue their formal education can benefit the business. Decisions in the areas of pay raises and promotions can be influenced by information indicating an employee's willingness to continually improve job skills.

Medical Records

Records relating to non-confidential medical information should also be maintained. This category includes information concerning dates of employee physicals, special job related work restrictions, allergies, and the person to be notified in case of an emergency. The emergency notification information should be updated whenever necessary and should be readily available at all times.

Supplier Records

Maintaining records on suppliers is important for ensuring the adequate supply of appropriate merchandise in a timely, cost effective manner. Supplier records should include the supplier's name, address, telephone number, and Fax number. Try to obtain and maintain a catalogue indicating the principal products or services available from each supplier. A special notation should be made on the supplier record regarding the primary contact person(s), including telephone numbers.

Helpful information to have about suppliers includes the number of employees; size; and location of their facilities; adequacy of production equipment; references from other customers; and financial status.

The supplier records should also include any agreements with the supplier. Special payment terms, discounts, and other considerations should be clearly indicated. And, finally, your company's experience with the particular supplier should be recorded. Information regarding speed of deliveries, condition of merchandise and level of backorders can be useful. Complete, accurate, and well maintained supplier records improve the efficiency of ordering merchandise.

Customer Records

There are several reasons to maintain customer records, the most obvious being to maintain billing information for credit customers. Even if credit sales are not involved, however, information on customers can be helpful for advertising, pricing, and deliveries.

Records should include customers' names, addresses, and telephone numbers. Demographic data like age group, family status, and income can be especially useful in selecting merchandising and planning marketing strategies. Credit account information should include credit references, checking account references, items purchased, date of purchase, and complete records of payment.

Additional customer record information which can be helpful includes complaints about service or quality, method of doing business, frequency of purchases hobbies and interests. Such data can help you improve your approach to your market.

Inventory-Related Record keeping

Inventory records are vital for ensuring that adequate quantities and types of merchandise are available for sale. There are two basic methods. The first, the perpetual method, keeps track of each item available for sale. As each item is sold, the inventory is reduced. The perpetual method works well with big ticket items.

More suitable for businesses selling large quantities of inexpensive items is the periodic inventory method. This method relies on a physical count of all merchandise available for sale periodically with inventory records adjusted to reflect the actual counts. The difference between the items on hand and the items purchased for sale represents the amount of items sold (although adjustments for shrinkage-shoplifting, employee pilferage, and the like-have to be made).

Inventory records should include the name, description, amount, and cost of merchandise in stock and on order. Also needed is supplier information, the dates items were ordered and received, and the name of the person who placed the order. For periodic inventory systems, the records should also include the date of the last physical inventory count and the names of the persons who conducted the inventory.

As noted earlier, there is a growing trend to use computerized inventory systems. Many software programs exist which are designed for specific businesses. You should make a complete study of available programs and check with individuals using the systems before making a decision to purchase a standard software inventory program or to have a custom program designed.

Understanding that inventory can be a liability rather than an asset and knowing how to plan and control your inventory are both crucial to your profit picture. The relationship of inventory to profit and loss will only be visible with an accurate records keeping system.

Book keeping of Financial Records

The bookkeeping of financial records of a company are vital for determining the profitability of the business. Without financial records, an owner/manager does not have the information necessary to evaluate the operating effectiveness of the business; to decide on how much additional capital might be needed; to determine realistic prices for merchandise; to expand operations or file for bankruptcy; or to answer a myriad of other questions dealing with the financial health of the business. This discussion provides an introduction to various recordskeeping practices

The Accounting Equation

The basis of accounting, the accounting equation, is Assets = Liabilities + Capital. An asset is anything a business owns that has a dollar value. Some common assets are cash, accounts receivable, buildings, and inventory. A liability is a debt. Anything owed by a business is classified as a liability. Some common liabilities include accounts payable, notes payable, and mortgages. Capital is the difference between assets and liabilities-between what is owned and what is owed.

For example, let's assume that Mr. Smith owns a house (an asset) worth $125,000 and owes a mortgage (a liability) of $100,000. Using the accounting equation, we see that:

Assets = Liabilities + Capital

$125,000 = $100,000 + ?

Mr. Smith's capital (or owner's equity) in this instance is $25,000. The important thing to remember is that assets always equal liabilities plus capital.

Financial Records

The financial records of a business begin when a transaction or event, measurable in dollars, takes place. A purchase of merchandise to sell, the payment of an electric bill, and the sale of merchandise are all financial transactions that need to be recorded. Some sort of written record-sales slips, check stubs, petty cash receipts, etc.-should be kept for each transaction.

The Journal

Transaction information should be recorded from the base documents into a journal, which is simply a record of the daily transactions of the business. Each journal entry should show the date of the transaction, a brief description of it, the amount of money involved, and the accounts affected. The journal, then, contains a record of all transactions.

The Ledger

Information is more usable, however, if it is categorized. Items recorded in the journal are later transferred (posted) to a ledger account. An account is a category within the broader categories of assets, liabilities, capital, income and expense. A book or file in which a number of accounts are kept together is called a ledger. An example of a ledger would be an Accounts Receivable file and an account would be Mr. Smith-Accounts Receivable. The number of accounts used depends on the size and complexity of the business.

Double Entry Accounting

The accounting system used in most businesses is called double entry. This means that at least two entries are made for each transaction-as a debit entry in one account and as a credit entry in another. Either the debit or credit entry may be broken down into several entries, but the total debit and credit entries for each transaction must equal each other. Each account sheet in the ledger has a column for the date, a brief description of the entry, the posting reference (where it came from in the journal), and two columns (debit and credit) for dollar amounts. Debit entries are always entered in the left-hand column and credit entries are entered in the right-hand column.

When balancing an account, total the debit column, then the credit column. If the debit column total exceeds the credit totals, the account has a debit balance and vice versa. The total of all debit balances in the accounts must equal the total of all the credit balances.

Trial Balance

Usually, at the end of each month, a trial balance is taken to make certain that the sum of the debit balances does equal the sum of the credit balances. A trial balance is also taken prior to preparing financial statements.

In simple terms, a trial balance is the adding of all debit balances, adding all credit balances, and comparing the two. If no errors have been made, the two totals will be equal.

Financial Statements

The journal provides a complete chronological record of all transactions of the business, but the information is not readily usable. The ledger accounts are useful because they organize information into categories. The information contained in the ledger accounts can be grouped so that financial statements can be prepared.

There are two basic financial statements vital for meeting the decision-making needs of the owner-manager.

The Balance Sheet is a reflection of the basic accounting equation: Assets = Liabilities + Capital. The Balance Sheet shows the balance between assets on the one hand and liabilities and capital on the other at a particular time.

The Profit and Loss Statement (also called the Income Statement) summarizes the revenue and expenses of a business over a certain period of time and indicates the profit or loss that resulted.

Petty Cash

It is advisable to establish a petty cash fund to make what small payments are necessary in the course of doing business. A fixed amount of money is put into the petty cash fund. Each time money is paid out of the petty cash fund, a petty cash slip is completed. The petty cash slip indicates the date, amount, purpose, and accounts to be charged.

The slips are kept with the petty cash. The balance in petty cash, reflecting the total of cash on hand and petty cash slips, should match the fixed amount initially put into the fund. When the cash in the fund gets low, the slips' total is used as the basis for writing a check to be cashed to replenish the fund. The petty cash slips are the base documents for making journal entries, debiting appropriate accounts, and crediting cash. The petty cash slips should then be marked to prevent them from being used again. Examples of uses of the petty cash fund are local taxi fares, or quick purchase of light bulbs, paper towels, etc.

Sales and Cash Receipts

Every cash receipt and every charge sale must be recorded, regardless of whether you use a cash register, sales slip, or both. At the close of business each day, the actual cash on hand is counted and balanced against the total receipts recorded for that day.

Daily Summary

The Cash Receipts portion of the Daily Summary records all cash received during the day. The cash sales total is taken from the cash register tape or by totalling the cash sales slips.

Total payments by customers on accounts receivable should be entered in the collections on account category. Receipts or other paperwork indicating customers' payments should then be held for posting to the customers' accounts in the Accounts Receivable ledger. Cash receipts that cannot be classified as cash sales or collections on account should be entered on the Daily Summary as "Miscellaneous Receipts." Examples of Miscellaneous Receipts include refunds from suppliers for overpayments, advertising rebates or allowances, etc. Total Receipts, then, is the total of all cash received on that day.

The second section of the Daily Summary of Sales and Cash Receipts is a count of the cash actually on hand. The money in the cash register or till is counted in the categories of coins, bills, and checks, then recorded and totalled on the Daily Summary.

Because petty cash slips represent cash on hand that has been paid out, but will be replaced, they are totalled and included in the cash on hand section. The cash on hand is then totalled.

The Daily Summary then records the petty cash slips on hand in the category, less change and petty cash funds. The coins and bills category reflects a combination of change that will be available for use and not deposited. The combined change and petty cash fund is kept on hand for use in the next day's operations and the balance of funds is deposited in the bank. It is not uncommon to have the amount to be deposited and the total receipts for the day not balance. Human error in making change may result in cash short or cash over, and when this occurs, the appropriate entry should be made.

Sales and Cash Receipts Journal

The Daily Summary of Sales and Cash Receipts can be thought of as a worksheet for figuring and recording the results of the daily operations. The Sales and Cash Receipts Journal brings together on one page the information from a number of Daily Summaries. The Journal provides a more comprehensive, permanent record and displays the information in a format that is easier to work with. Normally, total sales, charge sales, collections on account, and total cash deposits are entered on the same line of the Journal.

Cash Disbursements, Purchases, and Expenses

All business expenditures should be made by checks drawn on a business account. A typical business writes checks for purchases of merchandise, salaries, rent, utilities, etc. When a check is written, record on the stub or in the register the date, payee, amount, and the purpose of the payment. A running balance should always be maintained. Voided checks should have "VOID" written across their face; they should be stapled to the back of the checkbook and "VOID" should be written on the stub.

Never write a check without supporting documentation. An invoice, petty cash voucher, a payroll summary, or some other document should serve as the basis for writing a check. If no documentation is available, a memo should be written stating the purpose of the check. Supporting documents should be approved and signed by an authorized manager.

When a check is written, the supporting documents should be marked "paid" and the date and check number should be written on the document. The signer of a check should have the documentation available to verify when signing. It is advisable to require two signatures on all checks if the size of the business warrants it.

Cash Disbursements, Purchases, and Expense Journal

Each day's checks should be entered into the Cash Disbursements, Purchases, and Expense Journal. Make sure that each check number is accounted for in the journal. Voided checks should be entered by writing the check number and-in the description column-entering "VOID".

A Cash Disbursements, Purchases, and Expense Journal typically has amount columns for: Amount of Check, Merchandise Purchases, Gross Salaries, Payroll Deductions, Miscellaneous Income and Expense Items, and General Ledger Items. Again, in all entries in the journal, make sure that debits and credits are equal.

Accounts Payable

An unpaid bills file should be maintained for all bills and invoices received for merchandise purchased on credit. When a bill is paid, all packing slips, invoices, and statements relating to that transaction should be kept as supporting documentation.

At the end of each month, prepare a list of unpaid items showing the supplier and amount owed. The total amount owed is entered in the Cash Disbursements, Purchases, and Expense Journal as a debit to Merchandise Purchases and a credit to the general ledger account, Accounts Payable. Later, when a check is written to pay the supplier, the journal entry is a debit to Accounts Payable and a credit to Cash.

Bank Statement Reconciliation

A checking account statement is received each month with a list of checks cashed by the bank, deposit records, bank charges, and the ending balance according to the bank's records. It is important to reconcile your checkbook with the bank statement and account for all discrepancies. In order to make the reconciliation, you will need the preceding month's reconciliation, the checkbook stubs, the cancelled checks from the bank, and the bank statement. The process for reconciling a bank statement is as follows:

- Arrange all the cancelled checks in numerical order.
- Compare deposits listed on the bank statement with deposits listed in the checkbook. List in the first section of the reconciliation any deposits recorded in the checkbook during the month but not appearing on the bank statement.

- There may be cancelled checks from the previous month. Check these off the list of outstanding checks shown on the preceding month's reconciliation. Then list in the first section of the current reconciliation the checks still outstanding.
- On the check stubs check off all cancelled checks drawn during the month being reconciled. Add the checks recorded on the remaining stubs to the list of outstanding checks on the reconciliation.
- If errors in amounts are discovered in the preceding steps, list them in the second section of the reconciliation as adjustments to be added or deducted.
- Examine the bank statement for service charges, interest, or other adjustments to the account and enter them in the second section of the reconciliation.
- Compute additions and subtractions as shown on the bank reconciliation. The adjustment balance given by the bank statement should equal the adjusted balance in the checkbook.

Bank Errors

Occasionally, a bank may make an error in the account. Such errors should be reported at once. When the next month's bank statement is received, make sure that bank errors from the previous month have been corrected.

Adjustments to the checkbook resulting from the Bank Reconciliation must be entered in the checkbook and also in the journals. Some typical errors and ways to correct them include:

Check records in the wrong amount. Enter the amount of the adjustment in the Amount of Check column of the Cash Disbursements Journal. Enter the same amount in the other column in which the check was originally entered. If the check was recorded as less than the correct amount. simply enter the adjustment in the two columns. This will have the effect of an addition. If the check was recorded as more than the correct amount, enter the adjustment as a deduction (circled or in red).

Deposit recorded in the wrong amount. Enter the amount of the adjustment in the Total Cash Deposit column of the Cash Receipts Journal. If the adjustment can be identified with a specific receipt, it should also be entered in the column for that type of receipt. It is more likely, however, that the error was made in balancing the day's work.

In this case, it should be entered as a cash short or over. If too small an amount was recorded, the adjustment should be entered in the journal as an addition; if too large an amount was recorded, enter a deduction.

Bank service charges. All bank service charges should be entered in the Amount of Check column of the Cash Disbursements Journal and as a debit in the Miscellaneous Income and Expense column. The checkbook balance should be corrected by adding or subtracting the net adjustment.

Merchandise Inventories

One of the most important steps in the preparation of financial statements is determining accurate inventory figures. There are a number of methods for keeping perpetual (continuous) inventories, but a truly accurate inventory can be obtained only by actually counting all the merchandise on hand-a physical inventory. If a perpetual inventory has been kept, a comparison of the two inventories can reveal shortages or overages.

Many small businesses, however, do not want to maintain a perpetual inventory. In such cases, the inventory can be estimated for monthly statements and a physical inventory conducted only at the end of the year.

Estimating Inventory

Inventory can be estimated by using the gross margin method. Under this method, it is assumed that the gross margin (sales less cost of goods sold) for the period will be a certain percentage of sales. The gross margin percent for the period between the last two physical inventories is most often used for this. The cost of sales for the current period will then be the cost of sales percent (100 percent less the gross margin percent) times the sales for the period. Ending inventory is then computed as in the following example.

Suppose that sales for the month are $10,000, that the beginning inventory was $3,000, and that the merchandise purchases during the month amount to $6,000. Assume that gross margin is estimated at 25 percent of sales. The ending inventory can be computed as follows:

- Beginning inventory $3,000,
- Merchandise Purchases 6,000,
- Merchandise available for sale $9,000,

- Estimated gross margin percent 25,
- Cost of sales percent (100-25) 75,
- Sales for the month $10,000,
- Cost of goods sold (75% of $10,000) $7,500,
- Ending inventory $1,500.

If the gross margin method of computing inventory is used, it should be applied separately to each category of merchandise. While this method cañ give fairly accurate results for monthly financial statements, the fact remains that the resulting amount is only an estimate. A physical inventory could should be determined whenever possible.

Conducting a Physical Inventory

The frequency of conducting a physical inventory depends upon the type of business and whether it has a reliable inventory system. In all cases, a physical inventory should be taken at least once each year, normally at the close of the fiscal year.

To ensure accuracy in counting, care should be taken to see that merchandise is in good order on display and in storage. It is often impractical to try to conduct a physical inventory during normal business hours, so the actual counting may be done at night or on a weekend. The orderly arranging of merchandise, instructing personnel on the methods to be used, and perhaps counting some reserve stocks, however, can be done ahead of time.

A part of the planning for a physical inventory is to establish shipping and receiving "cutoffs"; that is, making certain that all items entered in the books as purchased before the inventory have been received and are counted and all items recorded as sold before the inventory are removed and not counted.

If the merchandise being counted requires weighing or any other kind of measuring, the equipment needed should be available.

In some kinds of business, a complete description of each item is needed. In these cases, inventory tally sheets showing this information should be prepared in advance, so that the only writing necessary while taking inventory is to record the quantities counted. A tally sheet should have a space for inserting the unit prices and extending the dollar value of the stock. The order of the items on the list should follow as closely as possible the order in which the items are arranged in the store.

If tally sheets are not necessary, inventory can be taken on "tags." A tag is placed with each different item in stock before the count. The description of the item and the number of units in stock are then entered in the tags by the counters. It is advisable to include a space for the price and extension.

If a large number of tags is to be used, they should be numbered. This is necessary to make sure that none are lost or misplaced after the inventory count is made and before the final summarizing of the inventory value.

In some cases, a complete description of the items is not necessary; the number of items and the price might be enough for the counters to enter.

Inventory Valuation

After the physical count of the inventory is completed, each item must be priced. A generally accepted method of pricing inventories is valuation of the items at cost or market, whichever is lower.

The price at which the item was purchased is obviously the "cost." Theoretically, this would be the invoice price, plus "freight-in", less any purchase discounts taken. In a small retail business, however, the factor of freight-in is generally not significant and is often ignored in pricing merchandise. Discounts may not be significant, either. If a small cash discount is applicable to most of the purchases, a percentage reduction in the overall inventory could be made instead of trying to reduce the price of each item.

Inventory valuation using "market value" consists of applying one of the following:

1. The replacement price of the item;
2. The current selling price, less normal gross margin, if the item has been marked down; or
3. The scrap or salvage value, if the item is no longer salable at retail.

Computing the cost of each item can be avoided by using the retail method of valuing inventory. Under this method, retail prices are entered on the tally sheet or tag as the count is made. The retail value of the inventory is then totalled and reduced by the year-to-date gross margin percentage. In the case of marked-down items, the marked-down retail price should be used.

Another method of inventory valuation is called "coded cost." This method involves marking the merchandise with a coded cost, as well as retail price, at the time it is made available for purchase. For example, a letter code can be devised using a ten letter key word with no letter repeated, like the following:

1	2	3	4	5	6	7	8	9	0
P	U	R	C	H	A	S	I	N	G

Using the above code, an article that cost $3.17 and sells for $5.00 would be marked "RPS $5.00." When taking inventory, the counters enter the decoded cost on the tag or tally sheet.

The practice of marking merchandise with a coded cost is common in gift shops, jewellery stores, and other stores where inventory turnover is comparatively slow and items have a fairly high gross margin. It serves primarily as a guide to the owner/manager in making markdowns and in bargaining with customers. The coded costs methods used in inventory valuation is made less attractive by the work involved in coding the merchandise in the first place and the fact that decoding of prices by the inventory counters can be confusing and subject to errors.

After all inventory items have been priced under the inventory valuation method selected as most suitable, the total dollar values are computed by multiplying the prices by the quantities. This may be done on the tags or on the tally sheets containing the quantities counted.

Perpetual Inventory

Some businesses maintain a continuous, or perpetual, record of their inventory. One type of perpetual inventory involves keeping records at both retail and cost. Purchases are added to the beginning inventory at retail, (with each invoice priced at the expected selling price), and all sales and markdowns are deducted. This results in a perpetual inventory at retail. At any time, this inventory can be converted to cost by dividing total purchases at cost by total purchases at retail, then multiplying the inventory balance by the result.

If these records are carefully kept, theoretically, they should provide a very accurate inventory. Inventory shortages, however, will not be disclosed. A physical count is still necessary at least once a year to determine inventory shrinkage. If this method is desirable, it is advisable to have a qualified accountant set up the system and explain it in detail.

Credit and Collection Methods

"Plastic" has become a way of life. Those wallet-size credit cards are accepted all over the world in millions of stores for many millions of products and services. To be competitive, you too must offer credit to your customers. After all, your own business purchases are probably on credit.

Management of Receivables

Credit and collection starts with managing receivables. As the operator of a small business, you must extend credit to customers on competitive terms so that sales will not be lost. At the same time, you must avoid long overdue accounts so that your capital will not be tied up and there will be less chance of accounts becoming uncollectible. If you manage your accounts receivable as suggested in this module, you will realize the marketing advantages of credit extensions and avoid the common problems noted above.

Section Objectives

This section has been designed to guide you in the management of your accounts receivable. In here, you will learn how to establish sound policies that will serve as guidelines in granting credit. You will be shown collection techniques that will minimize uncollectible accounts and reduce the volume of past-due accounts so that your credit sales are more quickly converted to cash. You will learn how to analyse your accounts receivable to determine whether or not a problem exists, if corrective action is needed, or if reevaluation of your credit and collection policies is necessary. You will learn how to evaluate credit applications so that many problems can be eliminated before they occur. You will learn how to initiate a collection program with all accounts, the delinquent and the not yet delinquent. You will learn how to follow up by mail and telephone to accelerate collections and the flow of cash to your business. You will learn when to resort to external resources such as collection agencies or the courts and how to use them to your advantage.

Benefits

If you apply the techniques you learn in this section to the management of your business, your dollars tied up in accounts receivable should be reduced, allowing for profitable application elsewhere. In addition, your credit losses should be reduced.

Credit Extensions

Many potential credit problems can be eliminated before they happen through investigation and prudent judgment when granting credit to customers. The need for sound judgment is particularly critical since credit extension policies should be neither too liberal nor too restrictive. Overly liberal policies invite excessive receivables and uncollectible accounts while overly restrictive policies cause lost sales.

Investigation

Before you decide, get the facts. Thorough investigation of credit requests protects you from the fraudulent applicant who has no intention of paying as well as the applicant who is extremely slow in paying.

Credit Applications

The basic source of information for decisions on credit extensions is the credit application. There are three major factors to consider in evaluating a credit applicant. The first is the applicant's ability to pay, based upon income and obligations. The second is willingness to pay, which can be determined from the applicant's credit history. The third factor is potential profitability of the account. You stand to lose your cost of the product or service sold to the customer if you cannot collect an account. If your cost is relatively high compared to the selling price, then you have to be particularly careful in assessing credit risks.

Application Evaluation

Your evaluation of any credit application will depend upon a number of factors. In the case of an individual applicant, you will want to consider the following:

- Employment history.
- Current position.
- Current income.
- Time on job.
- Job security.
- Monthly obligations (rent, loan payments, food, utilities, etc.)
- Bank balances.
- Personal assets (house, cars, stocks, bonds, etc.)
- Credit standing.
- Amount of credit desired.

Information Verification

Information on credit applications must be verified to ensure that it is correct, current, and complete. A good place to begin is the place of employment to verify that the applicant is employed and that income and time on the job have been reported accurately.

Bank references should also be verified. While laws restrict the amount of information that banks can disclose, checking on this information can protect you from obvious fraud and may give you some indication of the applicant's ability to pay. Most banks will confirm the existence of an account and disclose a broad idea of the average balance. The bank may also indicate whether or not the account has been satisfactory.

Credit Bureaus

An important source of information for retail credit is the local credit bureau, which generally provides information on credit applicants to firms that are bureau members. Annual membership fees usually depend upon the size of the business. Besides the membership fee, there is a nominal charge for each inquiry on a credit applicant. Your local credit bureau will provide you with details about services and costs.

Stability

In situations where the time or cost of a comprehensive credit check is prohibitive, professional credit managers have often found that a quick evaluation can be made based upon the applicant's stability. Stability is determined by the length of continuous employment and residence. This assumes that the person who has been employed for several years on the same job will most likely continue to be employed and therefore will be able to pay. Similarly, continuous residence indicates a desire to maintain standing in the community.

Summary

There are no hard and fast rules that can tell you who is a good credit risk and who is not. There are cases where the poorest of people pay their bills promptly, while the wealthy ignore them. As the owner of a small business, you must combine facts about the applicant with common sense to determine those risks that appear reasonable.

Commercial Credit

Commercial accounts should complete an application similar to that used for personal credit. Unlike individual credit applications, it is often difficult to verify information on income and expenses for businesses. It is also more difficult to make estimates of these factors for commercial accounts. There are situations where it may be reasonable to request a financial statement from the commercial account before extending credit, but these situations are not typical. Instead, you must rely more heavily upon references such as banks and suppliers with whom the applicant does business, the applicant's reputation in the industry, identity of officers, and so on.

The application should note the names of individuals who are authorized to purchase for the account so that fraudulent purchases can be detected. There should also be an indication of purchase order requirements so that you will be protected in the event of an unauthorized purchase.

Frequently, the commercial applicant with a marginal credit rating will list only those suppliers with whom a satisfactory relationship has been maintained. However, you can often use your own judgment and knowledge of your industry and locale to determine other suppliers with whom the applicant may have done business. If there is any doubt in your mind as to the credit worthiness of the applicant, it is always a good idea to contact these other sources to find out what their experience has been.

Commercial Credit Services

Commercial credit services maintain financial information and credit services for large and small companies throughout the country. The cost of this service varies with the detail and depth of information requested on any applicant.

Problem Detection

A successful credit and collection policy requires that all problems be detected and acted on as early as possible. The sooner a problem is detected, the sooner it can be corrected. This is particularly critical in receivables management where the sheer passage of time can aggravate any problem that may exist.

An important indicator of the effectiveness of your credit and collection policy is your average collection period. The average collection period is a ratio that expresses the total amount of receivables outstanding in terms of an equivalent number of average daily credit sales.

Figuring the Average Collection Period

The average collection period is calculated as follows:

$$\frac{\text{Accounts Receivable}}{\text{Average Daily Credit Sales}}$$

Or, viewed another way, the total amount owed by customers is equivalent to 45 days' credit sales, on the average.

For example, if a business had average monthly credit sales of $6,000 and outstanding accounts receivable of $9,000, the collection period would be calculated as follows:

$$\text{Average Daily Credit Sales} = \frac{\text{Average Monthly Credit Sales}}{30} = \frac{6{,}000}{30} = 200$$

$$\text{Average Collection Period} = \frac{\text{Accounts Receivable}}{\text{Average Daily Credit Sales}} = \frac{9{,}000}{\$200} = 45 \text{ days}$$

This indicates that, on the average, customers are taking 45 days to pay their accounts. (Some formulas for calculating the average collection period consider only net credit sales. These are determined by subtracting an estimated allowance for bad debts from total annual credit sales. While the result is mathematically more precise, it is being ignored here and the simpler formula, based upon total credit sales, is being used for instructional purposes.)

Comparisons

The average collection period can be compared with any of the following bases to determine whether or not a problem exists:

- *Payment terms:* If your terms of sale specify payment within 30 days and your average collection period is greater than this, it indicates that creditors are not complying With your terms and a problem exists.
- *Past history:* Comparison with your experience in previous periods indicates whether or not collections are improving or declining.
- *Industry averages:* Comparison with the experience of other companies in your industry will determine whether or not your credit and collection policies are as effective as those of your competitors. (Industry averages are usually available at your library or trade association.)

Determining the Extent of the Problem

The extent of the receivables' excess can be measured by comparing your actual receivables with a target level. For example, assume that your terms of sale specify payment Within 30 days, and your industry average collection period is approximately 30 days: A suitable target for your receivables Would then be 30 days' average credit sales.

If your average daily credit sales are $200, you could then calculate a target for receivables as follows:

Average daily Sales x Collection Period = Receivables.

$200 x 30 = $6,000.

If your actual receivables were $9,000, you would then know that you had an average of $3,000 ($9,000-$6,000) in receivables that require attention.

Corrective Action

A relatively high average collection period indicates that a problem exists and corrective action must be taken. Prompt attention should reduce the collection period, speed conversion of receivables to cash, minimize your capital tied up in accounts receivable and, at the same time, reduce the risk of uncollectible accounts.

Aging of Receivables

Analysis of your average collection period will help you identify and measure receivables problems in total. However, immediate corrective action requires identification of individual problem accounts.

Problems in individual accounts can be detected through analysis of your receivables by aging. A receivables aging divides each customer's account into amounts that are 0-30 days old, 31-60 days old, 61-90 days old, etc. The longer an account is past due, the more serious the problem. These can be identified quickly by aging, and corrective action can be initiated promptly.

For example, examine the receivables aging below. The first account shown, L. Brown, has a total outstanding of $775.02. Of this amount, $317.91 is 0-30 days old, $222.63 is 31-60 days old, $156.32 is 61-90 days old, and $78.16 is over 90 days old. Some prompt action seems required.

Totals are entered for each age group. It is often useful to calculate the percentage of total receivables in each age group to alert you whenever overdue receivables become excessive. For example, if you knew from past experience, or from industry averages, that receivables more than 90 days past due were seldom more than 5% of total receivables, the 19.9% would instantly alert you to a dangerous situation that requires immediate correction before you are faced with possible serious losses.

Internal Collection Procedures

The fundamental rule of sound receivables management is to minimize the time span between the sale and collection. Any delays that lengthen this span cause receivables to build to unnecessarily high levels and increase the risk of uncollectible accounts. This is just as true for delays caused by your billing and collection procedures as it is for delays caused by the customer.

Invoices

Proper collection procedures begin with invoice preparation. Invoices should be prepared promptly and accurately. Promptness eliminates one possible source of delay. Accuracy prevents those delays that occur when the customer disputes the invoice and returns it for correction, triggering a chain of events that is time-consuming and often costly.

Invoices should clearly state payment terms. Is payment due within 10 days? Thirty days? Are the days measured from the receipt of goods? Receipt of invoice? End of the month?

Cash Discounts

When selling to large accounts such as commercial, industrial, institutional, and governmental buyers, collection is often accelerated by the offer of a cash discount. The discount, usually 1% or 2%, is offered for payment within 10 days. Most large organizations take advantage of all such discounts. In so doing, they can sharply reduce your commitment of capital to accounts receivable. If your competitor offers cash discounts, it may be necessary for you to include the same provision to maintain your competitive position.

Specifying Payment Terms

Payment terms normally include discount terms and dating terms. Discount terms describe the discount available, if any, for prompt payment. Dating terms specify the time when payment is due.

Discount terms are usually described as follows: 2/10.

The number before the / is the discount percentage, in this case 2%. The number following the / is the number of days within which payment must be made in order to take advantage of the discount. In the example, the customer can take a 2% discount for payment within 10 days.

This leads to the next question, 10 days from when? And, if the customer lets the discount period pass, when is the net amount due? The answers to these questions are specified in the dating terms. Extending our previous example a little further, the terms might be expressed as follows: 2/10-n30. The "n" is an abbreviation for net. The "30" indicates that payment is due within 30 days. If no other date is specified, the 30-day period begins with the invoice date. For example, if the terms above appeared on an invoice dated September 2, the customer would be entitled to a 2% cash discount for payment by September 12. If the customer does not pay within this period, the net amount is due within 30 days, or by October 2.

Special Conditions

Large accounts often specify certain requirements for invoice preparation. They may require reference to a purchase order, proof of delivery, or a certain number of copies. Be certain that these conditions are met when the invoice is first prepared and submitted in order to avoid delays and duplication of effort.

Statements

To keep customers advised of their account balances, monthly statements should be submitted to all open accounts. The statement should summarize the amount owed and any activity in the account within the month.

Abbreviations are used to specify the beginning of dating periods that are different from the invoice date. Two common abbreviations are "EOM," End of Month, and "ROG," Receipt of Goods. In the first case, EOM, the discount and net periods begin at the end of the month, regardless of the invoice date. In the second case, ROG, the periods begin when the customer receives the goods, regardless of the invoice date.

Assume that an invoice issued on September 15 had the following terms:

2/10-n30 EOM.

The customer would be entitled to a 2% discount for payment by October 10. If the discount is forfeited, the net amount would be due October 30.

Your choice of payment terms will often depend upon customary practices in your business. In order to stay competitive, it is often necessary to offer payment terms that are equivalent to those offered by your competitors.

Delinquency Charge

In some businesses, a delinquency charge for late payment is used to discourage customers from allowing their accounts to become long past due. The delinquency charge normally involves a finance charge or service charge of 1% to 1.5% per month on all balances more than 30 days past due. For example, if a customer's statement at the end of June indicates a total balance due of $630, of which $417 is more than 30 days past due, the finance charge for June would be calculated as follows (assuming a 1% delinquency charge):

$417 x.01 = $4.17.

Most people recognize that a charge of 1% per month represents an annual interest expense of 12% (12 x.01). A charge of 1.5% per month represents an annual interest charge of 18% (12 x.015).

Follow-up

The best time to initiate pursuit of outstanding balances is immediately. As an account gets further behind, the balance often increases, while the chances of collection decrease. The person who owes a few hundred dollars today is not likely to be in better shape to pay next week or the week after than right now. Now is the time to start enforcing a rigid collection policy, making whatever arrangements are necessary to be sure that you receive the money due to you in a reasonable period of time.

Don't Be Reluctant

Many businesses are reluctant to enforce strict collection procedures. The reasons for this are several, and none of them are valid. Some people simply are embarrassed to ask for money even though it is owed to them. Others express concern that they might alienate a "good customer" and perhaps lose an account. The opposite is true. How good is an account if the bills are not paid? Even more important, the customer owing you a large balance may be reluctant to do more business with you until the account is cleared. You have not only lost your money, you have also lost a customer.

Some companies feel that rigorous enforcement of a collection policy can damage their reputation. Viewed logically, would you conclude that a person who owes you money is likely to spread this news around town?

Collection Follow-up

Whether or not your business chooses or use cash discounts or delinquency charges, a systematic follow-up procedure should be employed with all past-due accounts. Usually, this will take the form of a series of letters or telephone calls or both, as required.

First Collection Letter

When an account becomes approximately 15 days past due, the customer should be sent the first collection letter. Since the account cannot be considered seriously delinquent at this time, the tone of the letter should be moderate. Later letters should establish a firmer tone so that the customer is made aware of the seriousness of the situation.

The 15-day past-due letter should read about as follows:

Dear Mr. Adams:

According to our records, your current balance due is $473.25. Of this amount, $215.38 is more than 30 days past due. As you know, our normal terms require payment within 30 days after the invoice is sent to you.

Since you have established an excellent credit rating with us in the past, we are surprised to see a problem arise at this time. If there is some error, or you are unable to pay the amount due immediately, please contact me so that we can correct the situation or make suitable arrangements for prompt payment of this obligation.

Thank you for your attention to this request.

Very truly yours,
Jim Madison

Second Collection Letter

A second letter, 30 days later, might read as follows, if no response has been received from the customer:

Dear Mr. Adams:

We have not received any response from our statements of the last two months nor to our letter of September 15. Your entire account is now 45 days overdue, and you owe us a total of $473.25.

If there is some reason why this payment cannot be made immediately, please contact us so that we can make arrangements that will be mutually agreeable. Perhaps we can work out a payment schedule that would be realistic for your present circumstances.

Naturally, we do not want to endanger your credit rating or destroy the good relationship that we have maintained in the past. Therefore, would you please take care of this obligation immediately so that we will not have to file an unfavorable report with the credit bureau or resort to the use of a collection agency or an attorney.

We have enclosed a self-addressed envelope for your convenience. Please return it as soon as possible with your check for the balance owed.

Very truly yours,

Jim Madison

Third Collection Letter

If this is unsuccessful, a stronger letter should be sent in 30 days:

Dear Mr. Adams:

We still have no response from our statements of the past three months nor from the letters that we sent you on September 15 and October 15.

Your entire account is now seriously past due: It is obvious that our efforts to clear the account on a mutually agreeable basis have had no impact. Unless we receive payment from you within seven days, or can work out a mutually agreeable arrangement to discharge this obligation, we will have to report the matter to the retail credit bureau.

Subsequently, the account will be turned over to a collection agency or to our attorneys for further action. Since this is a costly procedure for both of us, and will cause serious damage to your credit rating, I would suggest that you call immediately so that we can clear the matter at once without resorting to such procedures.

Very truly yours,

Jim Madison

As you noticed, the tone of each letter became progressively stronger with suggestions of more serious action introduced in each case. The tone that you would want to establish in such "dunning letters" will often depend upon the type of relationship that you maintain with your customers. However, the ground rules should be clear. Past-due accounts should not be ignored.

Telephone

Frequently, an even more persuasive approach is through use of the telephone. The ground rules are basically the same. You must become progressively firmer with each call and indicate that stronger measures will be used if necessary to ensure prompt payment.

The telephone has the added advantage of flexibility since you can be more direct with better knowledge of the individual account.

You acquire this knowledge through asking questions such as the following:

- "What seems to be the problem? We never had difficulty with your account in the past."
- "How much would be a reasonable amount for you to pay each month? Perhaps $50, $60?"
- "How soon can we expect payment of this amount?"

Try to avoid questions that can be answered "yes" or "no." If the creditor gives you an answer such as, "I'll mail it today," answer with: "I appreciate that. Then I can expect it in two or three days. If I don't have it by then, I'll call you back." Be sure that the creditor realizes that you are totally aware of the situation and that you do not intend to ignore it.

External Collection Resources

If your own collection efforts fail, there are two courses of action that are left to you-the collection agencies and the courts.

Collection Agencies

Collection agencies are businesses established to collect past-due accounts receivable on behalf of creditors. The primary advantage that collection agencies offer is their superior knowledge of persuasive collection techniques. Additionally, creditors are usually anxious to clear invoices referred to collection agencies rather than further damage their credit ratings.

The collection agency's fee is usually based upon a percentage of each account collected. The percentage ranges from 25% to 50% depending upon the size of the account or the total dollar volume of accounts referred to the agency for collection. This approach, while often effective, can be expensive.

A business is committed to paying the agency's fee on any account referred for collection, whether payment is made to the agency or to the business. Although some creditors may resent making payment to a collection agency and prefer to pay the company directly, the company is still committed to pay the fee when the account is collected.

Courts

If the collection agency fails, your final recourse is through the courts. The matter may be resolved in a small claims court if the amount owed is small. For larger amounts, you may have to file suit to collect. In either case, you are faced with a costly and time-consuming procedure.

The best way of avoiding these time-consuming, costly procedures is to take prompt, strong action on your own as early as possible. In the long run, you will be doing not only yourself a favour but also the creditor. While your creditors may be unhappy at the time, you will have spared them costs, time, and the loss of their credit ratings.

Credit Cards

Many problems associated with credit can be avoided through the use of credit cards. In many businesses, particularly in the retail and consumer service fields, credit arrangements for customers are available through the use of these cards. Under these plans, there is little or no commitment of the business' own capital, and the costs and risks of administration and collection are almost entirely the responsibility of the credit card company or bank.

Credit card service is available from your regular commercial bank. Receipts from bank credit card purchases can be deposited daily and are immediately credited to your checking account. The bank assumes all credit risks provided that you follow instructions for approval of credit card purchases. Typically, these instructions require that you check the validity of the card against a master list of cancelled cards and contact the credit service before accepting the customer's card for purchase above a certain limit.

Credit card services are particularly vital for businesses with a large number of relatively small accounts. They eliminate the need for credit approval, invoice preparation, record maintenance, and collections. They also minimize your commitment of capital and virtually eliminate the risk of un-collectible accounts. From a marketing standpoint, the availability of instant credit could often encourage a customer to buy immediately, rather than postpone the decision to a later date or bypass it completely.

Credit cards are most often used for retail accounts. However, they have also been used successfully in selling to small commercial accounts. Businesses such as repair shops, supply firms, and stationery stores, which have a mixture of consumer and commercial accounts, often find it convenient and economical to extend credit card service to small commercial accounts.

Credit and Collection Policies

The establishment and execution of credit and collection policies can minimize problems associated with accounts receivable. As with all policies, they must be reevaluated from time to time in order to determine their effectiveness. If your business already has policies for receivables management, evaluate them according to the check list on the following pages. If you do not presently have credit and collection policies, you can use the check list as a guide in establishing policies.

Your answer to all questions should be "Yes" or "Not Applicable." If you have any "No" answers, you should consider revising your policy or have a strong and valid reason for not doing so. For example, you may have a "No" answer to the question, "Do you offer a cash discount?"

If your accounts are primarily personal, this might be a valid answer. If your accounts are primarily major industries, a "No" answer would suggest that you consider the possibility of offering a cash discount.

Credit and Collection Policies Check List

Credit Approval

1. Credit Approval:
   * Credit Approval.
     - Is a written application required with every credit request?
     - Do you have a standard form for credit applications?
     - Is it completed personally by the applicant?

- Is it reviewed for completeness?
- Is all information verified for accuracy and timeliness?
- Are applicants checked out with a credit bureau?
- Does your evaluation consider income?
- Does your evaluation consider fixed obligations?
- Does your evaluation consider job stability?
- Does your evaluation consider residential stability?
- Does your evaluation consider credit history?
- Does your evaluation consider bank balances?
- Does your evaluation consider other assets?

Invoices

- Are invoices prepared promptly?
- Is invoice preparation always accurate?
- Are payment terms clearly stated?
- Are customers' special instructions followed carefully?

Terms of Sale

- Do you offer a cash discount?
- Do you use a late payment penalty?
- Is the time limit for payment clearly stated?

Statements

- Are monthly statements submitted to all open accounts?
- Are statements prompt and accurate?

Problems of Identification

- Do you determine your average collection period on a regular basis?
- Do you compare your collection period with industry averages?
- Do you compare your current collection period with your previous experience?
- Do you compare your collection period with your payment terms?
- Do you have a monthly aging of all outstanding accounts?
- When a problem is identified, is corrective action prompt and firm?

Follow-up

- Do you have a systematic procedure for follow-up on slow accounts?
- Is there a standard sequence of follow-up letters?
- Is the tone of these letters progressively stronger?
- Do you use the telephone to contact delinquent accounts?
- Is your telephone technique effective?
- Do you offer special arrangements for collecting past-due accounts?
- Do you have a late-payment penalty?
- Do you put delinquent accounts on a C.O.D. basis?

External Resources

- Do you have a working relationship with a collection agency?
- Are accounts turned over automatically after a specific time period?
- Do you refer the most serious delinquencies to an attorney?

Summary

Sound policies for credit and collection can eliminate many problems before they occur and minimize those that do occur. In this module, you have learned the techniques of receivables management. If you apply these techniques to your own business, your profit will improve and your cash position will be strengthened. Profit will improve through fewer credit losses and lower costs of credit administration. Capital will be freed so that you will be able to meet your own obligations promptly and invest in those assets that offer a significant profit potential.

Financial Management Analysis: Watching your Profit (Checklist)

Making a profit is the most important-some might say the only-objective of a business. Profit measures success. It can be defined simply: Revenues-Expenses = Profit. So, to increase profits you must raise revenues, lower expenses, or both. To make improvements you must know what's really going on financially at all times. You have to watch every financial event without any kind of optimistic filter.

This financial management analysis Guide is a series of questions with comments to help you analyse your profits, their sufficiency and trend, the contribution of each of your product lines or services to them, and to help you determine if you have the kind of record system you need. The questions and comments are not meant to be definitive presentations on the subjects. They are meant to point to areas where further study might be-well-profitable.

Financial Analysis of Revenues and Expenses

Since profit is revenues less expenses, to determine what your profit is you must first identify all revenues and expenses for the period under study.

1. Have you chosen an appropriate period for profit determination? For accounting purposes firms generally use a twelve month period, such as January 1 to December 31 or July 1 to June 30. The accounting year you select doesn't have to be a calendar year (January to December); a seasonal business, for example, might close its year after the end of the season. The selection depends upon the nature of your business, your personal preference, or possible tax considerations.
2. Have you determined your total revenues for the accounting period? In order to answer this question, consider the following questions:
    - What is the amount of gross revenue from sales of your goods or service? (Gross Sales).
    - What is the amount of goods returned by your customers and credited? (Returns and Rejects).
    - What is the amount of discounts given to your customers and employees? (Discounts).
    - What is the amount of net sales from goods and services? (Net Sales = Gross Sales-Returns and Rejects + Discounts).
    - What is the amount of income from other sources, such as interest on bank deposits, dividends from securities, rent on property leased to others? (Non-operating Income).
    - What is the amount of total revenue? (Total Revenue = Net Sales + Non-operating Income)
3. Do you know what your total expenses are? Expenses are the cost of goods sold and services used in the process of selling goods or services. Some common expenses for all businesses are:
    - Cost of goods sold (Cost of Goods Sold = Beginning Inventory + Purchases-Ending Inventory).

- Wages and salaries (Don't forget to include your own-at the actual rate-you'd have to pay someone else to do your job).
- Rent.
- Utilities (electricity, gas telephone, water, etc.)
- Delivery expenses.
- Insurance.
- Advertising and promotional costs.
- Maintenance and upkeep.
- Depreciation (Here you need to make sure your depreciation policies are realistic and that all depreciable items are included)
- Taxes and licenses
- Interest
- Bad debts
- Professional assistance (accountant, attorney, etc.)

There are of course, many other types of expenses, but the point is that every expense must be recorded and deducted from your revenues before you know what your profit is. Understanding your expenses is the first step toward controlling them and increasing your profit....

Financial Ratios

A financial ratio is an expression on the relationship between two items selected from the income statement or the balance sheet. Ratio analysis helps you evaluate the weak and strong points in your financial and managerial performance.

Do you know your Current Ratio? The current ratio (current assets divided by current debts) is a measure of the cash or near cash position (liquidity) of the firm. It tells you if you have enough cash to pay your firm's current creditors. The higher the ratio, the more liquid the firm's position is and, hence, the higher the credibility of the firm. Cash, receivables, marketable securities, and inventory are current assets. Naturally you need to be realistic in valuing receivable and inventory for a true picture of your liquidity, since some debts may be uncollectable and some stock obsolete. Current liabilities are those which must be paid in one year.

Do you know your Quick Ratio? Quick assets are current assets minus inventory. The quick ratio (or acid-test ratio) is found by dividing quick assets by current liabilities. The purpose, again, is to test the firm's ability to meet its current obligations. This test doesn't include inventory to make it a stiffer test of the company's liquidity. It tells you if the business could meet its current obligations with quickly convertible assets should sales revenue suddenly cease.

Do you know your Total debt to net worth Ratio? This ratio (the result of total debt divided by net worth then multiplied by 100) is a measure of how company can meet its total obligation from equity. The lower the ratio, the higher the proportion of equity relative to debt and the better the firm's credit rating will be.

Do you know your Average Collection Period? You find this ratio by dividing accounts receivable by daily credit sales. (Daily credit sales = annual credit sales divided by 360.) This ratio tells you the length of time it takes the firm to get its cash after making a sale on credit. The shorter this period the quicker the cash flow is. A longer than normal period may mean overdue and un-collectible bills. If you extend credit for a specific period (say, 30 days), this ratio should be very close to the same number of day. If it's much longer than the established period, you may need to alter your credit policies. It's wise to develop an aging schedule to gauge the trend of collections (without adequate financing charges) hurt your profit, since you could be doing something much more useful with your money, such as taking advantage of discounts on your own payables.

Do you know your ratio of net sales to total assets? This ratio (net sales divided by total assets) measures the efficiency with which you are using your assets. A higher than normal ratio indicates that the firm is able to generate sales from its assets faster (and better) than the average concern.

Do you know your operating profit to net sales ratio? This ratio (the result of dividing operating profit by net sales and multiplying by 100) is most often used to determine the profit position relative to sales. A higher than normal ratio indicates that your sales are good, that your expenses are low, or both. Interest income and interest expense should not be included in calculating this ratio.

Do you know your net Profit to total Assets Ratio? This ratio (found by multiplying by 100 the result of dividing net profit by total assets) is often called return on investment or ROI. It focuses on the profitability of the overall operation of the firm. Thus, it allows management to measure the effects of its policies on the firm's profitability. The ROI is the single most important measure of a firm's financial position. You might say it's the bottom line for the bottom line.

Do you know your net Profit to net worth Ratio? This ratio is found by dividing net profit by net worth and multiplying the result by 100. It provides information on the productivity of the resources the owners have committed to the firm's operations.

All ratios measuring profitability can be computed either before or after taxes, depending on the purpose of the computations. Ratios have limitations. Since the information used to derive ratios is itself based on accounting rules and personal judgments, as well as facts, the ratios cannot be considered absolute indicators of a firm's financial position. Ratios are only one means of assessing the performance of the firm and must be considered in perspective with many other measures. They should be used as a point of departure for further analysis and not as an end in themselves.

Sufficiency Of Profit

The following questions are designed to help you measure the adequacy of the profit your firm is making. Making a profit is only the first step; making enough profit to survive and grow is really what business is all about.

- Have you compared your profit with your profit goals?
- Is it possible your goals are too high or too low?
- Have you compared your present profits (absolute and ratios) with the profits made in the last one to three years?
- Have you compared your profits (absolute and ratios) with profits made by similar firms in your line?

A number of organizations publish financial ratios for various businesses, among them Dun & Bradstreet. Robert Morris Associates, the Accounting Corporation of America, NCR Corporation, and the Bank of America. Your own trade association may also publish such studies. Remember, these published ratios are only averages. You probably want to be better than average.

Trend of Profit

- Have you analysed the direction your profits have been taking?
- Have you analysed the direction your profits have been taking?

The preceding analysis, with all their merits, report on a firm only at a single time in the past. It is not possible to use these isolated moments to indicate the trend of your firm's performance. To do a trend analysis performance indicators (absolute amounts or ratios) should be computed for several time periods (yearly for several years, for example) and the results laid out in columns side by side for easy comparison. You can then evaluate your performance, see the direction it's taking, and make initial forecasts of where it will go.

Does your firm sell more than one Major Product line or Provide Several Distinct Services? If it does, a separate profit and ratio analysis of each should be made:

- To show the relative contribution by each product line or service;
- To show the relative burden of expenses by each product or service;
- To show which items are most profitable, which are less so, and which are losing money; and
- To show which are slow and fast moving.

Mix of Profit

The profit analysis of each major item help you find out the strong and weak areas of your operations. They can help you to make profit-increasing decisions to drop a product line or service or to place particular emphasis behind one or another.

Records

Good records are essential. Without them a firm doesn't know where it's been, where it is, or where it's heading. Keeping records that are accurate, up-to-date, and easy to use is one of the most important functions of the owner-manager, his or her staff, and his or her outside counsellors (lawyer, accountant, banker).

Basic Records

Do you have a general journal and/or special journals, such as one for cash receipts and disbursements? A general journal is the basic record of the firm. Every monetary event in the life of the firm is entered in the general journal or in one of the special journals.

Do you Prepare a sales Report or Analysis?

(a) Do you have sales goals by product, department, and accounting period (month, quarter, year)?

(b) Are your goals reasonable?

(c) Are you meeting your goals?

If you aren't meeting your goals, try to list the likely reasons on a sheet of paper. Such a study might include areas such as general business climate, competition, pricing, advertising, sales promotion, credit policies, and the like. Once you've identified the apparent causes you can take steps to increase sales (and profits).

Buying and Inventory System

Do you have a buying and inventory system? The buying and inventory systems are two critical areas of a firm's operation that can affect profitability.

Do you keep records on the quality, service, price, and promptness of delivery of your sources of supply?

Have you analysed the advantages and disadvantages of:

(a) Buying from several suppliers,

(b) Buying from a minimum number of suppliers?

Have you analysed the advantages and disadvantages of buying through cooperatives or other systems?

Do you know:

(a) How long it usually takes to receive each order?

(b) How much inventory cushion (usually called safety stock) to have so you can maintain normal sales while you wait for the order to arrive?

Have you ever Suffered Because you were out of Stock? Do you know the optimum order quantity for each item you need? Do you (or can you) take advantage of quantity discounts for large size single purchases? Do you know your costs of ordering inventory and carrying inventory?

The more frequently you buy (smaller quantities per order), the higher your average ordering costs (clerical costs, postage, telephone costs etc.) will be, and the lower the average carrying costs (storage, loss through pilferage, obsolescence, etc.) will be. On the other hand, the larger the quantity per order, the lower the average ordering cost and the higher the carrying costs. A balance should be struck so that the minimum cost overall for ordering and carrying inventory can be achieved.

Do you keep Records of Inventory for each Item? These

records should be kept current by making entries whenever items are added to or removed from inventory. Simple records on 3 x 5 or 5 x 7 cards can be used with each item being listed on a separate card. Proper records will show for each item: quantity in stock, quantity on order, date of order, slow or fast seller, and valuations (which are important for taxes and your own analyses.)

Other Financial Records

Do you have an Accounts Payable Ledger? This ledger will show what, whom, and why you owe. Such records should help you make your payments on schedule. Any expense not paid on time could adversely affect your credit, but even more importantly such records should help you take advantage of discounts which can help boost your profits.

Do you have an Accounts Receivable Ledger? This ledger will show who owes money to your firm. It shows how much is owed, how long it has been outstanding and why the money is owed. Overdue accounts could indicate that your credit granting policy needs to be reviewed and that you may not be getting the cash into the firm quickly enough to pay your own bills at the optimum time.

Do you have a cash Receipts Journal? This journal records the cash received by source, day, and amount.

Do you have a cash payments journal? This journal will be similar to the cash receipts journal but will show cash paid out instead of cash received. The two cash journals can be combined, if convenient.

Do you Prepare an Income (profit and loss or P&L) Statement and a Balance Sheet? These are statements about the condition of your firm at a specific time and show the income, expenses, assets, and liabilities of the firm. They are absolutely essential.

Do you Prepare a Budget? You could think of a budget as a "record in advance," projecting "future" inflows and outflows for your business. A budget is usually prepared for a single year, generally to correspond with the accounting year. It is then, however broken down into quarterly and monthly projections.

There are different kinds of budget: cash, production, sales, etc. A cash budget, for example, will show the estimate of sales and expenses for a particular period of time. The cash budget forces the firm to think ahead by estimating its income and expenses. Once reasonable projections are made for every important product line or department, the owner-manager has set targets for employees to meet for sales and expenses. You must plan to assure a profit. And you must prepare a budget to plan.

Cost Cutting: How to Reduce Costs

Increasing profits through reduce costs and cost cutting must be based on the concept of an organized, planned program. Unless adequate records are maintained through a proper accounting system, there can be no basis for ascertaining and analysing costs.

Cost cutting is not simply attempting to slash any and all expenses unmethodically. The owner-manager must understand the nature of expenses and how expenses inter-relate with sales, inventories, cost of goods sold, gross profits, and net profits.

Reduce costs does not mean only the reduction of specific expenses. You can achieve greater profits through more efficient use of the expense dollar. Some of the ways you do this are by increasing the average sale per customer, by effectively using display space and thereby increasing sales volume per square foot, by getting a larger return for your advertising and sales promotion dollar, and by improving your internal methods and procedures. Profit is in danger when good merchandising and cost control do not go hand in hand. A big sales volume does not necessarily mean a big profit, as one retailer, Carl Jones, learned.

Jones's pride was stocking stylish and well assorted lines of merchandise. Each year, sales volume increased. This increase was attributed to good merchandise which Jones felt took care of the steady rise in expenses.

But Mr. Jones began to have doubts when he found it necessary to get bank loans more often than had been his practice. When he discussed the problem with his banker, Jones was advised to check expenses. As the banker said, "A large and increasing sales volume often creates the appearance of prosperity while behind-the-scene expenses are eating up the profit."

Paying the Right Price

Your goal should be to pay the right price for prosperity. Determining that price for your operation goes beyond knowing what your expenses are. Reducing expenses to increase profit requires you to obtain the most efficient use of the expense dollar.

Look, for example, at the payroll expense. Salesclerks are paid to sell goods, and their productivity is the key to reducing the payroll cost.

If you train a salesclerk to make multiple sales at higher unit prices, you increase productivity and your profits without adding dollars to your payroll expenses. Or, if four salesclerks can be trained to sell the amount previously sold by seven, the payroll can be cut by three persons.

An understanding of the worth of each expense item comes from experience and an analysis of records. Adequate records tell what has happened. Their analysis provide facts which can help you set realistic goals, you are paying the right price for your store's prosperity.

Analyse your Expenses

Sometimes you cannot cut an increase item. But you can get more from it and thus increase your profits. In analysing your expenses, you should use percentages rather than actual dollar amounts.

For example, if you increase sales and keep the dollar amount of an expense the same, you have decreased that expense as a percentage of sales. When you decrease your cost percentage, you increase your percentage of profit.

On the other hand, if your sales volume remains the same, you can increase the percentage of profit by reducing a specific item of expense. Your goal, of course, is to do both: to decrease specific expenses and increase their productive worth at the same time.

Before you can determine whether cutting expenses will increase profits, you need information about your operation. This information can be obtained only if you have an adequate record keeping system. Such records will provide the figures to prepare a profit and loss statement (preferably monthly for most retail businesses), a budget, break-even calculations, and evaluations of your operating ratios compared with those of similar types of business.

Break-even

A useful method for making expense comparisons is break-even analysis. Break-even is the point at which gross profit equals expenses. In a business year, it is the time at which your sales volume has become sufficient to enable your over-all operation to start showing a profit.

Once your sales volume reached the break-even point, your fixed expenses are covered. Beyond the break-even point, every dollar of sales should earn you an equivalent additional profit percentage. It is important to remember that once sales pass the break-even point, the fixed expenses percentage goes down as the sales volume goes up. Also the operating profit percentage increases at the same rate as the percentage rate for fixed expenses decreases-provided, of course, that variable expenses are kept in line.

Locating Reducible Expenses

Your profit and loss (or income) statement provides a summary of expense information and is the focal point in locating expenses that can be cut. Therefore, the information should be as current as possible. As a report of what has already been spent, a P and L statement alerts you to expense items that bear watching in the present business period. If you get a P and L statement only at the end of the year, you should consider having one prepared more often. At the end of each quarter might be often enough for some firms. Ideally, you can get the most recent information from a monthly P and L.

Regardless of the frequency, for the most information two P and L statements should be prepared. One statement should report the sales, expenses, profits and/or loss of your operations cumulatively for the current business year to date. The other should report on the same items for the last complete month or quarter. Each of the statements should also carry the following information:

(1) this year's figures and each item as a percentage of sales.

(2) last year's figures and the percentages.

(3) the difference between last year and this year-over or under.

(4) budgeted figures and the respective percentages.

(5) the difference between this year and the budgeted figures-over and under.

(6) average percentages for your line of business (industry operating ratio) when available, and

(7) the difference between your annual percentages and the industry ratios-under or over.

This information allows you to locate expense variation in three ways: (1) by comparing this year to last year, (2) by comparing expenses to your own budgeted figures, and (3) by comparing your percentages to the operating ratios for your line of business. The important basis for comparison is the percentage figure. It represents a common denominator for all three methods. When you have indicated the percentage variations, you should then study the dollar amounts to determine what line of operative action is needed.

Because your cost cutting will come largely form variable expenses, you should make sure that they are flagged on your P and L statements. Variable expenses are those which fluctuate with the increase or decrease of sales volume. Some of them are: advertising, delivery, wrapping supplies, sales salaries, commissions, and payroll taxes. Fixed expenses are those which stay the same regardless of sales volume. Among them are: your salary, salaries for permanent non-selling employees (for example, the bookkeeper), depreciation, rent, and utilities.

Taking Cost Cutting Action

When you have located a problem expense area, the next step obviously is to reduce that cost so as to increase your profit. A key to the effectiveness of your cost-cutting action is the worth of the various expenditures. As long as you know the worth of your expenditures, you can profit by making small improvements in expenses. Keep an open eye and an open mind. It is better to do a spot analysis once a month than to wait several months and then do a detailed study. Take action as soon as possible. You can refine your cost-cutting action as you go along.

Budgeting Systems

Budgeting is detailed planning for the allocation of funds in a business. It is sometimes referred to as the financial picture of the business; i.e, how the business plans to spend its financial resources.

Whether your business plan is for next year, for the next three years, or for the next five years, budgeting can help you keep on the right road. Once you've developed your business plan, preparing the first budget is easy — think of your budget as the financial picture of your future.

Because operating a small business is not a cut-and-dried affair, the first budget you prepare often uncovers problems with your business plan and helps you determine whether or not your financial goals are within reach. The budget will also help you focus and select from alternatives to help make your business plan realistic and achievable.

Your budget gives you answers to questions such as: What sales will be needed to achieve the desired profit? What will the equipment that is needed cost? Can you afford the marketing and advertising that you outlined in your plan?

When you complete your budget you will have one of the most effective management tools of all — a benchmark that you can use each and every month to check your progress towards your business goals.

Essentially, a budget is a translation of your business plan into numbers. In its simplest form a budget is a detailed plan of future receipts and expenditures-a projected income statement. Right from the beginning you can use your budget to validate the activities you have planned for the coming year. Will you be able to afford additional staff? Do you need to expand your facilities or equipment? When will be the best time to start your new sales campaign? Do you have a period where sales are slow and making ends meet is a challenge? Knowing what all your business activities will cost and when such expenses will occur will help prevent any unexpected surprises that could lead to financial problems down the road.

Once the period for which you have budgeted is completed, you can compare actual results with anticipated goals. Get into the habit of making this a regular part of your business routine. You may find it takes discipline at first, but the rewards are high. You don't have to do anything elaborate-just compare your budgeted figures to your actual results. Then, ask yourself why the numbers are different. If some of your expenses, for instance, are higher than you expected, do you need to look for ways to cut them or has business increased? If your sales aren't on track, what has happened to cause the difference? Use the information constructively so that you can make adjustments immediately, if needed, and improve your next budget.

Your budget can also be used to assess whether your present profit adequate. In a small business, the year end profit should be large enough to make a return on your investment and return on your own work, i.e., pay you a salary.

Value of Owner's Service

This is the net profit made in the business after taxes. Hopefully, it is a positive number, although for some start-up businesses that may take a year or two to achieve. Some people compare this number to the amount you could have earned if you worked at your trade for a pay check. That, of course, does not take into consideration the intrinsic rewards of working for yourself.

Return on Investment (ROI)

The year end profit is too low if it does not also include a return on the owner's investment. That investment includes the money you put into the firm when you started it and the profit of prior years that you left in the firm. You calculate Return on Investment by dividing the fiscal year's income by the amount of investment in the company. Investment also includes any long term debt you have taken on to support running the business.

Your Targeted Income

After you know what you made last year, you can set a profit goal for next year. Be sure that your goal includes payment for your services and a return on your investment as noted above.

You may need to make some changes to your record keeping system to ensure that you are collecting enough information in the right format to assist with your budget. Or, it may be that you need to produce a profit and loss (or income) statement at more frequent intervals to keep track of the seasonal fluctuations of your revenues and expenses. A good place to start is with your Chart of Accounts. Consider each expense category listed and estimate the amount that you will spend for this category in the next year. Last year's income statement is a good reference point, but don't rely entirely on it — consider changes in your markets, price changes, and cost increases, always going back to your business plan to make sure you are addressing all the goals and activities you want to accomplish.

The next step in preparing a budget is to determine whether you can achieve your profit goals. To do this, you must project your fixed costs and your variable costs. From these three figures — targeted profit, fixed expenses, and variable expenses — you can determine how much income you need to make to meet those goals.

As the name implies, fixed expenses generally stay the same over time. Some fixed expenses are rent, telephone, taxes on property, depreciation of equipment, interest on borrowed money, building maintenance costs, and office expenses.

Variable expenses usually change in relation to sales. In a business that produces a product, the cost of materials or goods for resale are the largest variable expenses. In some service businesses, the cost of labour is the biggest factor. Sales commissions, direct wages, payroll taxes, insurance, advertising, and delivery expense are other examples of variable expenses.

Once you have reasonable estimates of your expenses, you need to determine and evaluate your required revenues from sales. Calculate revenue from the ROI and expense estimates. Then take a realistic look at the revenues you will have to generate in order to make your targeted profits. If you're a service business, what is the hourly rate you will have to charge and is it realistic? Will you need to increase your customer base? If so, is this increase achievable? If you manufacture and sell a product, are you able to make and sell that many units with your current equipment? If these revenue projections aren't realistic, you will need to revisit your ROI and expense projections and adjust them.

After your budget is set, it becomes a marvelous tool to keep on top of what is happening in your business. Break your budget down into monthly amounts. This allows you to check for any discrepancies that may not show up readily in the annual figures. When many items are added together, it is easy for an error to creep into the totals or for you to overlook items.

During the year, the monthly budget provides you with an important financial management tools. By looking ahead at the coming months' budget you can anticipate peak periods and schedule stock and labour to handle sales volume. You can also plan vacations, special promotions, and inventory-taking for the slow periods.

A comparison of your monthly profit and loss statement to your budget indicates whether or not you are achieving your business plan goals. Set up a simple worksheet to compare actual expenses to your budget and get in the practice of reviewing a) where all the money goes, and b) any differences from the amounts you budgeted. Thus, you can pinpoint and work on the problems that have occurred during the month.

Here is sample copy of a budget to show how one is set up. The example is for an annual budget. Once you have the annual budget, projecting it monthly makes it even a more useful tool for monitoring throughout the year. Many financial software packages will provide you with templates to fill in for your budgets and reports to keep you on top of how you are doing at meeting your projections.

Bibliography

Anindya Bakrie & Morendy Octora.: *Schooling, Experience, and Earnings*, New York, Singapore National University, Columbia University Press 2002.

Baran, Paul A.: *The Political Economy of Growth,* New York, Modern Reader Paperbacks, 1975.

Bardsley, N., Cubitt: *Assessing Experimental Economics*, Princeton, Princeton University Press, 2009.

Basu, Kaushik. *Analytical Development Economics, The Less Developed Economy Revisited,* Cambridge, Mass.: MIT Press, 1997.

Bazilevskii, Y. Y.: *The Theory of Mathematical Machines*, Pergamon Press, Macmillan Co., New York, 1963.

Benería, Lourdes. *Gender, Development, and Globalization, Economics as if All People Mattered,* New York and London, Routledge, 2003.

Borcherding, K., : *Contemporary Issues in Decision Making,* Amsterdam, North-Holland, 1990.

Burke, Frank M., *Valuation and Valuation Planning for Closely Held Businesses*, Englewood Cliffs, NJ, Prentice Hall, 1981.

Caplin, A. and Schotter, A.: *The Foundations of Positive and Normative Economics*, New York, Oxford University Press, 2008.

Caviglioni O. : *Mapwise: Accelerated Learning Through Visible Thinking*, Network Educational Press, 2000.

Cohen, Lizabeth, *Making a New Deal, Industrial Workers in Chicago, 1919-1939* Cambridge University Press, 1991.

Commons, J. R., *Institutional Economics-Its Place in Political Economy*, The University of Wisconsin Press, Madison, Wisconsin, 1934.

Cootner, Paul : *The Random Character of Stock Market Prices*, MIT Press, 1964.

Copeland, Tom, Tim Koller, and Jack Murrin, *Valuation: Measuring and Managing the Value of Companies,* New York, Wiley, 1994.

Damasio, AR.: *Descarte's Error: Emotion, Reason and the Human Brain*, New York, 1994.

Daniel Kahneman, Amos Tversky.: *Choice, Values, Frames*, The Cambridge University Press, 2000.

Desmond, Glenn, and John A, Marcell, *Handbook of Small Business Valuation Formulas and Rules of Thumb,* Valuation Press, 1993.

Dimson, Elroy: *Stock Market Anomalies*, Cambridge University Press, 1988.

Fraser, Steven, *Labor Will Rule, Sidney Hillman and the Rise of American Labor,* Reprint ed. Ithaca, N.Y.: Cornell University Press, 1993.

Fruhan, W. E.: *Financial Strategy, Studies in the Creation, Transfer and Destruction of Shareholder Value.* Homewood, 1979.

Goleman D.: *Emotional Intelligence,* New York: Bantam, 1995.

Gowdy, J., *Coevolution Economics: The Economy, Society and the Environment*, Kluwer, Boston, 1994.

Granger, Clive W. J.: *Empirical Modeling in Economics, Specification and Evaluation*, London, Cambridge University Press, 1999.

Guala, F.: *The Methodology of Experimental Economics,* New York, Cambridge University Press, 2005.

Guarti, Luigi, *The Valuation of Firms*, Blackwell Publishing, 1994.

Gul, F. and Pesendorfer, W.: *The Foundations of Positive and Normative Economics*, New York, Oxford University Press 2008.

Harrigan, K. R.: *Strategies for Declining Businesses.* Lexington, MA: Heath, 1980

Hausman, D. M.: *The Inexact and Separate Science of Economics*, Cambridge, Cambridge University Press, 1992.

Hayek, F. A. *Individualism and Economic Order*, The University of Chicago Press, Chicago, 1948.

Hunt, E. K. *History of Economic Thought, A Critical Perspective.* New York, HarperCollins, 1992.

Janis, I. L., & Mann, L.: *Decision Making, A Psychological Analysis of Conflict, Choice and Commitment.* New York, Free Press, 1977.

Kasper, Larry J.: *Business Valuations, Advanced Topics*, Westport, CT, Quorum Books, 1997.

Knapp, C. L.: *Commercial Damages, A Guide to Remedies in Business Litigation*, Matthew Bender, 1993.

Lindblom, C. E.: *A Strategy of Decision: Policy Evaluation as a Social Process*, New York, The Free Press, 1970.

Link, Albert N.: *Evaluating Economic Damages, A Handbook for Attorneys*, Westport, CT, Quorum Books, 1992.

Lipsitz, George. *Rainbow at Midnight, Labor and Culture in the 1940s*, Urbana, Ill.: University of Illinois Press, 1994.

Loomes, G.: *Current Issues in Microeconomics*, New York: St. Martin's Press, 1989.

Magnussen, L., *Evolutionary and Neo-Schumpeterian Approaches to Economics*, Kluwer, Boston, 1994.

March, J. G.: *A Behavioural Theory of the Firm*, Englewood-Cliffs, Prentice Hall, 1963.

Marris, R. L., and Wood, A.: *The Corporate Economy*, London: Macmillan, 1971.

Martin, Gerald D.: *Determining Economic Damages*, Santa Ana, CA: James Publishing, 1995.

Meyer, M. W.: *Theory of Organizational Structure*, Indianapolis, 1977.

Mooney, J. D., and Reiley, A. C.: *Onward Industry*, New York, 1931.

Nelson, Judy A.: *Feminism, Objectivity and Economics*, London and New York, Routledge, 1996.

Peirson, G., Bird, R., Brown, R., & Howard, P.: *Business Finance*, Roseville, 1990

Pennings, J. M.: *Decision Making, An Organizational Behaviour Approach*, New York, Markus Wiener Publishing, 1983.

Pfeffer, J., and Salancik, G. R.: *The External Control of Organizations, A Resource Dependence Perspective*, New York, 1978.

Plous, S.: *The Psychology of Judgement and Decision Making*, New York, McGraw-Hill, 1993

Rappaport, A.: *Creating Shareholder Value, The New Standard for Business Performance*, New York, Free Press, 1986.

Ross, D.: *Economic Theory and Cognitive Science*, Cambridge, Mass., MIT Press, 2006.

Roth, A. E.: *The Handbook of Experimental Economics*, Princeton, Princeton University Press, 1995.

Santos, A.C.: *The Social Epistemology of Experimental Economics*, London, Routledge 2009.

Schumpeter, J. A., *The Theory of Economic Development*, Harvard University Press,Cambridge, Massachusetts, 1934.

Scott, W. R.: *Organizations: Rational, Natural, and Open Systems*, Englewood Cliffs, 1981.

Selznick, P.: *Leadership in Administration, A Sociological Interpretation*, New York, Harper & Row, 1957.

Smith, Gordon V., and Russell Parr, *Valuation of Intellectual Property and Intangible Assets*, New York: Wiley, 1994.

Smith, V. L.: *Papers in Experimental Economics*, Cambridge, Cambridge University Press, 1991.

Taylor, F. W.: *The Principles of Scientific Management*, New York, 1917.

Throsby, David, *Economics and Culture*, Cambridge University Press, 2001.

Tietenberg, Tom, *Environmental Economics and Policy*, New York, HarperCollins, 1994

Tinbergen, Jan.: *On the Theory of Economic Policy*; Amsterdam, North-Holland 1952.

Towse, Ruth ed.: *A Handbook of Cultural Economics*, Edward Elgar, 2003.

Trugman, Gary R., *Guide to Conducting a Valuation of a Closely Held Business*, New York, American Institute of Certified Public Accountants, 1993.

Ullman, D. G.: *Making Robust Decisions*, Trafford, 2006.

Warwick, D. P.: *A Theory of Public Bureaucracy*, Cambridge, MA: Harvard University Press, 1975.

Weber, M.: *The Theory of Social and Economic Organizations*, New York, Oxford University Press, 1947.

Weibull, J. W.: *Advances in Understanding Strategic Behaviour*, New York, Palgrave, 2004.

West, Thomas L.: and Jeffrey D. Jones: *Handbook of Business Valuation*, New York: Wiley, 1992.

Woodward, J.: *The Oxford Handbook of Philosophy of Economics*, New York, Oxford University Press, 2009.

Yegge, Wilbur M., *A Basic Guide for Valuing a Company*, New York, Wiley, 1996.

Zipp, Alan S., *Business Valuation Methods* New York, American Institute of Certified Public Accountants, 1990.

Index

D

E

F

G

H

I

□□□